T. Cullen Young: Missionary

and Anthropologist

Published by Christian Literature Association in Malawi (CLAIM)
Po Box 503, Blantyre, Malawi

First published 1989 by University of Hull

Distributed outside Africa by:
African Books Collective
www.africanbookscollective.com
abc@africanbookscollective.com

ISBN: 99908-16-64-6

Cover pictures: T. Cullen Young at Livingstonia with Mount Waller in the Background
                A Fowl House
                Loudon Church
                Zomba Market

Graphic design: Patrick Lichakala

Published with the assistance of Feed the Minds, Guildford, UK

Printed by Lightning Source

T. Cullen Young: Missionary

and Anthropologist

Peter G. Forster

Kachere Monograph no. 18

CLAIM
Christian Literature Association in Malawi
Blantyre
2003

Kachere Series,
P. O. Box 1037, Zomba Malawi
Email:kachere@sdnp.org.mw

This text is part of the Kachere Series, a range of books on religion, culture and society in Malawi. The other Kachere Monographs published so far are:

George Shepperson and Thomas Price, *Independent African. Jonh Chilembwe and the Nyasaland Rising of 1951*

Harry Langworthy, *"Africa for the African". The Life of Joseph Booth*

Matthew Schoffeleers, *Religion and Dramatisation of Life: Spirit Beliefs and Rituals in Southern and Central Malawi*

Joseph C. Chakanza, *Voices of Preachers in Protest: The Ministry of Two Malawian Prophets: Elliot Kamwana and Wilfred Gudu*

Ernst R. Wendland, Buku Loyera: *An Introduction to New Chichewa Bible Translation*

James . Amanze, *African Traditional Religion: The Case of the Bimbi Cult*

J. N. M. van Breugel, *Chewa Traditional Religion*

Silas S.Ncozana, *The Spirit Dimensions in African Christianity: A Pastoral Study Among the Tumbuka People of Northern Malawi*

Orison Ian Mkandawire, *Chiswakhata Mkandawire of Livingstonia*

The Kachere Series is the publication arm of the department of Theology and Religious Studies of the University of Malawi

Series Editors: J.C. Chakanza, F. L. Chingota, Klaus Fiedler, P. A. Kalilombe, Fulata L. Moyo, Martin Ott, Sharif Mahomed

Contents

Contents

Preface

The initial inspiration for the present volume arose out of a long secondment from the University of Hull to the University of Malawi for the period 1978-81. This formed part of a British Council link for sociology between the two universities. My main duties at the time involved the teaching of theoretical courses. However, I had been brought up on African material as an undergraduate and as an MA student at Manchester University, since I had been taught by Professor Max Gluckman and his predominantly Africanist anthropological colleagues. I had continued to maintain contact with African topics through teaching interests at Hull, but my research had tended towards the sociology of religion and social movements in Western societies. Personal experience in Africa soon reawakened my African interests, while the fields of my previous research led naturally to the study of missionary activity.

It also soon became apparent to me when I was in Malawi that there were greater potential areas of common interest between missionaries and anthropologists than might initially be supposed. In particular I noticed that, to a far greater extent than most other expatriates, many missionaries had developed a keen interest in African languages and cultures.

Further investigation revealed that this had also been so in the past, and this eventually led me to the work of T. Cullen Young. His studies of the Tumbuka for long provided the only published record of the ethnography and history of northern Malawi. Moreover, his interests subsequently developed into a broader concern with 'African culture', which had political implications in both the pre- and post-Independence situation. The story of Cullen Young's expulsion of Hastings Kamuzu Banda as a schoolboy and their subsequent reacquaintance and collaborative work has, too, a fascination of its own.

An attempt is made in the present study to bring these themes together and thereby to provide an overall vision of 'the man and his work'. This exercise is not to be confused with the old style of missionary biography, such as is seen for instance in the works of W.P. Livingstone.[1] Rather my concern has been to examine the thinking of one particular writer and to place his ideas in their historical and social context. Important though I see his work to be, I am not placing Cullen Young in the illustrious company of writers such as Marx, Weber and Durkheim: none the less, the study by L.A. Coser, *Masters of Sociological Thought*[2] probably comes nearest to a model for the methodology that I have adopted.

Chapter V makes certain comments on the political culture of Malawi under Dr Banda. To avoid misunderstanding, it should be stressed that the aim of the discussion is neither polemical nor hagiographic. Following Max Weber, I am concerned to engage in the exercise of *verstehen*, or the 'interpretative understanding' of social action[3]. In the case of Dr Banda, my contention is that this task can be eased to some extent by an awareness of his relationship with Cullen Young. Like so many others with Malawian connections, I am fully aware of the authoritarian nature of the Malawian political system yet at the same time feel that there is much in the country to be admired. Some insights into the national political culture might be of assistance in resolving this dilemma and at the same time might provide some broader indication of the potential for cultural nationalism in Africa as a whole.

Notes

1. See, for instance, W.P. Livingstone, *Laws of Livingstonia: a narrative of missionary adventure and achievement* (London, 1921).

2. L.A. Coser, *Masters of Sociological Thought: ideas in historical and social context* (New York, 1971).

3. Ibid., pp. 220-1; M. Weber, *The Theory of Social and Economic Organization* English trans. (New York, 1947) pp. 88-105.

Acknowledgements

Numerous people have contributed directly or indirectly to the writing of a work of this kind. I am particularly grateful to Professor Ian Cunnison, who gave continued support to the venture and who read the first draft of every chapter; to Professor George Shepperson, who encouraged my work at various stages; and to Mrs Margot Moffett, daughter of the subject of this study, who has displayed an informed interest throughout. Special thanks are due to the Sir Philip Reckitt Educational Trust and the Nuffield Foundation for providing the financial assistance which enabled personal interviews with Mrs Moffett in India. My wife, Suzie Rose (née Longwe), born in Mzokoto, and whom I married in 1979, has given me constant support and encouragement and has also helped me with numerous insights into Tumbuka culture.

I have also been stimulated by discussion of my work, both informally and in seminars, by colleagues at the Universities of Malawi, Hull, and Dar es Salaam. I have been assisted in tracing specific contacts and library material by Mr J. Benthall (London), Mr D. Bone (Dundee), Revd J. Campbell (Belfast), Revd W.P. Chibambo (Mzuzu), Revd G.L. Cowan (Glasgow), Mr A.M. Currie (Edinburgh), Dr G. Currie (Glasgow), Revd I.A. Elders (Edinburgh), Mrs C. Gascoigne (St Andrews), Revd A. Gilmore (Guildford), Mr R.D. Kermohan (Edinburgh), Mr F.J. Liabula (Blantyre), Professor J. Littlejohn (Edinburgh), Revd H.A. Mhone (Mzuzu), Mr D.J. Mothersill (London), Mrs B. Morrow (Zomba), Mr I.T. Nance (London), Mr J.M. Napier (Maidstone), Miss K. Ramsay (Edinburgh), Revd Dr A.C. Ross (Edinburgh), Mr P. Short (Paris), Miss E. Sloan (Edinburgh), Mr V. Syme (Stirling), Dr T.J. Thompson (Birmingham), Mr C.W. Turner (Glasgow), Dr. L. Vail (Cambridge, Mass., USA), and Professor A.F. Walls (Edinburgh).

Many people have given assistance by providing direct personal recollections of Cullen Young: these are listed separately in Section 2 of the Bibliography.

Mr M. Mann of the London School of Oriental and African Studies has provided useful advice on linguistic matters.

I have received considerable help from librarians, archivists and their assistants at the libraries of the Universities of Hull, Edinburgh, Aberdeen, and London (School of Economics and Political Science, and School of Oriental and African Studies); the Accountants' Libraries of Glasgow and Edinburgh; the Glasgow Public Library; the British Library; the Royal Commonwealth Society Library; the Imperial War Museum Library; the Public Record Office, Kew; the Selly Oak Colleges Library; Rhodes House, Oxford; the National Archives of Malawi; and the Society of Malawi Library. In particular the Hull University Library has provided much assistance with inter-library loans, and where this exercise was not practicable the Department of Sociology and Social Anthropology of the University of Hull has provided funds for travel within the UK. The secretaries of this Department have also been active in preparing numerous letters in connection with the research project. The staff of the Malawi High Commission in London helped to secure clearance to consult the National Archives of Malawi, and to arrange an interview with Dr H. Kamuzu Banda, Life President of Malawi.

The front cover illustration, and Plates 1 and 3, appear by courtesy of Mr R.B.C. Young (Cheltenham); Plate 2 is by courtesy of Dr A. Young (Edinburgh). Mr R. Wheeler-Osman of Hull University Library copied the photographs used for the plates, and Mr K. Scurr of the Geography Department prepared the maps. Dr J. Bellamy and Miss J. Smith of the Hull University Press have given much assistance in the process of preparation of the manuscript for publication.

Mention here does not imply approval of or agreement with the contents, for which I alone take full responsibility.

University of Hull　　　　　　　　　　　　　Peter G. Forster
August 1989

List of Maps, and Figure

....

List of Plates

Note on Orthography

References to the sources cited in this work will quickly reveal that there has been a certain amount of variation in the spelling of names of persons and places in Malawi. Cullen Young himself was not always consistent; for instance he sometimes wrote *Kamanga* and sometimes *Nkamanga*. Both these versions differ from *Nkhamanga*, as used on modern maps. Likewise the Ngoni Paramount Chief appears as *M'mbelwa* in modern form, but previous writers have frequently written *Mwambera* or *Mombera*. Some older works, too, prefer *Uzwangendaba* to the modern *Zwangendaba*, and *Chungu* to the modern *Kyungu*. The Ngonde appear as Nkonde or Konde in some writings. Again, the modern forms have been universally employed here.

In the case of Chichewa words and proper names, modern official guidelines exist and these have been followed. For Tumbuka the situation is more difficult since this language is no longer officially recognised or encouraged. The forms preferred in this work are those which avoid the use of diacritical marks or special letters: in particular, the bilabial implosive is represented by **b** rather than by **w** or **ɓ**.

It should finally be noted that in both Chichewa and Tumbuka the letters l and r are interchangeable (both being pronounced as l). It is important, however, to distinguish Paramount Chief Kalonga of the Chewa from Karonga, the Lakeshore settlement in northern Malawi.

Note on Place-names

There are numerous instances in which the name of a place referred to in the text has been changed in the course of the events described. In particular, after Independence a more authentically African name has sometimes been substituted for the previous English or anglicised version. The general policy throughout this work has been to adopt the modern name even when it was not in use at the time. Thus the name *Malawi* is also adopted when events during the British colonial period are described. The only exception to this policy are as follows:

(1) A particular historical event (e.g. the German East African Campaign) retains the title adopted at the time when it occurred.

(2) The term *Loudon* is generally used for the mission, and *Embangweni* for the village in which it is situated.

(3) In the bibliography, the name in use at the time of publication of the work in question is adopted. English versions of Continental place-names have however been used where they exist.

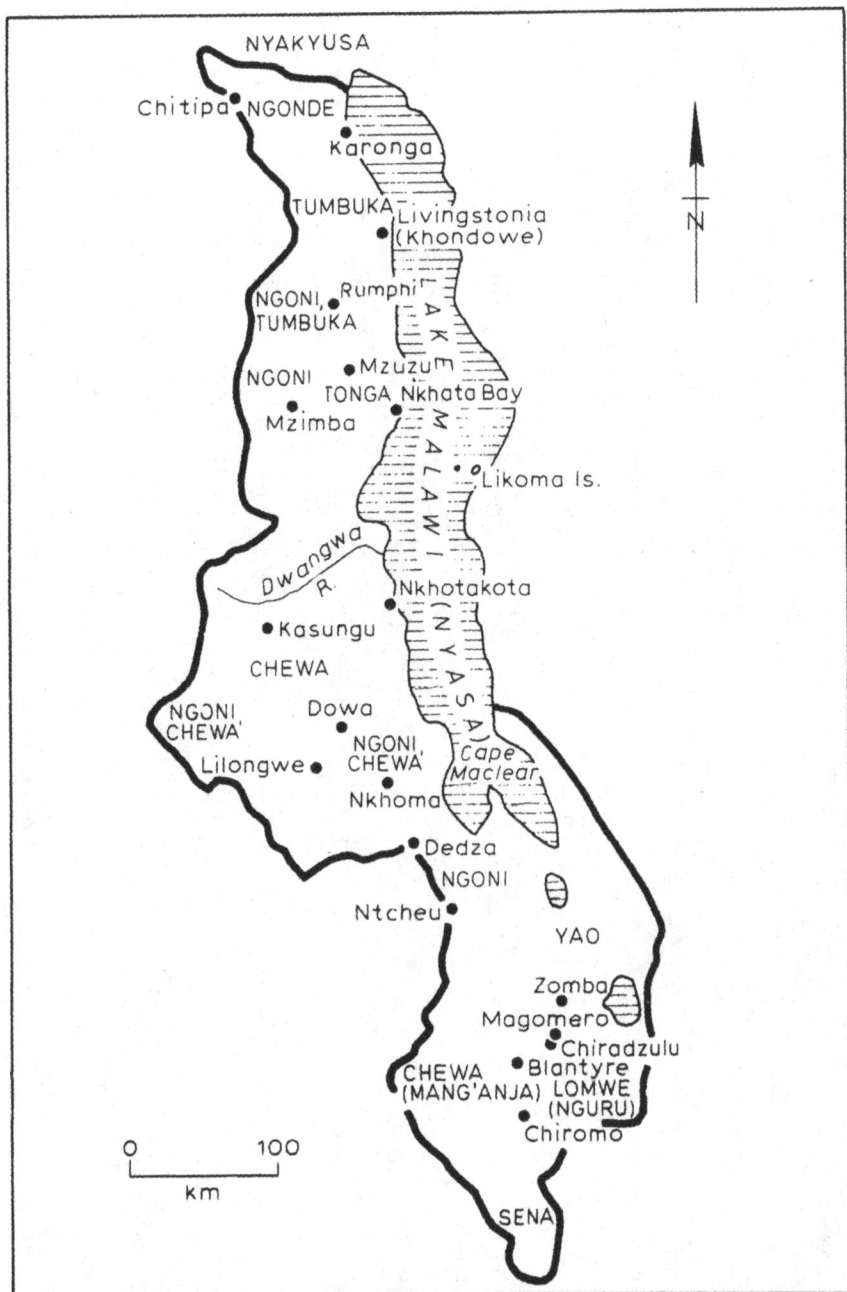

MAP 1 :   Malawi, showing principal places referred to in the text, and modern
           ethnic divisions.

List of Abbreviations

DC   District Commissioner

MNA   Malawi National Archives

NLS   National Library of Scotland

PRO   Public Record Office

RTS   Religious Tract Society

SOAS   London University, School of Oriental and African Studies

UMCA   Universities Mission to Central Africa

UMCB   United Missions in the Copperbelt

USCL   United Society for Christian Literature

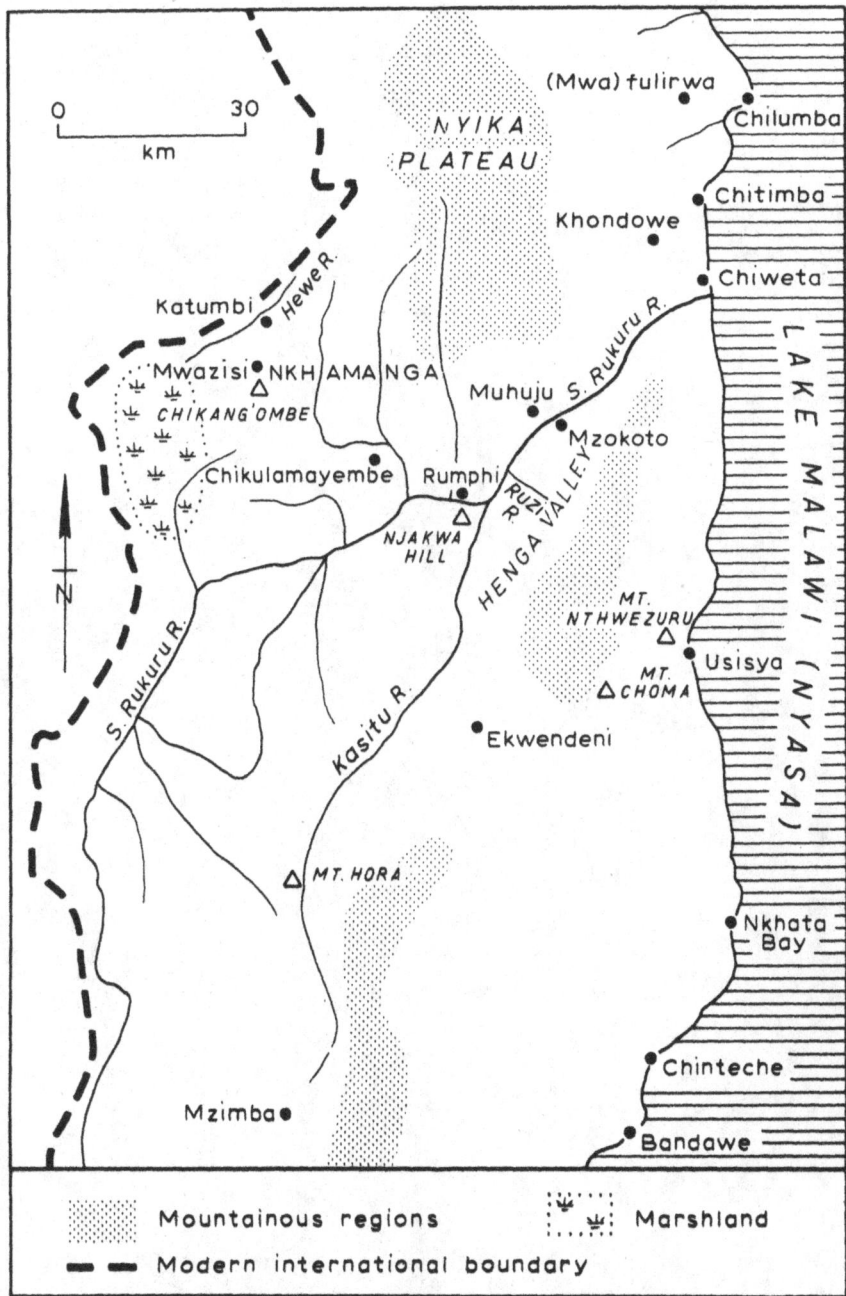

MAP 2:   Northern Malawi, showing places mentioned in the text.

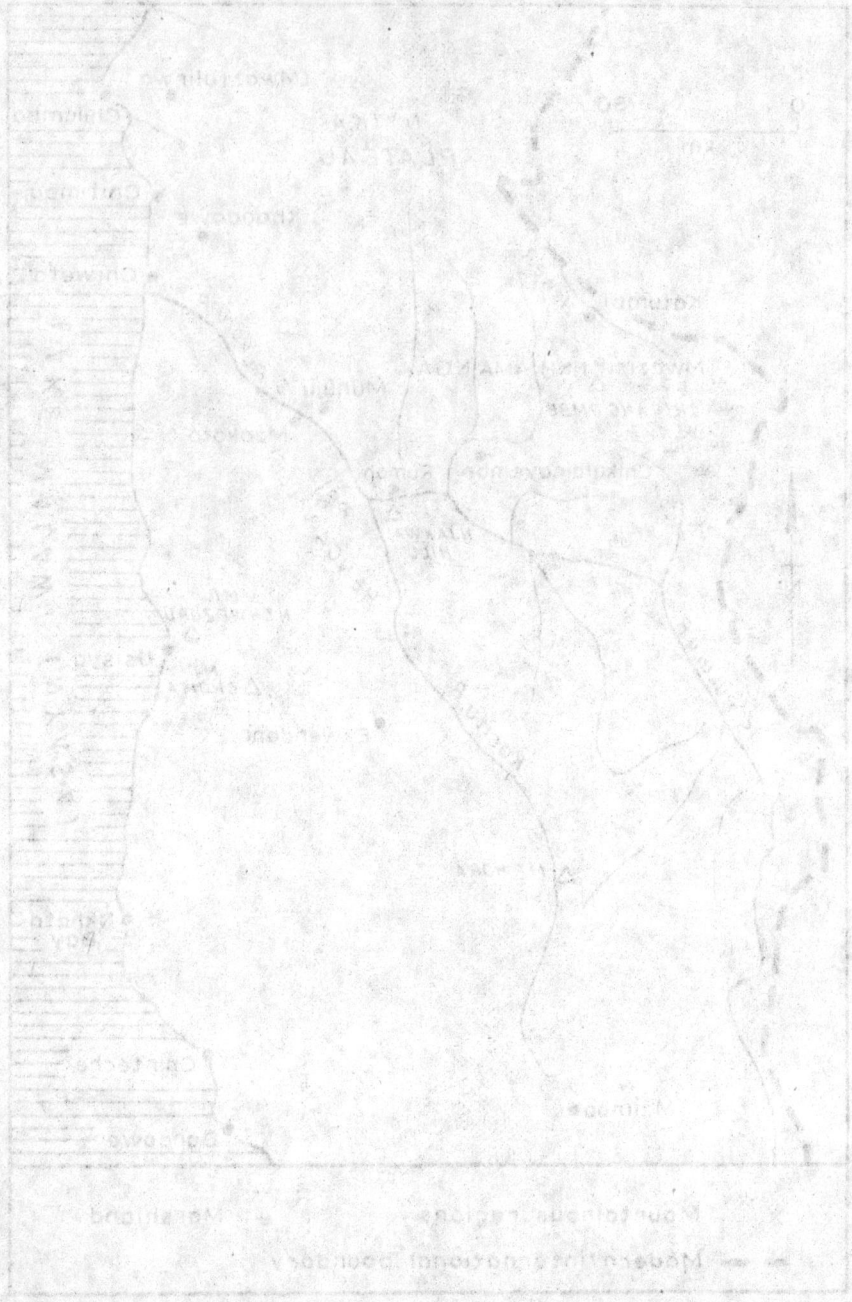

I

The Man and his Times

The second half of the nineteenth century was a period when missionaries and their activities received considerable public attention. Missionary literature had a wide circulation, and the influence was all the greater since the literate population was growing. Missionary reports were among the earliest sources of information on non-European peoples, especially for Africa. Accounts were sometimes provided by missionaries concerning the people whom they were evangelising, and much of this documentation is now generally recognised to be highly distorted. No rigorous professional standards for the conduct of anthropological inquiries had been proclaimed, and social-evolutionary theories which put Africa at or near the bottom were highly influential. Indeed, there was often a premium upon distortion, since a more sensational picture of the customs of the people to be evangelised could show a greater need for the mission. This could lead to greater support, especially financial, from the home country. Missionary accounts and the distortion contained in them often influenced theories of social evolution[1].

It thus appears that the relationship between the missionary and the anthropologist could be uneasy and potentially hostile: all the more so since the Darwinist critique of Christianity was in full development at the time of missionary expansion from Britain. But there was never an absolutely uniform pattern of response on the part of missionaries towards indigenous cultures; moreover, there was a gradual change towards a more accommodating attitude in the twentieth century. From the beginning, it had always been difficult for the missionary to remain totally aloof from those whom he was trying to convert. He had to learn the vernacular, not only well enough for ordinary communication, but also to a sufficient standard to translate the Bible. Linguistic studies led sometimes to a greater understanding of culture, and to an interest in anthropology. Certain missionaries, such as Edwin Smith, became not merely favourable to anthropology, but went further and themselves made important contributions which met exacting scientific standards.[2] Greater political and medical security for missionaries in the twentieth century encouraged a more patient attitude towards local cultures. An increasing concern became apparent to preserve and accommodate to what was 'good' in African culture (though it was still Europeans and not Africans who were the arbiters of such value). The policy of 'adaptation' became the keynote to African missionary effort at an influential conference of Protestant missionaries which was held in Belgium in 1926.[3] A growing appreciation of at least some aspects of African culture led to overtures with anthropologists: the International African Institute, founded in 1926, was itself partly initiated by missionaries. A further development came as a response to rapid change in Africa. Not only missionaries, but even some anthropologists, began to see Christianity as having a potential social 'function' in a situation where widening geographical horizons were likely to make traditional religions redundant. Thus the distorted account was likely to give way to more rigorous investigation though the former was not entirely eliminated.

It must be remembered, too, that apart from their directly religious contribution, missions brought other kinds of change. The expression 'legitimate commerce and Christianity' was popularised by Livingstone, and the particular aim in question was to abolish the slave trade. British missions were likely to encourage colonialism as a form of protection for their own activities, and also as a logical extension of missionary effort. 'Legitimate commerce' often had the effect of creating (sometimes quite consciously) new wants and eventual dependence upon European employers. Missionaries frequently brought medical services with them, generally as a way of attracting attention to the mission. But especially significant has been the missionary contribution to education. All missions advocated some measure of education, since an ability to read the Bible in the vernacular was an essential requirement for effective conversion. But there was much debate as to how far education should proceed beyond that level. Questions arose as to how appropriate it was that education and other missionary activities should be 'adapted' to indigenous practices. There were debates about the relative merits, with limited resources, of educating a small elite (needed as a source of African ministers and teachers) or of a policy of mass education with restricted aims. Another controversial matter was that of the appropriate mix of religious and secular education; and with the consolidation of colonial rule the issue arose as to how far government support of education was desirable, since this would also involve a measure of control. Although missionary policies varied considerably, their sympathies for the provision of secondary education were on the whole greater than those of the colonial government (as far as British colonies were concerned). A consequence of this was that the new elites of Africa, whose first generation were to lead their countries to independence, went through and were strongly influenced by mission schools.

In discussing British missionary effort, it is important to be aware of differences between England and Scotland. The particular concern here is with Scotland, where, in Blantyre in 1813, David Livingstone was born. His activities inspired admiration and very occasional emulation in both England and Scotland.[4] The area of mission interest under consideration here - northern Malawi - became so much a focus of Scottish activity that it could easily be thought of as a Scottish colony. It is as well at this juncture to note certain relevant aspects of Scottish history and culture, especially in relation to religion.

Livingstone was not unusual in Scotland in his ability to combine a strong religious outlook with an equally strong scientific commitment: indeed, his sponsors feared at times that the latter was in danger of outweighing the former. Scotland shared with France an Enlightenment tradition, but the eventual consequences for religious commitment were different in each case. The key issue in the Enlightenment was not so much an anti-religious commitment as a concerted opposition to what had hitherto been accepted on authority, especially in intellectual matters. But whereas in the French, Roman Catholic tradition it was difficult to distinguish between opposition to religious authority and opposition to religion as such, in Scotland the situation was different. Here the claims of reason and religion seemed already to have been reconciled, and Presbyterianism could be seen as a democratic form of ecclesiastical organisation. As was seen with the work of Adam Smith and Adam Ferguson, the Scottish Enlightenment was favourably disposed to the development of social science; and Livingstone's works show important sociological insights. Livingstone's attitudes towards race were progressive for his time, and in his relations with Africans he was often quite liberal. He was most unusual for a medically-qualified missionary in his preparedness to respect traditional doctors as professional colleagues.[5] He wrote of degradation in Africa, but he tended to stress the idea of degradation *as a consequence of the slave trade*, rather than suggesting that African society was degraded as such.

The Scottish churches had long been non-missionary, and missionary activities could easily be felt to be opposed to the notion of a national church.[6] None the less, the urgings of Livingstone did attract attention, and Scotland was to play an important part in the British missionary zeal.

The educational system in Scotland was another significant factor. Scottish education even at elite level preferred the day to the boarding principle. It was academic rather than athletic, and the 'muscular-Christian' ethos of the English public schools penetrated only slowly and incompletely into Scotland. The emphasis throughout was upon a high level of academic attainment.[7] It was stern, and there were no short cuts; but it was relatively democratic in that a Scot from a poor background, by dint of extremely hard work, was in a better position to obtain education up to university level than was his counterpart in England.[8] This ethos was to have implications for missionary activity; David Livingstone came from a very poor background and this was not unusual among Scottish missionaries. Typically they were those who had obtained a university education through self-help and considerable sacrifice, though missionaries from a clerical background were a major exception to this generalisation. Other family links between missionaries were also quite common. Candidates for the overseas mission service were however few in number.

The Calvinist tradition, with its strong work-ethic, also exercised its pull. Philanthropic activities at home could be suspect, seen as a form of subsidy to those who had failed through every fault of their own. Overseas mission was rather different. Those who had never heard of the Christian gospel had had no chance to fail, and were thus seen as more worthy objects of charity.[9] Calvinist businessmen could also be attracted by the idea of 'legitimate commerce and Christianity'. They were an important source of financial support, though were never as generous as the missions would have liked. Mission activities in the north of Malawi were closely associated with Livingstone's ideas of 'legitimate commerce'. In 1878 was formed the Livingstonia Central Africa Company, which after 1881 was known as the African Lakes Company.[10] Its directors and most of its original subscribers were members of the Glasgow Livingstonia Subcommittee. As managers were appointed two brothers, John and Fred Moir, Christian businessmen who had been influenced by the evangelical movement. The African Lakes Company did however expect a reasonable dividend, and its intention was not to give its profits to the mission.

Livingstone in his famous phrase had directed attention to Africa. This was by no means the only or the most significant mission field in which Scottish Presbyterians were destined to work. India and China were other important places for mission activity, and there were major differences between attitudes towards Asian and African indigenous culture. Unlike India and China, Africa had a non-literate culture; it was more likely to be seen as an 'uncivilised' continent, and not all of the degredation was necessarily attributed to the slave trade. Africa could easily be seen as a *tabula rasa*, with nothing to contribute, but at the same time with no major cultural barriers to mission penetration. The view could easily be taken that Africa was in a better position than were literate civilisations to absorb European culture. European culture might even be seen, as by the Blantyre (Malawi) missionary Clement Scott, as 'modern' culture, which Africans like anyone else had the right to share in.[11]

One complication was that Scottish Presbyterianism was not a unified phenomenon. In 1843 the Disruption had taken place, over the issue of the infringement of popular rights by patronage. This had led to the formation of the Free Church as a rival to the Established Church. Also in 1847 was formed the United Presbyterian Church, from two other schismatic bodies, the Secession Church and the Relief Church. Again the key issue had been patronage. However, most of the Free and the United Presbyterian Church came together in 1900 to form the United Free Church, and, in 1929, most of the United Free Church joined with the established Church of Scotland. Whenever there was an amalgamation, however, some dissidents usually formed a 'continuing' church with the original name.[12]

However, in the mission field, a relatively ecumenical spirit prevailed, which could extend beyond Presbyterianism. Two Presbyterian Scottish churches, the Church of Scotland and the Free Church, set up missions in Malawi to commemorate Livingstone. One, in central Malawi, was named Blantyre after Livingstone's birthplace; while the other, in the north, was named Livingstonia. Livingstone had also called for commercial operations in association with mission stations, and, particularly at Livingstonia, educational activities extended to commercial and industrial matters. No temporal powers were sought at Livingstonia, though they had been at Blantyre, with unfortunate results.[13] For this and other reasons, colonial rule was welcomed by the mission. High standards were soon established at Livingstonia for the most able pupils; an academic education was seen as being within the reach of the most able Africans, just as if they were Scots. But education was a lengthy process, and as a consequence there were long delays before the first Malawians were ordained. Yet both Blantyre and Livingstonia missions promulgated an optimistic view of African potential; and there were members of both missions who were interested in anthropology.

It is relevant to some subsequent events to note that the Presbyterian Scottish churches were not the only ones to begin work in Malawi as a response to Livingstone's call. The Universities Mission to Central Africa (UMCA), a High Anglican body, set up a station in Magomero in 1861. After opposition and failure it removed to Zanzibar in 1864; but Malawi was not lost sight of. In 1885 Likoma Island in Lake Malawi (Nyasa) was chosen as the new UMCA headquarters, and there were spasmodic contacts with the Scots at Livingstonia.

As Cullen Young was a member of Livingstonia mission, it will be to this that subsequent attention will be devoted. Livingstonia began with the arrival in Africa in 1875 of a pioneer party which included Dr Robert Laws, son of an Aberdeen carpenter;[14] through hard work, Laws had become qualified in both medicine and theology. He and his party originally attempted to set up a station at Cape Maclear, to the south of Lake Malawi; but this proved unsuccessful and the move north was made to Bandawe, still on the lakeshore, in 1881. This site was to be followed by several stations in northern Malawi. Livingstonia mission concentrated its efforts in the Northern Region, with the Tumbuka language as its chief means of communication. In 1894 was established the centre at Khondowe, and this was the place which the name Livingstonia came to designate. The school there was known as the Overtoun Institute, after Lord Overtoun, a Scottish industrialist who was a major benefactor of the mission.[15] The educational activities there were wide-ranging, and one area of study offered was a commercial course. This had been instituted as a direct response to a request from Cecil Rhodes, who had expressed a wish for qualified Africans to assist him in his plans for a Cairo-to-Cape telegraph. The mission was well established in 1904, when a layman was sent out to assist Dr Laws with the mission accounts; he was also expected to teach commercial subjects, in response to the demand for such training. The person who undertook this work was Thomas Cullen Young.

Thomas Cullen Young was born on 27 October 1880,[16] in Edinburgh. He was the eldest in the family, and had a non-identical twin brother, John. He was eventually to have four other brothers and one sister. He was a missionary from a clerical background: his father was the Revd John Young, who at the time of his birth was serving in Edinburgh as Minister of Newington United Presbyterian Church. The ancestry of the Young family was linked to the Borders. Cullen Young's father [17] was born in 1844 at Berwick-on-Tweed, on the English side; likewise his grandfather, another John Young, was born in Norham, also just in England. The senior John Young had his own business, and was involved in church and municipal interests. His son John (Cullen's father) grew up to experience political controversy from an early age, and soon became acquainted with movements for civil liberty. He took a keen interest in the life of the Borders, and the 'Riding of the Bounds' in Berwick made a particular impression. This was and is an annual municipal event when the boundaries of Berwick are traced by riders on horseback. This custom evidently also impressed Cullen Young, since he made repeated references to it in his writings. Cullen Young was also impressed from an early age with the significance of boundaries between different cultures.

The junior John Young was very successful at school, but he experienced discrimination on religious grounds when he attempted to secure a scholarship at Durham University. He had obtained the best marks in the examination, but was passed over because he was a Dissenter. He still read widely, including works on African discovery, and various boys' magazines. Having experienced discouragement in the English educational system, John Young went to board at Irvine in Scotland, and at the Academy of that town he obtained a broad education, with little specialisation. On leaving school in 1860, he began an apprenticeship as a merchant and taster of tea, in Edinburgh. While serving his apprenticeship he was heavily involved in church life, maintaining particular association with the church at Broughton Place. He became interested in the temperance and the missionary movements, and also formed a church literary society. He read extensively, taking a particular interest in missionary biographies. His church interests overtook his business concerns so that on completion of his apprenticeship he decided to enter the ministry of the United Presbyterian Church. With this in view he studied for and completed the M.A. degree of Edinburgh University, followed by classes at the Theological Hall. While studying theology he became very friendly with Robert Laws.

In 1872 John Young married Mary Robertson, but in 1876 he was widowed. His second marriage, in 1880, was to Catherine Copeland Cullen: he had been acquainted with her family through his church activities in Edinburgh. One of the firstborn twins was given his father's name John (the name given to the first son of the family for several generations); the other was christened Thomas Cullen, after his maternal grandfather. Cullen Young seems not to have used the name Thomas extensively, and his father was referring to him in letters as 'Cullen' by the time he was showing interest in mission service. The Youngs were strict disciplinarians at home; there was however no evidence of pressure to follow the same occupation, though informal influence will have been considerable. One other son of the family, William Paulin (born 1886) was eventually ordained.

It appears likely that Cullen Young first attended school in Edinburgh, though records are only available for the time when the family had moved to Glasgow. Thus in 1891 it is recorded that he began attendance at the Glasgow Academy. All the boys of the family received the same school education. The Academy covered classical subjects, but was more 'modern' in emphasis than the Glasgow Grammar School.[18] Games were played, but without the preoccupation with sporting achievement that characterised the English public schools. Cullen Young participated actively in these, and continued sporting links with the Academy after he had left. He did not go on to University, but in 1899 he began an apprenticeship with the firm of Moores, Carson and Watson, with a view to becoming a Chartered Accountant. He completed his training successfully, and passed his final examinations in 1902. He was admitted as a member of the Institute of Accountants and Actuaries in Glasgow in 1904. He remained active in church affairs, and was a supporter of the 'Student Volunteer' movement, which aimed at evangelisation of the world in one generation. On qualifying he decided to follow the family tradition and make the mission service his career. He embarked on theological training in preparation for this. His first year's studies were at Glasgow Theological Hall; after one year the family moved to Edinburgh, and he continued his studies for a further year at New College, Edinburgh. He completed his studies without difficulty, taking courses in New Testament Theology, Systematic Theology, and Church History. The issue of the relative merits of Darwin and Genesis was still a live one, though science and religion eventually established some sort of uneasy truce. After these studies, Cullen Young's destination was to be Livingstonia. Robert Laws had no accountancy training, and had devised his own system of book-keeping out of necessity. There was also the demand for commercial training, that had originated from Cecil Rhodes. Cullen Young was now well qualified to look after both the business side of the mission and commercial education.[19] John Young was by now Home Mission Secretary of the United Free Church, and he realised that his son's position at Livingstonia might be a little difficult at first. But he knew that his old friend Robert Laws would be of assistance.[20]

Before sailing to Africa, Cullen Young was one of twelve new missionaries presented to the United Free Church General Assembly, and it was noted at the time that as many as eight were children of the Manse. The new missionaries were advised by the Moderator to show patience; they were first to learn the language and habits of the people, so as to feel in sympathy with them. He pointed out that there would be a sowing and a reaping time. Cullen Young evidently followed all this advice very closely. Before sailing, he was interviewed by Lord Overtoun, and wished godspeed.[21] He sailed on 23 May 1904, the journey to Livingstonia taking three months.

On arrival at Livingstonia, Cullen Young soon absorbed himself in the problem of sorting out the mission accounts. He was very impressed by Laws's ingenious system of book-keeping, but none the less it was a relief to all that the accounts could now be put on a more professional footing. Laws was also pleased about the time saved. Certain difficulties had been experienced with Laws's attitude to financial matters; he had for instance a reputation with the African Lakes Company for delaying payment of bills. But Cullen Young succeeded in taking the accounts in hand, and he was congratulated for his first statement in 1905. A book-keeping problem that Young highlighted was the fact that Livingstonia was both a producer and a consumer. He also began teaching the commercial course, which initially had eight pupils. One of these was Levi Mumba, whose name will appear again in this account. He enjoyed the teaching side of his work, though felt it important from the start to look for 'character' as well as for ability to absorb the coursework. He remarked in his early report that Africans possessed brains but also, guile. But on the whole he was impressed by his pupils' aptitude for a completely new subject.

Cullen Young's recreations were various sporting activities, which he greatly enjoyed. He also obtained a gun licence and began some game shooting. He was asked by the Mission Board in Scotland to record his first impressions; but he felt that these could be misleading, and refused. He was also idealistic enough to suggest that his salary be reduced to £100 per annum. This was politely declined by the authorities in Edinburgh; though it was noted that his brother William Paulin had begun to show interest in mission work, and the possibility of their sharing one salary was not excluded.[23]

On the whole Cullen Young followed the advice he was given, and he learnt patiently. He admitted in one of his reports that initially he had possessed a certain amount of revolutionary zeal, but that this had given way to a deeper understanding.[24] In this connection it can be noted that, at Livingstonia, a tradition already existed of recording details of customs and beliefs. Much of this had emerged from study of the local Tumbuka, Tonga, and Ngoni languages. Dr George Steele had already been working on Tumbuka vocabulary, but had died in 1895. Walter Angus Elmslie (1856-1936) had also worked on the Tumbuka language. He produced some material on customs, though his more popular work was rather sensational.[25] Alexander Gillon MacAlpine (1869-1957) had provided some dispassionate studies of the Tonga for the *Livingstonia News*.[26] The influence of serious study of African custom by Blantyre missionaries (MacDonald and Scott) was also important.[27] In 1900 and again in 1904 there had been mission conferences for the whole of Malawi; at these the study of custom was urged, and emphasis was placed upon the existence of an indigenous morality in Africa.[28] Significantly, too, the Overtoun Institute had its Literary Society, where debates took place on subjects such as witchcraft, and the merits or otherwise of betrothal payments.[29] A concern had begun to be felt by the missionaries about the consequences of change, whether caused by their own activities or not. Donald Fraser was a missionary who had declared his opposition to a 'Gospel which denationalises'.[30] But the acceptance of the value of African customs was very selective. In common with nearly all other missionaries, the Livingstonia staff condemned polygamy. There was also opposition to beer-drinking, which tended to accompany economic activities, especially as a reward for agricultural labour.[31] But its function was not appreciated by the Scottish missionaries, who despaired of the apparent lack of a work ethic. On other matters, however, there could be a certain amount of openness towards African customs. At the time of Cullen Young's arrival, Fraser was relatively sympathetic to indigenous tradition, and certainly more so than Elmslie.[32] Young was quite impressed by Fraser's outlook, but saw himself as merely a learner in his early days at Livingstonia. He patiently set to work at mastering the Tumbuka language. He took an examination in it in 1906, which was set by Elmslie, Fraser, and MacAlpine. He passed with the high mark of 88 per cent.[33]

One missionary whom Cullen Young found already at Livingstonia was Miss Jessie Fiddes; she had arrived only slightly earlier (in May 1904). She was born in 1876, and originated from an Aberdeen family with a strong Protestant outlook; her father was a grocer. She was adventurous enough to qualify as a 'Lady Literate in Arts', at St Andrews University, in 1900. This was a qualification akin to a degree, except that women were not admitted to the usual degree

courses and so a special provision was made.[34]   On completing this
she decided to enter the mission service, and studied for two years at
the Burnbank Missionary Training Home, in Glasgow.   Her duties
were to include work for the medical side of the mission, and in
preparation she did two years' dispensing for a doctor brother in
London.   She was finally accepted as a missionary in December,
1903.   She soon became closely involved with work among girls at
Livingstonia.   Like most other missionaries, she tended to see work as
something new to Africans: she claimed to be teaching the girls the
virtues of manual work.   She particularly enjoyed visiting villages.
Jessie Fiddes was very open, almost gushing in her religiosity: she
was congratulated by the mission secretary in Scotland for her vivid
and picturesque writing.   This contained frequent reference to doing
the work 'for His sake' and 'in His name'.   When, in 1905, she saw
an African die, she wrote 'I shall never forget watching the life ebbing
away from one heathen man.   I stood transfixed for nearly half an
hour afterwards, wondering where the man's soul had gone to'.[35]   On
the other hand, about the death of Miss Jordan, a fellow-missionary,
she commented 'After three short days of fever she passed through
the Gate .... Her friends said they saw her *eternal life* shining through
....'[36] (italics in original).

Jessie Fiddes accepted that patience was necessary, and she too
devoted much attention to learning the Tumbuka language.   She took
the examination at the same time as Cullen Young, and obtained the
high mark of 79.5 per cent.   She also had dealings with Young in a
professional capacity, since she was advised to consult him regarding
her annuity on completion of mission service.   The next report after
her success in the language examination in 1906 was that she and
Cullen Young had become engaged.[37]   Both left Livingstonia for
furlough in July 1907, arriving in Britain on 29 September.   They
were married on 24 June, 1908, at the Grand Hotel, Aberdeen: Cullen
Young's father assisted in the service.[38]   Mrs Young was thereafter
counted as a 'missionary's wife': the mission did not employ married
women in their own right.   During furlough Cullen Young attended a
further session at New College; he also visited Fred Moir, of the
African Lakes Company, to discuss the mission accounts.   On this
occasion he had to be reprimanded for changing the appointment at
the last minute, apparently having become unused to Western
attitudes to time during his stay in Africa.[39]

The Youngs sailed back to Africa in July 1908, and their initial duties were to be at Karonga, in the far north of Malawi near the Tanzanian border. Here Cullen Young was to serve as locum tenens for Dr Frank Innes, who was going on furlough. He taught in and inspected primary schools there, and it was during this period that he began to develop an awareness of the importance of recent history of the area for throwing light on the present. He was now working among the Ngonde, who evidently disliked the mission's policy of using the Tumbuka language as the medium of instruction. Young understood that there was a historical reason for this, as Tumbuka was the language of the Henga who were intruders into the area. He gradually began to have more success with the Ngonde, though he still considered them to be less hard-working than the Henga. He reported with dismay that two teachers had lapsed into 'flagrant sin': though he was reassured to note that this was now disapproved of by Africans as well as by the mission. He began at this point to comment upon aspects of educational policy.[40] He took the view that it was appropriate to charge fees for education, seeing these as leading to more enthusiastic attendance. He also commented in the *Livingstonia News* on an article about Indian experience in education; he argued that the dangers there outlined of developing disregard for indigenous culture by the newly educated had important lessons for Africa.[41]

It was while the Youngs were in Karonga, in 1909, that their son John was born. 1910 saw a further move, this time to Loudon (Mzimba district, now Embangweni). Here Cullen Young was to be the colleague of Donald Fraser, who eventually became one of the most prolific writers about the Livingstonia Mission. Fraser had been in Malawi since 1896; he was influenced by Elmslie and remained quite close to him on a personal level. But Fraser seemed much more relaxed and open in his dealings with Africans. He was not liberal about all aspects of indigenous culture; he found certain dances disgusting, and was particularly contemptuous of traditional medical practitioners. Fraser expressed some of his views in *The Future of Africa*, a textbook for mission study circles, which was published in 1911. Although this contained much condemnation of African custom, some aspects he saw as admirable, and he perceived in Africa some 'broken lights of God'. A further important publication by Fraser appeared in 1913, under the title *Winning a Primitive People*.

This again contained a fair amount of condemnation, especially of dancing and beer-drinking; there was also some reporting of history and folklore, in tones that were not very sympathetic. This work adopted a clear tendency to praise the Ngoni conquerors and their centralised state system, and to condemn the institutions of the Tumbuka, whom the Ngoni had invaded successfully. Fraser praised social control, while condemning 'idleness' and polygamy. He was active at the 1910 Nyasaland Mission Conference; he argued there that some elements of heathenism were avenues towards Christianity, though expressing concern that in traditional cosmology God was an absentee. Like many other missionaries, he was less censorious about African customs when addressing more restricted audiences.[42]

Fraser and Young worked together till Fraser's furlough in 1912. Fraser left confident that the station would be run by someone who knew the people and the work. Young was particularly interested in the fact that this field of Livingstonia's activity was on the boundary of two culture-areas: that of the (by now) patrilineal Ngoni/Tumbuka of the north, and the matrilineal Chewa of the Central Region. His own Borders origin awakened in him much interest in the significance of such situations.

His comments on educational policy continued to stress the importance of fee-paying, and of the development of 'character'. He reported in 1912 that 20 out of 230 teachers had 'fallen', and that it was difficult to know when a boy was trustworthy. He also noted certain competing attractions. He expressed concern about 'Ethiopianism', i.e. the establishment of independent African-led churches not of European mission origin. Such movements had begun to exercise influence in Malawi, but Young saw them as proving attractive to those not of sound character, who could be tempted by offers of free books, and by a 'mistaken nationalism'. Many older Livingstonia missionaries discussed this phenomenon in mission publications. Young also noted that some Ngoni were hostile to the mission, since they deliberately held dances at times which would conflict with school requirements. He did not object to the dances as such, but he maintained rather that there was ample time for both work and play.[43] His anthropological interests were further stimulated by other factors. In 1909 he was chosen as the recipient of an anonymous manuscript dealing with Tumbuka history. In 1912 he witnessed a Chewa initiation ritual, and listened carefully to the explanation of the procedures, which the old men provided. In reporting on this in the *Livingstonia News*, he noted parallels between Western marriage customs and those of the Chewa.[44]

Another development, in 1910, was the appointment of Cullen's brother William Paulin to Livingstonia. He was ordained in 1911, and proceeded to the station at Bandawe; in 1912 he moved to teach at the Overtoun Institute. W.P. Young was later to have an important influence on the mission's educational policies. He feared that the 'industrial mission' philosophy which Livingstonia had adopted had the danger of neglecting village needs, and that it served the interests of planters first and foremost. He remained on his first tour till the outbreak of war in 1914. He then returned to enlist in the Royal Scots, and was to have a distinguished war record.

Mission policy at this time was by no means totally negative regarding African culture. Yet there was a continued concern with the importance of producing a conviction of sin; and Cullen Young shared with many other missionaries the fear that schooling was relatively easy to obtain. But 'good character' was a different matter. Dismissals and expulsions were frequent in the mission schools, and where one student was expelled there were always plenty more to take his place. With regard to the setting up of an indigenous church, there were steps forwards and backwards. On the one hand, the first Malawians were ordained by Livingstonia Synod in 1914. These were Yesaya Zerenje Mwasi, Jonathan Chirwa, and Hezekiah Tweya. But on the other hand, Levi Mumba was required to leave his position as Elder for having taken a second wife. Another development concerning Mumba occurred in 1912, when he became a founder member of the North Nyasa Native Association, which was set up with the full encouragement of Robert Laws. These various developments were quite consistent with the standpoint of the Livingstonia Mission. High standards were insisted upon, with no short cuts: But when the time was ripe, Africans could certainly be the political, religious and educational equals of Europeans.[45]

The Youngs again took furlough in August, 1913. Cullen Young was in great demand during his leave, as a speaker for the interests of Livingstonia. He was felt to be particularly suitable for this work since he was young, strong, and full of zeal. He was especially pleased to have the chance to speak about Livingstonia in the Borders area. He was now advancing in seniority in the mission.[46] In 1913 he joined the Mission Council. In 1914, he was nominated as Livingstonia Mission Council's Representative Elder to the General Assembly, and the same Assembly approved his ordination.

During this General Assembly, Cullen Young expressed his views on certain aspects of mission in Africa. He remarked that while literate civilisations such as India and China could be studied and learnt, for Africa only the 'human documents' were available. He also noted that, while certain social practices were to be seen by the outsider as cruel, for those involved there was a strong weight of social and supernatural authority behind such actions. He did not appear at this stage to have any awareness of functionalist theories of society, which in any case had barely been developed at that time for analysing anthropological data. But his outlook was evidently such as to be highly receptive to functionalism when it became known to him. He did not wish to preserve the existing order of things in Africa, but rather suggested that the mission was helping to remove the fear on which such apparently cruel practices were based.[47]

There was initially some debate as to whether Cullen Young's ordination should be unconditional, or whether it should be limited to the mission field (a frequent condition for the ordination of missionaries). It was eventually agreed that his ordination should be unconditional. There was unqualified approval of his character and demeanour, while his academic qualifications were regarded as 'quite satisfactory'. He was seen to have completed the ordinary curriculum apart from Hebrew and theology.[48] The ordination service took place at Broughton Place church, with which, as has been seen, there was a family connection.[49] While on furlough Cullen Young renewed this link. In February 1914 he had spoken there of his work at Livingstonia; and he had also been involved in conducting the 'Cannongate Sabbath Afternoon Bible Class for Young Men'. The ordination took place on 16 June: his father was one of the speakers at the service.[50] It was subsequently noted that, although fully ordained, Cullen Young disliked the title 'Reverend'.[51]

The Youngs sailed soon afterwards, on 9 July; but their journey back to Africa was impeded by war. Mombasa was reached after only a month, but the overland journey to the final destination (Tamanda, a sub-station across what is now the Zambian border) could not be completed till December. While his steamer was waiting in Mombasa, Young paid a rapid visit to Dr J.W. Arthur, a former school-mate who was in charge of Tumutumu mission.[52]

Cullen Young spent about six months in Tamanda, before moving to the larger station, Loudon, where he had worked previously. Around this time, Laws applied for a licence for Cullen Young to conduct marriages under ordinance. During 1915, Young paid a visit to Kasungu station, where a remarkable incident took place. He had been called upon to invigilate an examination for pupil-teachers who had hopes of going on to the Overtoun Institute. Young wrote the questions on the blackboard: his writing was small, suitable for postcard correspondence (of which he was fond). One sixteen-year old pupil was small in stature, but had been placed at the back of the examination hall. At one point he stood up in order to see the questions over the shoulder of the pupil in front of him. Cullen Young immediately suspected him of cheating; and, in accordance with the strict policy of the mission, excluded him from the examination room and debarred him from further participation. The boy concerned was named Hastings Kamuzu Banda.[54] At the time Cullen Young seems to have had no further thoughts on the matter, but it will be shown that Young and Banda were to meet again. Moreover, after Young's death, Banda was to become Head of State in an independent Malawi: but consideration of this matter will be deferred for the present.

In 1914 war broke out in Europe, and it almost immediately began to impinge upon Malawi, as a British colony with German East Africa (Tanzania) to the north. The war had its repercussions on the mission in at least two important respects. In the first place, resentment of recruitment of African troops in the service of a 'European' war was to lead to support for the first major rebellion against colonial rule in Malawi. In the second place, the missionaries themselves, as well as many of their followers, found themselves liable to call-up for the German East African Campaign. Cullen Young was affected by both developments.

The rebellion in question was led by John Chilembwe.[55] Chilembwe had received some theological training in the United States, with the assistance of Joseph Booth. Booth was a highly unorthodox kind of missionary. English-born but with experience of living in Australia and the United States, Booth had in 1892 set up the Zambezi Industrial Mission. Chilembwe had accompanied him to the United States in 1897, and he had attended a Negro Baptist seminary

for two years. On his return to Malawi Chilembwe set up the
Providence Industrial Mission, at Chiradzulu, fifteen miles from
Blantyre. In the years preceding 1914 a cumulative series of
grievances against Europeans had developed. These related
especially to the Bruce Estates, where conditions for African
employees were particularly bad, and where African churches had
been burnt. He plotted a rising, in which the aim would be to kill the
European masters, and then to set up an independent African state. In
this the only Europeans allowed to remain would be deprived of
political authority. His campaign might have remained fairly
localised were it not for the outbreak of war in 1914. Soon African
carriers and soldiers began to lose their lives in a war which was a
European concern. Moreover, the depletion of able-bodied men from
the villages had implications even for those not directly involved in
the fighting. Eventually, on 23 January 1915, Chilembwe began an
attack on Europeans in the Shire Highlands; there were also attacks in
Blantyre and Ntcheu. Three Europeans were killed, but there were
many African casualties, and Chilembwe himself was among the
dead. The rising was a failure, and had been extinguished completely
by 3 February 1915. But it shook European complacency in the
Protectorate: it also led the colonial government to become suspicious
of missionaries, not only those of smaller bodies but also the well-
established Scots. A Commission of Inquiry was set up, and began its
investigations in May 1915. Livingstonia was far from the place
where the rising occurred, but Elmslie and Fraser were interviewed
and Cullen Young sent written evidence. His comments related to the
deleterious consequences of labour migration, and also to the dangers
attendant upon employment of Africans of 'bad character', who had
not completed their courses at the mission. The tone of his comments
was paternalistic, but Europeans rather than Africans were the object
of such criticism.[56]

Meanwhile, since the outbreak of the war there had been clashes in
German East Africa (Tanganyika). The Protectorate was not well
prepared for war, though all Europeans there eventually volunteered
for military service. Participation in the German East African
Campaign was not always enthusiastic, and some preferred to
volunteer for France. African carriers and soldiers were recruited,
and there was some resistance to this. Paramount Chief Chimtunga of
the Ngoni refused to cooperate with recruitment; as a consequence,

the colonial authorities deposed and imprisoned him, not releasing him till 1920.[57] There was also Chilembwe. The missionaries found the war an embarrassment; they had preached peace, but now two Christian European nations were fighting one another. Livingstonia mission cooperated in making available provisions for the supply line for the north, though Dr Laws always insisted on payment of the full market price. Missionaries' services were soon called upon for the war effort: their acquaintance with the language, region and people made them particularly well equipped for supervision of carriers and scouts.

Cullen Young heard news of the war as soon as his ship arrived in Mombasa. Like most other missionaries, he regretted the war but accepted the military exigencies of the situation. Moreover, he disliked German methods of missionisation and colonisation. Livingstonia was concerned with transport northwards, using carrier corps known as *tenga tenga*. Captain Barton, based in Karonga, used Europeans with close African links for intelligence work, and Cullen Young was called upon in this capacity. His particular concern was to provide competent African interpreters; these he recruited and controlled, together with scouts, runners and guides. The mixed group of which he was in charge varied from 120 to 160 in number, and the aim of this body was to pick up talk of the countryside regarding enemy movements.[58] In noting Young's involvement in the campaign, the Livingstonia authorities in Scotland expressed the hope that he might also be able to do some religious work among the troops, though there is no record that he engaged in this. He wrote extensive notes on the campaign, and the unpublished typescript is still available.[59]

Young's initial experiences in the campaign did not seem to present many difficulties. The Nyasaland Field Force, as it was known, was lucky in marching northwards to the Tanzanian border at the Songwe river, undetected by a German column marching southwards towards Karonga. It appears that subsequently German forces were on a slow retreat. The Nyasalanders marched towards Neu Langenberg (Tukuyu) and were reinforced by troops from the Rhodesias and South Africa. There was a further move north towards Njombe. There were some casualties, but also periods of inactivity, during which game hunting was a popular sport, and Young participated. In due course operations became more risky, but he was

---

unharmed in the campaign. Towards the end the troops on the ground were assisted by an aeroplane. There was a southward movement, and German forces were eventually defeated by a cooperative effort involving all Belgian and British forces in the area. The Nyasaland Field Force ceased to exist as a separate entity in May 1917, and soon afterwards Young was allowed to return to mission work: he was one of the first to be released.

The war obviously left a deep impression upon Young, though it was not a subject that he talked about extensively. But he prepared the long typescript which deals with his experiences, and long afterwards he published two articles about incidents during the war.[60] He made several important observations regarding Africans' participation in the campaign.

In the first place, he singled out the African carriers for particular praise. He had a great respect for the askari, but noted that soldiering was after all their job, and he did not fear that their contribution would be forgotten. But the *tenga tenga*, he urged, had a special claim to the white man's gratitude: 'without exaggeration, they carried us to victory on their backs', he commented. He also noted their versatility as compared with wagon transport.

He noted, secondly, that during the campaign South African troops were involved in a racially-mixed force. He hoped that this experience would not be forgotten by the South Africans, especially in view of the bravery displayed by the askari. He seemed not to have enjoyed his acquaintance with the white South African troops: he commented unfavourably on their lack of 'natural aptitude for the coloured races' (and also deplored their frequent recourse to bad language).

Thirdly, he commented that the African soldiers would not forget their experiences; survivors would return to their villages full of the things they saw and did. It is not certain what he had in mind here, but the effect of war experience upon the growth of nationalist consciousness has been widely commented upon.

One experience had a rather different, personal effect on Young. While hunting game in 1916, he killed an elephant. A second elephant was wounded on the same hunt, but escaped further attention from the hunters. But it returned later to die next to the beast that had already been killed (Young speculated that they were twins). The scene had an emotional impact, and he never again agreed to hunt

Cullen and Jessie Young at Loudon

The sons and daughter of Dr John Young, shortly after the end of World War I

elephant.[61]

A further personal matter was that not only Cullen, but all his brothers were involved in the war; his sister May also served as a nurse. This was an obvious time of anxiety for their parents, but in the end all survived remarkably unscathed. A group photograph of them all in uniform was taken to commemorate the fact (see Plate 2). William Paulin Young was particularly active in the war; he was wounded in France, and in 1918 was taken prisoner-of-war. He was awarded the Distinguished Conduct Medal. William Young wrote an account of some of his experiences, with a religious message, entitled *A Soldier to the Church*. His unconditional support for the war was very forthright here: while deploring division between the churches, he expressed regret that the churches had not spoken with a corporate Christian voice in support of the war. When the war was over he nearly decided to remain in the armed forces, as a chaplain in the Royal Air Force; but eventually he decided to work for the Student Christian Movement before returning to Livingstonia in 1922.[63]

Cullen Young returned to mission work direct from the war; he was sent to Kasungu to relieve the Revd George Prentice. He remained there till his furlough in 1919. In the early stage of the war, he had missed the birth of his daughter Marguerita Catherine Mary (Margot). He suffered considerably during this period from blackwater fever. He was fortunate that his wife had sufficient nursing training, since otherwise he would have died. One incident of note occurred in 1918, at a meeting of the Mission Council which Young attended. Members present were saddened to accept the resignation of Jonathan Chirwa, one of the first Malawians to be ordained. The resignation was on the grounds of adultery; the Presbytery treated Chirwa as a sinner who was able to be forgiven, and eventually (in 1924) he was restored. But Donald Fraser was deeply distressed by the incident, and he appreciated Young's efforts to keep him cheerful on this occasion.[64]

Before furlough in 1919, Jessie Young wrote an article for publication in the *Record of the Home and Foreign Missionary Work of the United Free Church of Scotland*, about village work especially among women. When they visited the villages together, Cullen Young would check the teachers' work, while Jessie tried to make friends with the women. Cullen Young also made their visit a popular occasion by shooting for the pot. The Youngs both shared the view that women's work was important for the success of the mission.[65] Jessie Young was able to help in collecting anthropological material on the life of women, which her husband would not have been able to obtain easily.

The family sailed to Britain in April 1919, arriving early in May. Cullen Young took on the work of secretary to the Mission Study Council while on furlough; this was acceptable to the Livingstonia Committee as long as the duties involved left Sunday free for deputation work. As on his previous furlough, Young made an important contribution to the United Free Church General Assembly (1920), on the subject of Livingstonia. His address was this time rather more political in content. He argued that Jesus was acceptable to Africans, but not in the form in which he was being presented by the missions. He also pointed out that the whites were now trying to deny Africans their share of the life which Christ promised, and that anti-white feeling had been spread by the war. He went on to express the fear that industrial enslavement was now replacing the slavery which the mission had helped to abolish. His contribution to the Assembly was greeted with acclamation.[66]

A problematic factor for Cullen Young's missionary career was the presence of his two children. There was a home for Church of Scotland missionaries' children known as Cunningham House, in Lauder Road, Edinburgh, and this was where the children were placed. Conditions were not unattractive in the home as far as institutional life goes, but the long separation was a strain for parents and children alike. The situation was such as to lead to the Youngs' eventual permanent departure from Africa. Even in 1920 Cullen Young returned to his duties at Livingstonia in September of that year; but his wife stayed behind with the children and did not sail till a whole year later. Difficulties of this kind were of course common in the early stages of European penetration of tropical Africa.

When he sailed in 1920, Cullen Young's destination was Livingstonia. He was to fill the position of Headmaster of the Overtoun Institute till 1925. He was often ill around this period, and it also appears that his work at the centre of Livingstonia's activities was not really to his liking: he was later to request that he should be given duties in the villages. But his work at the Institute did have the advantage that he could discuss his growing historical interests with educated converts at the school. Jessie Young, still in Scotland, was concerned for her husband's health, especially since he refused to use a hammock: he found it very distasteful to see eight to ten men sweating over carrying him through the bush. Mrs Young therefore urged the mission authorities in Edinburgh to provide her husband with a bush-car, pointing out that it was almost unheard of for anyone to return to the tropics after having suffered from blackwater fever.[67]

During this time Cullen Young began to see the growth in the mission of practices that he was to condemn in due course. He had seen that segregation of the races was unlikely as long as the European community was small, but that when Europeans reached a significant number they were likely to segregate themselves from the rest of the population. In Khondowe itself, Africans did not stay in 'European' houses. In 1924, Dr J.E.K. Aggrey, a West African member of a group studying educational practices (the Phelps-Stokes Commission) came to visit Livingstonia: it appears that he was the first black African to be treated as an equal by the Europeans.[68] (Koyi, Elmslie's helper from South Africa, had however, drawn a full missionary's salary, but Malawians were not normally accorded equal status).[69] In 1924, the General Mission Conference took place in Livingstonia, and mixed eating was introduced for all participants. Livingstonia members of the gathering seem to have accepted this arrangement; however, representatives of the Dutch Reformed Church who were present found it most embarrassing. It was feared that negotiations to federate the Presbyterian churches in Malawi would thereby be placed in jeopardy, and the arrangement was discontinued after two meals.[70]

A formal complaint was put forward by Yesaya Chibambo, a teacher who eventually became a historian of the Ngoni, and who was ordained in 1929. Chibambo complained in 1921 to the Livingstonia Mission Council, regarding inferior conditions of service for African employees of the mission. He drew attention to lack of security of tenure, lack of pensions and gratuities, and lack of travel expenses. He pointed out that African employees were not seen as colleagues, and that missionaries commonly called them 'boy'. He also indicated that disagreements in the Presbytery nearly always split along racial lines. Chibambo claimed that he spoke also for many other African mission workers. He received a courteous reply, but almost nothing was conceded.[71] Cullen Young's specific comments on incidents of this kind have not been recorded, but he certainly condemned such practices in a general way.

There were at this time certain other policies that were becoming popular among outside bodies, which could lead to segregation even if their implications were not necessarily illiberal. A growth in educational policies which stressed 'adaptation' to village needs was in evidence; and there was also a slow but steady growth in influence of the policy of 'Indirect Rule' in local African government. Neither policy automatically led to a segregated society, but in both cases the danger existed that the African educated along Western lines would be excluded from decision-making. Cullen Young's contribution to debates about education will be considered in Chapter IV; the relationship of his historical works to claims under Indirect Rule will be considered in Chapter III.

After his long reticence during his junior years at Livingstonia, Young now began to have the confidence to commit some of his thoughts to writing. His particular concerns were those of language and history. He presented these together, apparently incongruously, in the volume *Notes on the Speech and History of the Tumbuka-Henga Peoples* (1923). He had already shown himself to be successful at studying the Tumbuka language, from an earlier stage in his Livingstonia career. Senior missionaries, especially Elmslie and MacAlpine, had helped him in this task: he was also stimulated by the dictionary of Mang'anja compiled by David Clement Scott of the Blantyre Mission. This was much more that a dictionary in its first edition, and contained many perceptive observations about customs. Wartime experience with troops who spoke various Bantu languages helped to broaden his linguistic interests.[72] Another influence upon Young was Madan's work *Living Speech*.[73] This work stressed the importance of verbs in Bantu languages; it also urged that Bantu languages be seen in their own terms rather than through Western eyes. In his exposition of Tumbuka grammar, Young followed an approach which avoided the over-use of Western categories. He stressed the amateurish and tentative nature of his work, but his lack of too many preconceptions could have stood to his advantage here. He did, however, reiterate some of his prejudices about 'laziness'. Commenting on the fact that some verbs had contracted forms, he referred to 'the African, with his usual dislike of any unnecessary work, discarding the initial syllable'.[74] His exposition showed a sensitivity to dialectal variation, and he constantly checked and rechecked information.[75] He also showed interest in proverbs and folk tales (the latter field of investigation having also been one of Donald Fraser's interests).

Cullen Young's most influential work was on Tumbuka history. This interest had been awakened in his earlier years at Livingstonia, when he had noted the historical roots of the differential response by Tumbuka-Henga and Ngonde pupils, at the school in Karonga. And while he taught at the Overtoun Institute, he found numerous articulate informants. These were anything but impartial, since the legitimacy of claims to chieftainship had become highly controversial after the establishment of the British Protectorate.[76] The Ngoni conquest had eclipsed the importance of traditional Tumbuka authorities, and initially Ngoni chiefs had had remarkable autonomy within the framework of British rule. But Ngoni privilege was beginning to wane by wartime, and in the post-war situation many educated Tumbuka began to defend the claims of Chikulamayembe, the Tumbuka chieftainship. Cullen Young was teaching John Gondwe, son of the Chikulamayembe, when working on his historical study, and was influenced by the claims that he pressed. These seemed to confirm the standpoint of an earlier spokesman on this subject. It has already been noted that in 1909 Young was chosen to be the recipient of an anonymous contribution to Tumbuka history.[77] The author of this later turned out to be Saulos Nyirenda, a former teacher who had become a telegraphist. Nyirenda had moved south to Zomba for his work and, feeling homesick, had written a history of the Tumbuka on blue forms used by the Telegraph Company. Nyirenda was concerned to press the claims of the Tumbuka against the Ngoni, and especially those of the Chikulamayembe-ship. Thus when in 1923 Young committed to writing his first thoughts on historical matters, they provoked much discussion and unwittingly provided support for the Chikulamayembe cause.

As yet, Cullen Young had written little on Tumbuka custom, though some of his earlier thoughts were being published. Livingstonia had long encouraged investigation of this topic. A further contribution had come from Meredith Sanderson, a medical practitioner who initially worked in the north. Young's interests were mainly in Sanderson's historical comments.[78] He also tended for a long time to be sceptical about local wisdom, but an incident in 1924 was to change his mind. A rainmaker had warned him of an impending storm, but Young dismissed his prediction as nonsense. The storm came and many of Young's cattle were killed as a consequence. He respected the rainmaker after this event.[79]

One topic which recurs in Young's writings is the question of the difference between old and young. His strict upbringing had inclined him towards a respect for the wisdom of elders, and this attitude was transposed by him to the African situation. He observed that, though the old were deeply embedded in pagan beliefs and practices, the quality of their response to Christianity was encouraging. He mentioned that groping Christianity made quite an impression on the old people, whereas for many of the young even advanced Christian knowledge seemed to make little difference.[80] A corollary of that was his unease about the impact of modernising forces, and about the uncertain future heralded by the perspectives of younger Africans.

Personal factors again intervened in Young's missionary career. Jessie Young duly returned to Africa in September 1921, but she had left the children behind in Cunningham House. The long separation from the children began to take its toll on her mental health. But furlough was due in 1925, and the Youngs sailed at the beginning of October in that year. After arrival in early November, Cullen Young made contact with the Religious Tract Society (RTS), and there a proposal was discussed which would accord with Young's interests while at the same time ensuring that the family could be kept together. The idea was that he would take extended furlough, during which he would serve as joint secretary for Scotland with the Revd John Knox. A particular concern in this appointment would be advocacy of the cause of vernacular literature.[81] This cause was very dear to Cullen Young's heart. He had always found an attractive feature of village life to be the 'talking-place', which was set apart for discussion of village affairs of all kinds.[82] This functioned effectively in the village setting, but especially with the impact of labour migration some were destined for wider experiences. Young saw that vernacular literature, whether of religious or wider interest, could be a useful alternative to the talking-place; and in any case he saw it as important to provide the newly-literate with something to read.

Young proposed to take extended furlough till the end of March 1929. This was to be financed by the RTS, but he needed permission from the United Free Church authorities to remain in Britain for an extended period. Permission was duly granted, though there was a misunderstanding with the Livingstonia Committee, who did not see his RTS work as a logical extension of mission work, in the way which Young conceived of it.[83] Young began as intended, but for reasons that are not apparent from the records, he resigned from his RTS work early, in December 1927, and immediately rejoined the Livingstonia staff. In February 1928 the Youngs sailed again for Malawi.

An extended presence in Britain did enable Cullen Young to attend an international conference of Protestant missionaries, on the subject of 'The Christian Mission in Africa'; this was held at Le Zoute (Het Zoute) in Belgium, in 1926. This, incidentally, was apparently his only visit to the European continent. He was accompanied by his wife; his brother William had also hoped to attend but was indisposed. The Le Zoute conference was a more ambitious event than a previous Protestant missionary conference that had been held at High Leigh, in England, in 1924. At this Lord Lugard, the exponent of 'Indirect Rule', had been present, also the missionary-anthropologist Edwin Smith. Concern had been expressed at High Leigh as to the danger of cutting off the African from his past. At the same conference, the value of linguistic and anthropological research was emphasised. The Le Zoute conference continued these themes, and placed them on a firmer footing. Donald Fraser of Livingstonia was chairman of this gathering. The conference urged that a much more positive attitude to African customs be taken in future. Though polygamy was strictly condemned, many customs were seen as not necessarily incompatible with Christianity. Both anthropological research and vernacular literature were supported by the conference, and it was also urged that missionaries be thoroughly conversant with the vernacular. Educational philosophies stressing 'adaptation' to local conditions were also advocated. The theme of fulfilment rather than destruction was approved of by the majority of the delegates.[84] Cullen Young is not recorded as having made any distinctive contribution to the discussions, though he was clearly in accord with many of the views expressed.

In 1927, before returning to Africa, Young published an article entitled 'The New African', in the Scottish mission periodical *Other Lands*.[85] Here he articulated many of the ideas that he was now beginning to formulate more clearly, about mission policy and the broader social context of the mission. He stressed that Africans were much more able than Europeans had originally thought; that the Gospel could be seen as fulfilment; and that the mission had many unintended consequences. He noted that Laws's attempts to meet Cecil Rhodes's needs had led to the growth of a significant white-collar class among mission converts, and that there was no justification for refusal of genuine partnership between the races. He also commented upon the responsiveness of Africans to Christianity. He remarked that the African 'is really not so much a convert from heathenism as a man upon whose waiting and groping grace the Messiah has at last come. He is a proof of the universal application of Jesus' own words: I have come not to destroy, but to fulfil'.[86]

He noted with approval the manner of Africans' response to Christianity; Europeans did not share their openness, and he reiterated the point that there should be nothing of Western ways to stand between the African and the message of Jesus. He stressed the fact that Africans were perfectly at home in thinking that human life was in direct control from outside. This appears to have been something to which Cullen Young also responded enthusiastically; while he fully favoured a scientific outlook, this was not to exclude the awareness of 'other' forces in the world. In 'The New African', Cullen Young pointed out that the Bible was particularly influential in Africa, since many families had no other book. But he urged that this situation should change with the growth of literacy. He thus strongly supported the cause of literary production for and by Africans. He also urged the importance of training missionaries in anthropology.

The Youngs sailed for Livingstonia on 24 February 1928. Completing their journey by train from Beira, they met J.H. Oldham, secretary of the International Missionary Council. He and his wife were travelling in the opposite direction on a train which crossed the one from Beira at Chiromo. The Youngs' ultimate destination was again Loudon. Cullen Young now began to take a serious interest in anthropology, having joined the Royal Anthropological Institute as a Fellow in 1928. Young was not alone among missionaries in taking anthropology seriously. The Le Zoute meeting had encouraged this; moreover the International African Institute, which Oldham had played a leading part in founding, had further stimulated anthropological interests among missionaries. One consequence was an increasing tendency for missionaries to publish their work in secular journals to be assessed by secular criteria.

Young continued to develop his interest in customs; and he was able to further the cause of vernacular literature. At this point he was doing work very much to his liking, but personal circumstances were soon to bring it to an abrupt end. The problem lay again with the enforced separation from the children, a matter which was causing further psychiatric problems for Jessie Young. This led Cullen Young to resign from the mission: this decision was accepted in Edinburgh with understanding but with deep regret. In Malawi too, regret was expressed in various quarters: the Northern Province Annual Report was one such place. On the Legislative Council the Governor, Sir Shenton Thomas, paid tribute to Cullen Young. He was praised for his educational zeal, his linguistic ability, and his genial personality when dealing with both Africans and Europeans.[87] It thus appears that by diplomacy and personal charm, Young had succeeded in enjoying good relations with both the colonial administration and with the Tumbuka themselves. The Youngs left Loudon on 14 April 1931, arriving in Southampton on 28 May. They were never to return to Africa.

Cullen Young was by now becoming prolific as a writer. In 1931 he published an article on Tumbuka proverbs; and also his book, *Notes on Customs and Folklore of the Tumbuka-Kamanga*.[88] For many years ahead his output was now to be considerable. But he was still only 50, and required regular gainful employment. His interest in religious publishing stood him in good stead, and even before leaving Malawi it seems that he anticipated securing employment in this area.[89] His qualifications as an accountant also enabled him to tackle the business side of publishing with confidence. On 31 May 1931, just three days after his return to Britain, he was one of the speakers at the annual Missionary Breakfast of the RTS. He was interviewed for a post in that organisation shortly afterwards.[90] Although he would have preferred to be based in Scotland, his wife in particular having a higher regard for Scottish education, he eventually agreed to reside in London so as to work for the RTS central headquarters. His work was to be concerned with propaganda, collection of funds, and superintendence of district secretaries: particularly appropriately, he was to deal with the supply of literature to Africa and with administration of the Africa Fund. He was appointed with effect from 23 July, 1931, at a salary of £600 per annum. There was some debate initially as to the appropriate title for his post, but the designation

'Deputy Secretary and Home Superintendent' was eventually agreed upon.[91]

Till now Cullen Young had lived in a remote place for most of his adult life. He valued his colleagues, both European and African, at the mission; but in such a situation contacts with the world of science were obviously limited. London stood in sharp contrast to this, and Young profited from the chance to make contact with scholars, especially those interested in Africa. He became a frequent visitor to the London School of Oriental and African Studies, and discussed linguistic and other matters of common interest with the staff. He participated in the activities of the Royal Anthropological Institute, the Royal Empire (now Commonwealth) Society, and the Royal African Society. His special interests seem to have been social anthropology, and the politics of Empire in Africa. He was now in tune with many aspects of contemporary thought which had hardly penetrated into the African situation. His religious orientation was now to be challenged, not as previously by pagan belief, but rather by secular humanism. He seems to have managed this situation without too much difficulty as far as religious matters were concerned: he still remained secure in the belief that there were mysterious forces at work in the world, which were not reducible to scientific propositions. In any case, the world of African Studies was not exclusively secularistic, and included other retired missionaries too. Rather more difficult for Young to absorb were certain new intellectual trends. Freud, for instance, disgusted him; he saw the problems raised by Freud as things to be overcome by 'sublimation' (a favourite word of his). He had always been very open and responsive to new and possibly subversive ideas *in an African context*, but this did not extend to certain trends in Western thought. He was diplomatic in handling delicate situations, and this extended to his intellectual output. He preferred to avoid mentioning matters which would prove deeply divisive. In religious matters, some compromise was becoming possible through the functionalist approach. According to this perspective Christianity could be seen as better adjusted to modern Africa than pagan religion, since the latter tended to assume limited geographical horizons.

By 1932, Young's main intellectual output on the Tumbuka had been achieved. In the previous year, as already noted, his work on customs had been published. His work on speech and history was now expanded into two volumes, both of them fully revised. The historical work took account of the response among the Tumbuka to its first edition. One noteworthy feature of the discussion of customs was his aim to defend the work of the traditional doctor (*ng'anga*). Most Livingstonia missionaries (though not Livingstone himself) had been particularly hostile to this functionary, who offended religious susceptibilities by being a pagan, and scientific susceptibilities by being a quack - and who could also be a competitor with the mission hospital. Young showed rather that the *ng'anga's* activities were concerned with safety, such as preserving a new village from evils.

Young extended his interests beyond the Tumbuka, to examine more generally the nature of 'Africanity'. He stressed the importance of the communal bond, and was particularly attracted by the notion of the 'good village'. One article which he contributed to *Africa* for 1934 was exclusively devoted to this theme.[93] He defined the 'good village' in the words of a Tumbuka informant: A good village is where the headman and the elders are respected by all: and where they too have regard for all, even for the children. It is a good village where the young respect parents and where no one tries to harm another. If there is even one person who belittles another person or works harm, then the village is spoiled.[94]

This was a theme to which Young constantly returned; the expression 'good village' was important to him and also influential among other missionaries. He constantly stressed the idea that there were moral values regulating behaviour in African village life, and he opposed those who saw there mere 'savagery'. He did however see traditional values as destined to belong to a new unity which was to incorporate elements of Western influence. He was particularly critical of anything that could impair such a growth. Accordingly he was opposed to the proposal to 'christianise' traditional rites such as initiations, which in the Malawian context had become popular among Dutch Reformed missionaries. He spoke on this theme at the International Congress of Anthropological and Ethnological Sciences in London in 1934, and the text appeared in *Africa* for 1935. His particular objection was that European members of missions would not go through such rites, and thus the inevitable consequence would be the segregation that he deplored.[95] He opposed any practice which would deny comradeship, so central to African existence, and he advocated joint progress based on mutually contributing cultures.

A major part of Young's work with the RTS was the business of vernacular publishing. This happened to be particularly strongly supported in Malawi by the Dutch Reformed missionaries, with whom Young disagreed on some other important questions. A convert of the Dutch Reformed Mission, Samuel Y. Ntara, won the prize for a Chichewa publication, offered by the International African Institute in 1932. Young translated the Chichewa text into English in 1934, with the title *Man of Africa.*[96]

While he was working for the RTS, Young initially stayed in a boarding-house in Bloomsbury. He eventually found a permanent abode at 26 Belsize Park Gardens, where his daughter Margot joined him till 1939. His son John had by now qualified as a medical doctor, and he set up practice in Midlothian. During his long service with the RTS, Cullen Young attended committee meetings regularly, though no distinctive contribution has been recorded except when African business was being discussed. He also became a regular attender at the Church of Scotland in Pont Street. In 1933 the Kirk Session decided to ordain a number of new elders, and Cullen Young was one of them. He was not particularly active in the Eldership, as he was often away on RTS business: and in the church as a whole he seems to have kept a low profile. He did however give a talk to its literary society in 1935, on the subject of 'Fragments of History'.[97] It was during this period, also, that he took an interest in the Society of Friends. He still retained his ministry in the Church of Scotland, but his religious orientation was now such that he became attracted to a broader form of religiosity. He found Quakerism very appropriate; it made few doctrinal demands, but fostered the awareness of spiritual forces, in a way that Young found significant. He might also have seen Quakerism as being opposed to the double standards that he had found in the practice of the missions, especially regarding racial segregation. In a review of a book edited by Isaac Schapera, *Western Civilization and the Natives of South Africa*, he noted with approval a criticism voiced there of failure to live out Christianity in everyday contacts.[98]

Various other matters relating to Africa continued to attract Young's attention. He was critical of certain aspects of colonial policy, especially with regard to taxation and labour migration. He was actively involved in schemes to promote book centres in the Zambian Copperbelt. It was in this context, particularly, that he articulated his ecumenical concerns. He was strongly opposed to divisions between the churches in any case, but especially so in the mission field. He was concerned about the fact that there were different organisations in Britain for the supply of religious literature: not only the RTS, but also the Christian Literature Society for India and Africa, and the Christian Literature Society for China. He engaged in much negotiation behind the scenes to ensure the ultimate amalgamation of these bodies, which duly took place in 1935. The new organisation became known as the United Society for Christian Literature (USCL).[99]

He continued to publish extensively in the thirties. He did various book reviews for *Man* and the *International Review of Missions*. He constantly stressed the high level of African thought, and saw it as having something to teach Western civilisation. He also urged the advancement of educated Africans, and noted that one consequence of Indirect Rule was their likely exclusion. He now felt sufficiently experienced to be able to articulate a broad vision of 'Africanity', and he devoted two major works to this theme. These were *African Ways and Wisdom*, based on a course given at a Church Missionary Society training school, and appearing in 1937; and *Contemporary Ancestors*,[100] which appeared in 1940. Much of the ground covered is similar to that appearing in *Notes on Customs and Folklore of the Tumbuka-Kamanga Peoples*, but his work does reflect wider reading, also his experience of matrilineal/patrilineal differences at Loudon. His work was directed at administrators as well as at missionaries. Young never expressed opposition to colonialism as such, but he was critical of many of its aspects. His interests were reflected in a collaborative work written with Frank Melland, a British administrator who had retired in 1927. Melland was a devout Christian, and was also interested in anthropology, especially its insights into the phenomenon of witchcraft. He produced a full-length study, *In Witchbound Africa*, in 1923, based on his experiences among the Kaonde of Zambia. The collaborative work by Young and Melland was the collection of essays entitled *An African Dilemma*, dealing with various aspects of colonial and missionary policy; it appeared in 1931.[101]

Cullen Young also developed his theological reflections. He had long considered it appropriate to play down the importance of the Old Testament, when working in the African situation. He saw this as belonging to a non-African past, and felt that it would be better to look for elements in the past of African societies which had anticipated the Messiah. He was also aware of a dampening down of conflict between science and religion, in contrast to the time when he had studied theology in Edinburgh. Already in *Contemporary Ancestors* he had analysed parts of Genesis and had suggested parallels to them in different myths of origin. He continued this theme in 1941 with the publication of the small volume *The Genesis Mosaic*.[102] He was stimulated to produce this work by a debate in a certain friendly society as to whether the expression 'our legendary mother Eve' would be appropriate. Not wishing for unnecessary confrontation between science and religion, he thought that light could be thrown on the matter by comparative study. He also saw the younger churches as having a freer mind, and as not being rooted in old mission techniques.

In 1939 a new event, of crucial importance, was to take place in Young's life. He was in Scotland on business, and happened to meet an African outside Edinburgh University. They got into conversation, and Young was interested to discover that he was a Chewa from Malawi. His name, it transpired, was Hastings Kamuzu Banda; he was the boy whom Young had debarred from further participation in an examination, in 1915. Banda had none the less succeeded in obtaining an education up to university level, and he was now at Edinburgh so as to obtain the licentiates which would qualify him for practice as a physician in the British Empire. Young had totally forgotten Banda and the incident concerned: Banda clearly remembered Young, but did not reveal his own identity till a few years later. After the reacquaintance, although living in different towns, Banda and Young frequently consulted about matters of Chichewa translation. Discussion of language led to discussion of broader issues of custom, and the collaboration culminated in the production in 1946 of the collection *Our African Way of Life*. This consisted of three short stories translated from Chichewa; Banda and Young wrote a short introduction, explaining the story of the examination room and the subsequent reacquaintance. Here Young commits to print the expression 'by what we call chance', referring to the occasion of their renewed acquaintance in Edinburgh.[104] This was one of Young's favourite phrases, reflecting his belief that there were 'other' forces at work in the world, which cannot be traced scientifically. The joint introduction develops the theme that European ways are not necessarily better than those of Africa, and are sometimes worse.

The relationship with Banda will be considered further in Chapter V. It is worthy of note at this point, however, that they both shared a dislike of proposals to establish a white-dominated Federation in Central Africa. Young was able to draw a comparison between Nazism and racist imperialism, and this topical subject was developed in his booklet *Herrenvolk and Sahib-Log*.[105]

Wartime events were to have a significant impact on the work of the USCL. Evacuation to Horley took place in 1939. In 1941 the London offices were heavily bombed and most records were destroyed. Young himself was promoted in 1940 to the position of General Secretary. The staff were depleted through military service, but Young was at 61 obviously too old for any more activities in that direction. He had further success in his effort to unify organisation. He enabled both the London and the Scottish committees of the Christian Literature Society for China to combine with the USCL by 1942. He then saw the Society through the war years, but eventually he expressed the wish to retire. He gave 'family reasons' when he presented his proposal to the Committee in 1945. His wife had continued to suffer from increasingly serious symptoms of arteriosclerosis which had been building up for many years; and Young needed more time to devote to her. But in any case, he was to reach his 65th birthday in October 1945, and normal retirement thus became possible. He finally left the service of the USCL in March 1946.

Cullen Young was a long-standing, senior, and dedicated employee, and his retirement was commemorated accordingly. On 26 March 1946, a function in the USCL office was held, attended by its President, Lord Luke. In the tributes paid to Young, his work for Africa was one contribution particularly singled out for attention. The office meeting was followed by lunch at Derry and Tom's Restaurant, in Knightsbridge. A silver fruit bowl was presented to him, inscribed with the words 'Guide, Philosopher and Friend', while Jessie Young was presented with a handbag and a bouquet. Appreciation was expressed of his work for the society during the war, and for his vision, wisdom, and steadiness; his wider mission interest was also praised, especially in relation to African authorship and other African affairs.[106] Cullen Young replied with humour and modesty, describing his work for the USCL as 'fifteen years of undetected crime'.

Cullen Young had resided in London purely for his work. He was proud to be a Scot, and had the habit of making 'pawky' remarks about the English. He naturally took the opportunity to return to his native country on retirement. He settled in Midcalder, near where his son was working as a general practitioner, but then moved to Edinburgh. He did not totally relinquish his interest in publishing, and he was paid a retainer for some continued editorial assistance for the USCL. He was immediately appointed to the Central Committee of the USCL for Scotland. His wife's health problems prevented him from attending frequently, though he often apologised for absence: it was 1949 before he first put in an appearance at the committee. At one point he considered the possibility of returning to Malawi; he had a strong longing to go there, and his wife might have been helped by their return. But in the end nothing came of this plan.

Young's interesting life attracted the notice of an academic anthropologist. Dr Ralph Piddington, of Edinburgh University, had long sought a rapprochement between missionaries and anthropologists, and he had already had occasion to praise Young's insights into African wisdom.[107] He therefore decided to propose Young for the honorary degree of M.A. This proposal, supported by the Dean of Divinity, was accepted by the University authorities, and the degree was conferred in 1950.

Though latterly Young had been paying more attention to Chewa language and culture, he continued to interest himself in Tumbuka. A major task for him in the last few years of his life was the preparation of the Tumbuka translation of the Old Testament. His domestic affairs were however becoming increasingly problematic. Jessie Young continued to suffer from arteriosclerosis, and her mental health was such that she could be incoherent and at times even violent. John Young (Cullen's brother) was a near neighbour in Edinburgh, and his wife was a psychiatrist. They all eventually agreed that Jessie Young should be admitted to a mental hospital, and there she remained till her death in March 1954. Cullen Young too was by now beginning to have serious health problems, and when his wife was admitted to hospital he agreed to go to the Church of Scotland Eventide Home in Gargunnock, Stirling. He continued to concern himself with translation and writing. He became somewhat reflective about the past, and published two articles about his wartime experiences. One was about the last elephant that he shot, and the other dealt with the 'Battle of Karonga', at the beginning of the war[108] He also reiterated his thoughts as to the relationship between old and new in Africa, in almost identical terms to those used in his 1927 article 'The New African'. He wrote of colleagueship between European and African staff, noting that this had now been achieved but that unfortunately in the past such an aim had not been pursued with any great urgency. He wrote of the death of two mission employees, Edward Bote Manda and Yuraya Chatonde Chirwa, who had both been able to remember Livingstone. He recollected with approval the remark of an old headman, who had commented that missionaries *complete* what the old folk taught.[109] The notion of the Christian message of completion was important to Young, as it expressed his belief in fulfilment rather than destruction.

After his removal to Gargunnock, Young began to fade away from the publishing scene. He attended the Central Committee of the Scottish USCL only twice between 1951 and 1954. He gradually succumbed to cancer of the pancreas, and evidently saw the end approaching. He donated many of his books to the Nyasaland Society Library (Blantyre).[110] His existence in Gargunnock was rather lonely; he sometimes remembered the names of his old Malawian servants and tried to call them. He took to the habit of going on long country walks and claimed that on one occasion, when he began to suffer pain, Jesus Christ had walked beside him and he had felt comforted. On 30 September 1954 he left Gargunnock, and went first to Edinburgh, then to nearby Kirknewton, to the home of his son John. There he remained till his death on 14 June 1955; a few days before then he had been looking forward to helping with missionary training in Edinburgh.

He was shortly afterwards cremated without formality, a common practice in the Young family. He death was however widely reported, and there were numerous tributes paid to his missionary work, his writings, and his interest in publishing. On the Scottish USCL committee, his concern for the inward sources of religion rather than forms and titles was noted.[111] *Life and Work*, the Church of Scotland monthly periodical, praised his concern for publishing, and for laymen's witness, and also noted his self-sacrifice for his wife in his latter years.[112] A collection was immediately begun for a permanent memorial. Young had maintained a continued interest in book centres on the Copperbelt. A new bookshop in the chain was just being opened up at Kitwe, and it was agreed that the memorial should be situated there. It was decided that the most suitable memorial would be a reading room to be used by all races. A collection of £2000 was called for, to cover the cost of furnishing the room, and of providing a memorial plaque. Most of the money was collected in Scotland, but some was received through St Columba's Church, Pont Street.[113] The plaque was dedicated at a memorial service at Broughton Street Church on 26 November 1956. The inscription was as follows:

TO THE GLORY OF GOD
AND IN HONOUR AND LOVING MEMORY OF
THOMAS CULLEN YOUNG, C.A., Hon. M.A. Edinburgh
Missionary, Author, Organizer
Who died 14th June 1955
Having served for 25 years in Nyasaland and
in many capacities in Scotland and London as
General Secretary of the United Society for
Christian Literature

"He was worthy ... for he loveth our nation" (Luke 7: 4-5).

The plaque was shipped to Kitwe, and was installed at a service on 27 August 1957.[115]

Cullen Young's son John died in 1981 and was not therefore able to contribute material for his father's biography (though *his* son, Robert, has contributed photographs). Cullen Young's daughter, Margot Moffett, resides in Dehra Dun, India, and has provided a wealth of personal detail for this account.[116]

II

The Anthropological Contribution

Cullen Young had no effective preparation for anthropological research in the field. Professional anthropology had not been developed (in the way that it is now practised) at the time of his departure from Scotland: and in any case, the use of anthropology by missionaries was a much later development (albeit one which Young was to advocate). However, he was not devoid of some kind of appropriate orientation. Livingstone's works were familiar to him, and Elmslie's book on the Ngoni was available. He took note of the advice given to him before departure; he showed patience, and learnt the language to a high standard. His initial excursions beyond the linguistic field were more historical than directly anthropological; he displayed an interest in oral history, and examined the historical roots of varying reaction to the mission. But both history and linguistics contain sociological dimensions, and the customs of the Tumbuka and neighbouring peoples became an absorbing interest for Young. He was soon able to hold his ethnocentric prejudices in check; he learnt quickly how to sit back unobtrusively, and he became intrigued with local activities. Certain practices, such as the destruction of a child whose mother had died, and those concerning treatment of twins, were things that he clearly wished to change; but first he saw it as important to understand their social roots.

Young was not the first missionary to show a serious ethnographic interest in the Tumbuka and their neighbours, though he was more systematic in his presentation of findings than were his predecessors.[1] The earliest missionaries in the north of Malawi had been aware of ethnic diversity, since the Ngoni had migrated northwards and had made many Tonga and Tumbuka their subjects. Consequently the mission had found itself in the difficult position of preaching to both sides in a situation of conflict. African customs became topics of discussion at mission conferences. Elmslie was the first missionary to write a major book-length work about the people in the Livingstonia mission area. He was a medical doctor, and was ordained in 1897. His work *Among the Wild Ngoni* appeared in 1899.[2] This contains some ethnographic information, but is mostly concerned with the message of promoting the victory of Christianity over barbarism. Lord Overtoun's introduction is particularly sensational, but Elmslie too is highly critical. He admits that he was concentrating on the study of customs which hindered missionary work, and that not all Ngoni customs were bad. Indeed, he goes on to suggest that it was necessary to study the soil into which the seeds of Christianity were being cast. Even some of the customs which hindered missionary work were not reported by Elmslie, since he regarded them as 'too disgusting to be described'. He was particularly concerned to attack 'laziness', and above all, begging. Like many other medically-qualified missionaries, he singled out for condemnation the work of the traditional medical practitioner (the *ng'anga*). None the less, he admitted that such practitioners were shrewd and thoughtful.

Other aspects of Ngoni life were seen by Elmslie in more neutral or in favourable terms. He was relieved to note that the Ngoni believed in God, thus seeing no insurmountable barrier to communication of spiritual truths. The Ngoni also fully recognised the existence of a spiritual world, and the missionary task was therefore to promote a correct understanding of its character. The Ngoni were viewed more favourably than the Tonga and the Tumbuka; some Ngoni values, and their practice of authoritarian rule, accorded more with Western susceptibilities. On the other hand, the Ngoni were less responsive to the mission than were their subjects, who saw the mission as a welcome source of protection. Elmslie's work is informative in places, but is marred by sensationalism. He clearly experienced a culture-shock as a consequence of the contrast between Ngoni values and those of Victorian Scotland; but it was exaggerated for the benefit of the likely readership, who if shocked about what they had read would hopefully be more likely to give support to the work of the mission. A further limitation of the value of Elmslie's study was that much of his work was about activities of the missionaries themselves, rather than about the Ngoni.

Another contributor to the study of the local culture was Fraser, mentioned in Chapter I: he and Young were colleagues at Loudon between 1910 and 1912. Donald Fraser (1870-1933) had joined the mission in 1897. He was initially shocked by the 'obscenity' of certain dances (Elmslie quoted him with approval on this point), and this attitude persisted in many ways. None the less he was of Highland origin, interested in Celtic prehistory, and this enabled him to feel a certain amount of affinity with the local culture. Elmslie, by contrast, had at times viewed Highland and Ngoni beliefs with equal contempt. Fraser encouraged the use of traditional Ngoni tunes for church music; he was interested in history and folk tales, and in traditional medicine. He tried to discourage the practice of the latter, though admitted that some such medicine was effective. Like Elmslie, Fraser admired the Ngoni conquerors rather than their subjects. Yet, while his writings were extensive, there was remarkably little of anthropological interest: 'true adventure stories' dealing with the activities of missionaries in the bush predominated, and there was little systematic documentation. In any case, Fraser did not begin to publish his chief works till Young was already settled at Livingstonia; but as a colleague he will have exercised an important influence.

More objective investigation was carried out by the Revd Alexander Gillon MacAlpine, who arrived at Livingstonia in 1893, and who immediately set about the task of familiarising himself with village life before beginning serious missionary work. He produced some ethnographic material in article form, in the Livingstonia periodical *The Aurora*, the series beginning in 1905. The articles concerned were remarkably devoid of sensationalism, and could be seen as the first really systematic study of the culture and the region. Particular attention was paid by MacAlpine to religious beliefs of the Tonga, and he provided a full account of mortuary rituals. This material was appearing at the time when Cullen Young was beginning to settle at Livingstonia, and would almost certainly have stimulated his interest in serious ethnography.

Cullen Young's Tumbuka informants must early have realised that

he would lend a responsive ear to their view of the past and their
preoccupations of the present. As already noted, in 1909 Saulos
Nyirenda had chosen Young as the trusted recipient of his account of
Tumbuka history. Young later refers to an account by a different
author, entitled 'Habits and Customs of the Olden Days among the
Tumbuka-Kamanga People'; this was published by Young in 1936,
but it is not clear when it was written. Young's contribution to the
Livingstonia News for 1912 on the Chewa *Uzamba* ceremony shows
that he was by then sufficiently confident to put his observations on
record. He had stumbled on this event by chance, while on duties
concerning the school. The ceremony was for a girl, and consisted of
a combination of coming-of-age and marriage. Young felt that a
record of the event was important since such customs were fast
disappearing. One part of the ceremony involved the bridegroom. He
was required to shoot an arrow into a tree stump, this being a token of
what would befall anyone who might interfere with his wife. Young
felt that it would be useful to pursue possible parallels with Western
marriage customs.

Young paid little further direct attention to *Chewa* ethnography,
though his position at the border between Chewa and Tumbuka
territory kept him constantly aware of differences and similarities
between the two peoples. For the moment, his main concern was with
the Tumbuka. He particularly respected the old ways, and clearly
found old people easier to deal with than the young. Eventually he
corrected this bias, and became open to the needs of change as well as
tradition. Indicative of his concern with Tumbuka values were his
studies of proverbs and folk tales. This interest was shared by others.
As already noted, Donald Fraser had looked into this topic; but there
were also some more systematic students, who published their
findings. One was Dr Meredith Sanderson, who arrived in 1910 in
Malawi. Sanderson eventually became an authority on the Yao
language,[3] but his earlier work was in northern Malawi. He served
there as a government medical officer. He was a careful observer, and
published some ethnographic material: eventually he specialised in
tropical hygiene. Another student of proverbs and tales was the Revd
Matthew Faulds. Faulds had initially been suspicious of the idea of
missionary work, and even after he took a different view he was never
a typical missionary. He was one of the few who stayed in villages, in
traditional housing, and his impact by doing this was considerable.[4]

Faulds collected extensive material on proverbs from Karonga, and made it available to Young.[5] Finally, William Paulin Young arrived in 1912; he was less close to the people than his brother, but he concerned himself with folk-tales; he published some of the material that he had collected, though on a much smaller scale than Cullen Young.[6]

Jessie Young also showed an interest in aspects of Tumbuka culture, and concerned herself particularly with women's activities. She frequently used to admire the beads that the women wore; she was then often given them as a present, and this eventually led to a large collection. She donated the collection to museums in London and Edinburgh after her return to Britain. Her own published writings appeared earlier than her husband's, though they never got beyond the 'travellers' tales' variety.[7]

Educated converts of the mission grew in numbers, and became an important source of information regarding beliefs and customs. It was in this capacity that Levi Mumba wrote on 'the Religion of my Fathers', and Young sponsored the appearance of this material in the *International Review of Missions*, for 1930.[8] Mumba was concerned to draw attention to the hierarchy that existed both in the natural and in the spiritual world, in Tumbuka traditional religion. He showed that appeal to the spirits went through the family head; and that the ancestral spirits were able to mediate with God. God, however, showed himself only in *general* manifestations of disapproval, such as pestilence. The spirits were concerned more directly with guardianship of the living, but this concern could be suspended if relations among the living were not kept in accordance with tradition. But with repentance and sacrifice, guardianship would be resumed. Mumba showed how the Tumbuka carried on a constant communication between the dead and the living, especially through dreams. Certain ritual experts, including the much-maligned traditional doctor, were able to deal with supernatural forces. The supernatural was all-pervading; everything was controlled, nothing happened by chance, and every happening had a purpose to fulfil. Taboos existed, whose purpose it was to refine and maintain social development. Mumba expressed his own view that it was desirable to follow traditional beliefs for as long as the new religion had not been assimilated. Young expressed some concern with Mumba's account, seeing it as indicative of the fact that Christianity could be taught

while not being fully absorbed. He also observed that Mumba had
failed to recognise any vitally unique feature in Christ. But Young
was influenced positively by Mumba's comments on clan solidarity,
the pervasiveness of the supernatural, and the relationship between
the living and the dead. Young was subsequently to express strong
and repeated criticism of the view that there was such a thing as
'ancestor worship'.[9] He preferred to speak rather of a conclave
between the living and the dead. On the question of the supernatural,
Young had already expressed the view that Africans were less self-
conscious in acknowledging publicly the existence of such a sphere;
and that Western reticence on the subject should not be allowed to
spill over into the mission field.

It has been noted that Young had displayed a special interest in the
establishment and subsequent expansion of the Chikulamayembe
dynasty. It was in connection with this that he made excursions into
the slowly-growing field of scientific anthropology, which was at the
time 'general' rather than 'social'. In the grave associated with
Chikulamayembe Young had, with the help of a British army captain,
discovered a number of iron 'tridents' of uncertain origin. He had
become a Fellow of the Royal Anthropological Institute in 1928, and
in 1929 he wrote a note on the subject of his discovery to its
periodical *Man*.[10] A correspondence developed on this subject
though nothing conclusive emerged.

It was after his return to Britain in 1931 that Young began to
publish his major contributions to the anthropology of the Tumbuka.
Most of this appeared quite rapidly, and the bulk of his later
contributions were concerned with the general question of 'African
customs' (albeit with a heavy debt to Tumbuka materials). In 1931
Young contributed to *Africa* an article on Tumbuka proverbs. In the
same year, published in Livingstonia, appeared his *Notes of the
Customs and Folklore of the Tumbuka-Kamanga Peoples*; and in 1933
appeared his article 'Tribal Intermixture in Northern Nyasaland', in
the *Journal of the Royal Anthropological Institute*. This had been
presented as a Communication to the Royal Anthropological Institute
in the previous year.[11] Also in 1932, Young contributed a further
item to that Institute's *Journal* on the subject of medicine-men in
northern Nyasaland.[12] Much later, in 1950, Young contributed an
article to Edwin Smith's collection *African Ideas of God*. This dealt
with northern Malawi but was not confined to Tumbuka material.[13]

The discussion of *tribal intermixture* covers much ground which had been considered in Young's other works, particularly with regard to early historical references to the Tumbuka by travellers, and to details of intrusions into the area. This article clearly displays his sensitivity to the contrast between the Chewa and the Tumbuka, especially concerning descent and marriage. He maintains that the original condition of the Tumbuka was not unlike that of their southern neighbours, the Chewa, in that matrilineal and uxorilocal conditions had prevailed. This situation was however disturbed by incomers known as the Balowoka, who came from across the Lake, and who by virtue of their superior commercial acumen were able to dominate much Tumbuka territory by setting up a new royal dynasty, that of Chikulamayembe. Royal descent was patrilineal, and the commoners followed this example. The patrilineal setup was subsequently strengthened by the Ngoni incursion, particularly with regard to the payment of bridewealth on marriage. The general adoption of the Ngoni custom in this respect was reinforced by the first British magistrate. His previous experience was among the Zulu, and hence he was familiar with the workings of such a system. In 1908 he summoned a meeting where he explained that in future he would recognise only those marriages in which bridewealth had been paid. Young also includes in his article on tribal intermixture some details of marriage procedures, drawn from the text 'Habits and Customs of the Olden Days'. There are also some details of traditional medicine and magical and religious beliefs. Unique to this article are certain speculations about the prehistory of Malawi: not only the 'tridents', but also some cave paintings are alluded to.

The discussion of *proverbs* can also be briefly dealt with. Most of these had been collected by Faulds from Karonga. Young did however observe that nearly all of them had parallels in the southern part of Tumbuka territory, thereby appearing to come from a common stock. He noted that much of the content of the proverbs related to wisdom which was already familiar to the student of Bantu societies, but that the Tumbuka findings were useful in contributing new material. In the list, some proverbs related to animals or natural objects; others related to specific historical incidents; while others were simply aphorisms. In his discussion of the proverbs, Young noted certain linguistic peculiarities.

It remains to consider Young's major contribution to the study of custom, namely his *Notes on Customs and Folklore*. As always, Young disclaimed any specialist knowledge of a scientific kind, and saw his contribution as merely 'notes'. The text has, as will be seen, some significant biases and omissions, but it is quite devoid of 'travellers' tales'. There is almost no reference to the activities of Young himself and of fellow-missionaries, and there is at least some systematic attempt to portray various aspects of Tumbuka life. Throughout the study there is a stress upon the values and standards that permeate Tumbuka culture, the aim being to refute accusations of 'savagery' that the less well-informed commentators on African society might be inclined to make. He was aware that changes were taking place and that these would also be worthy of anthropological study; but at the same time he argued that old people in the very rural areas were only superficially changed as a consequence of recent developments. None the less, it is likely that Young's tendency to concentrate upon key informants about 'olden days' would have contributed to giving his work a certain antiquarian flavour.

The key notion in Young's exposition of Tumbuka values was that of the 'Good Village'. He showed that this ideal had to be constantly sustained, otherwise the village would be 'spoilt'. He refers to the idea of 'building a village' (*kuzenga muzi*). This referred to the goal to be aimed at in Tumbuka villages: the possession of a contented group under one's control. Sharing and open-handedness were virtues, and selfishness was a vice, in such a scheme of things. This was expressed by the proverb *ufumu nkuwoka* (chiefship is of the hand, or, more freely, give and it shall be given) - the Tumbuka version of *do ut des*, the principle of reciprocity. A corollary of the ideal of building a village was the desirability of *increase*: many children result in a large following.

To ensure the continuance of the 'good village' various safeguards were required. These included, firstly, the correct magical protection of the village by the *ng'anga*, whose concern was to invoke power against danger. Young notes that the removal of a village required various ritual safeguards, since it was a hazardous enterprise. The site had to be encircled before it could be declared satisfactory. The village headman would nominate a man and a young girl to perform this task; the man was expected to be of 'quiet heart', and the girl 'ignorant of evil'. The *ng'anga* would carry two antelope horns, one containing magical medicine, the other being used as a trumpet.

When the site was proclaimed satisfactory, all villagers and their houses would be smeared with a small amount of medicine.

If the resiting of a village was hazardous, the same was also true of key events in the life cycle. In view of the importance of 'increase', correct procedures were required for the socialisation of the child and the adolescent. Marriage, which was to result in 'increase', was a group and not an individual concern. Death, which was a passage from the world of the living to that of the ancestors, was an occasion upon which other concerns had to be halted; and the sense of obligation to attend a funeral was particularly strong.

For the Tumbuka, a child was a group possession, not just the concern of its parents. Correspondingly, all adults had their say in a child's upbringing. Certain births, such as those of twins or illegitimate children, would be ominous; they would lead to segregation and ostracism, followed by later readmission to the village. Otherwise the birth of a baby would be greeted with ululation: this was longer for a girl than for a boy, since the birth of a girl meant a greater possibility of 'increase'. After the birth, mother and baby would be secluded for a week, being in a dangerous state before performance of rituals by the midwives. After one week the baby could be brought into the sun, but the mother was still dangerous for a month after the birth. The husband would then give the midwives a present, the mother would be shaved, and the child named. There were further customary procedures with regard to teething, and if the child cut its upper teeth first, great fear was expressed. After infancy, certain restrictions were begun according to the sex of the child. A girl was not now to use her father's sleeping-mat, and a boy was not to put his hands in a cooking-pot, or to lean on the doorposts of a hut.

Cullen Young's account continues with discussion of socialisation to the time of coming of age. For boys, physical maturity was recognised at some time between fifteen and eighteen; for girls, between eleven and fourteen. He points to the separate arrangements made for boys and for girls, and notes with approval that instruction on matters that are not publicly discussed in the West is specifically provided for among the Tumbuka. Thus, after the age of eleven, a girl would go to live with other girls for the purpose of instruction; while on reaching physical maturity she would be placed in seclusion in the bush, then brought back. Special food compounded with medicine and salt would be used to secure continuance of the mature state; during seclusion, no contact with men was permitted, and instruction would be given by the older girls. Beer would be hidden in the bushes before her return; when she came back from her seclusion, the hidden beer would be sought and drunk; then an *Uzamba* dance of the kind initially observed by Young among the Chewa would follow. The time for marriage would be announced at this point; gifts would be exchanged with the prospective in-laws, and further instruction, regarding marriage, would be given by the midwives.

For a boy, the procedure would begin with the onset of puberty. The boy would report to an older unmarried boy what had happened, and this boy would tell the first boy's father. Puberty medicine would now have to be prepared and administered by the *ng'anga*, and till then the boy could neither eat salt nor speak with an elder. The boy would be given a spear, arrow or staff to throw over a hut, and it would be a good omen if it came down on its end. He would then be introduced to the marriageable lads, and an older man would be told to give instruction as to his future behaviour.

The next stage in the life-cycle would be marriage itself; Young devoted three chapters to this important institution. He showed how the various incursions into northern Malawi had brought about considerable change in the customs associated with marriage. He maintained that in the aboriginal state, the Tumbuka had practised a matrilineal system similar to that of the Chewa, for instance. He argued that certain elements of the southern Tumbuka (the upper Rukuru basin, and the hill country of the upper Kasitu and Mzimba rivers) provided evidence for this, since they had been furthest removed from the intruders and also retained certain important matrilineal features. In this area, children appeared to belong to the mother's kin-group and succeeded to the estate of the mother's brother. They also took the clan-name of the mother's kin. Evidence for this state of affairs seems to have been drawn from the text on 'Habits and Customs of the Olden Days'. Information from this source seems also to have been used for material about negotiations for marriage. The system outlined there is one in which marriage is uxorilocal. The process described would begin when either the boy or the boy's parents saw a suitable girl. The boy himself would first watch the girl's behaviour so as to see, for instance, whether she was a good worker. After obtaining the agreement of his mother, negotiations would then be placed in the hands of a messenger, a man of the boy's clan, who would then invite the elders of the girl's village to discuss the matter. If they agreed on the match, the boy would then have to keep away from the girl's village; goods would have to be offered and accepted before a right of cohabitation could be established. The boy would be expected to live with his wife's kin, and his kin-group would always expect to receive requests for payments.

Arrangements began to change with the coming of the Balowoka; in particular, marriage now became virilocal. A husband took his wife at her village, but could then carry her to his own. There were also variations in the nature and extent of gift-giving. This system continued to prevail in areas which, while clearly under the influence of the Balowoka, had not come under Ngoni domination. The areas where the Ngoni had established themselves showed a further move in a patrilineal direction: full bridewealth (lobola) was paid in the form of cattle or their equivalent. The effect of this transfer was to confirm full rights upon the husband. Young saw this development in terms of an evolution from a matrilineal system, which eventually came to prevail only on the Chewa fringes; through the Balowoka period, which marked the transfer of importance from females to males; then finally came the full *lobola* system. He attributed this change to the expansion of outside interests (the theme of expansion of horizons recurs in various parts of his work). Thus the Balowoka era meant that the male had to face the world as a trader, while in the Ngoni period he did so as a warrior; accordingly, Young argues, matriliny eventually disappeared. The magistrate whose job it was to record marriages found the *lobola* system easier to manage, as already noted. He also found that it led to less litigation, since compensation for the death of a wife by her kin was less likely in a situation where her child-bearing capacity had been transferred to the man's kin-group.

Such were Cullen Young's prime interests when describing marriage patterns. Before leaving the question of socialisation and the life cycle, however, it is appropriate to mention the importance of folk tales. These were carefully documented by Young and recorded together with the customs. Young was particularly intrigued by the fact that these were told to children at a set time of day, namely at dusk; the 'moral lesson' had a special period set aside for it. The tales emphasise the values of family bonds, obedience, and respect for the wisdom of the elders. Punishment for folly could be a lonely death, and excessive wealth was also something to be disapproved of. There were thus various anti-social actions whose effect would be to 'destroy the village'. Young noted, none the less, that moral codes were not applicable to members of other clans, and he saw Christianity as important in extending such restricted loyalties. He shared the interest in folk-tales with his brother, William.

As is the tendency with missionary-anthropologists, Young naturally paid attention to beliefs held by the Tumbuka about God and the spirit world, and also to magical practices. He noticed, in the first place, that there were numerous taboos. Children were constantly admonished to behave in accordance with these, so that by adulthood conformity had become instinctive. Young noted that such practices could breed confidence and optimism, provided that only known situations were encountered. One of his favourite themes was that Tumbuka culture possessed value but that in many cases it made sense only within the confines of a relatively small area. The taboos recorded by Young accompanied situations such as pregnancy, childbirth and the handling of children; procedures regarding maturity, betrothal and the early stages of marriage; and matters concerning sitting-places, posture and the use of domestic utensils. In some cases there were taboos relating to food. These applied for instance to abstinence from salt, which was expected of a betrothed couple directly after maturity; there were also taboos as to who could eat with whom (e.g. it was inappropriate to eat with one's parents-in-law). Summarising his findings, Young maintains that taboo was a combination of common sense and 'sympathetic magic', though he is not totally uncritical on the subject. He suggests that obedience to taboos would produce confidence, but that disregard for them would produce depression. He indicates that the sanction for disregard for taboos would be the wrath of the ancestors. He sees the ideal of the 'good village' as again at work in the development of this kind of belief and practice.

Continuing the theme of the supernatural, Young goes on to discuss the significance of omens and spells. In the case of omens, the Tumbuka saw the animal world as significant. Warning could be given, for instance, by the bark of a fox or by a snake crossing one's path. It would then be the responsibility of the village elders and the *ng'anga* to discover the danger so announced. The spirit world would be the source of certain omens. If a particular species of eagle fell to the ground for no obvious reason, this would show that the spirits needed attention, and the *ng'anga* would be called to find out why.

Spells were seen to be widely known, but Tumbuka people were reluctant to admit extensive knowledge of these, except in the case of the *ng'anga*. Medicines could be used for protective purposes, especially against theft and the related crime of adultery. Spells could be lifted only by the *ng'anga* who had cast them. A spell could be used as a way of extracting a confession, thus serving as a form of social control. Thus a *ng'anga* would threaten to cast a spell if nobody made a confession. Young noted the 'law of similarity' in operation; tubers on poles, used to protect a garden, could serve as the symbol of the swelling of the body that would occur in anyone who might attempt theft. Spells could also be used to inflict harm, though Young cites fewer examples. Thus a person with a grievance would place certain objects round his enemy's crops; a public inquiry would then be needed to see who put them there. The aggrieved party would then have the opportunity to put his case to the Council of Elders, and the food could not be used till the removal of the objects. Magic was also available to ensure safe housebreaking. Finally, Young noted that love magic was becoming increasingly popular, and that this was especially the province of the younger, educated *ng'anga*.

Young now turns to the whole question of the cosmology of the Tumbuka. He examines, among other things, beliefs concerning the celestial objects, God, and the ancestors. Again he stresses that Tumbuka beliefs reflected a limited area, a world of people bounded by the coming together of the earth and the sky. He notes, however, that this world is not a sealed chamber; rather it is believed to be surrounded by pillars, and little old folk have the responsibility of preventing woodpeckers from alighting on these; if this were to happen, the pillars would crash down and there would be eternal darkness. The sun and the moon, in Tumbuka cosmology, are lights of the sky, with a path over and under the world. An eclipse would be reacted to by the use of every noisy object that could be found. The moon is male and has two wives, one of them being meticulous over preparation of food and the other being casual. Various 'astronomical' omens were postulated; a falling star was a warning of a relative's death, while an earthquake was the sign of the impending death of a chief. A comet would be a general indication of impending destruction for mankind overall.

Young also pays attention to the Tumbuka conception of God, a matter that he was to pursue later, in more general terms, in his contribution in 1950 to the collection *African Ideas of God*, edited by Edwin Smith. In his more specific account of Tumbuka cosmology, he considers the question of the likeness or otherwise of Tumbuka and Christian notions of God: in particular, he considers whether Christianity could build upon indigenous conceptions or whether it would be necessary for the missionary to overthrow them. He notes the tendency, which is common throughout Africa, for the cult of the ancestors to be all-important, and for direct approaches to God to be rare. Only in the case of severe break with ordered routine - plague, epidemic, or unexpected drought - would there be a communal direct approach to God. Otherwise God could not be related to, and indeed seemed rather frightening; thus he 'takes' children if they die, and he is manifested in eclipse, earthquake and plague: the Tumbuka God is not seen as all-loving.

He stresses the essentially *localised* nature of traditional Tumbuka religion; this is evident even in some words for God, which relate to particular sacred sites. But the key element in Tumbuka traditional religion is the cult of the *vibanda*, the spirits of the ancestors. When people die, it is believed that they have the same position and character as they had on earth: thus some spirits are friendly while others are irascible. A spirit can return and visit its old body. Worship (a term used by Young in *Notes on Customs and Folklore* but later severely criticised by him) occurs on certain special occasions. Thus prior to a journey or a venture, the *ng'anga* uses divining instruments to indicate whether it is appropriate to proceed; if the response is favourable, then one of the spirits of the ancestors should be approached with offerings, to ensure cooperation. If a venture is successful, the spirits receive in the form of sacrifice some of the profits, spoil, or meat. Another occasion for 'worship' is when sudden danger is faced. In such a situation there is no time to secure offerings; an invocation is made, and gifts are later offered at graves if the danger is surmounted. Dreams may also be a prophetic warning, indicating displeasure by the *vibanda*, for reasons such as neglect.

Beer would then be placed on the fork of a stick, and the ancestors would be seen to have been appeased when they had taken some; all elders would be able to partake after this.

Illness can also indicate displeasure of the ancestors, and a diviner is accordingly consulted to indicate which of them is angry. When this has been discovered by asking questions, flour is laid by the grave of the ancestor concerned and apologies are proffered. If the flour has been disturbed the next morning, then the spirit has partaken; if not, further inquiries are necessary. If the ancestor actually appears in the sick patient's dream, then this is sufficient to explain the neglect and there is no need for divination by the *ng'anga*. In the case of a calamity or special community need, worship would take place by the group concerned at the grave of the greatest remembered ancestor, with appropriate offerings. Such a procedure is also followed when a headman takes over on the death of his predecessor. Worship also takes place when success has been realised, or danger delivered from. Gifts will in such cases be presented at the graves of the ancestors. When crops are ripened, the *ng'anga* is summoned; he would boil samples of each crop with medicine, and gardens could only be touched after this ceremony.

As already noted, Young's thoughts on the subject of Tumbuka religion continued to develop. In his contribution to *African Ideas of God* he notes the importance of the social structure in the formation of religious ideas; he remarks that diversity in theology may follow diversity in social structure. He continues the theme that ancestral presence and ancestral power are all-important, with only minimal reference to God occurring. He is concerned here with unravelling the area of operation of the Deity and that of other powers, commenting as follows: 'I am forced to the conclusion that our path towards appreciation of an African idea of God, so far as my own area is concerned, must lie apart from the scrub and undergrowth of charm, spell, and tabu'.[14]

He notes occasions for approach to the ancestors, not now referring to 'worship', but rather suggesting that they are symbolic sharers of a common meal; this reflects the notion of a conclave of the living and the dead which, as will be seen, is pursued further in Young's general discussions of African culture. On the matter of God, he remarks that in twenty-seven years in northern Malawi, he heard direct, spontaneous reference to God on only four occasions in circumstances that were unrelated to imported belief. These were: firstly, instinctive reaction to the unexplainable, such as a miscarriage (where the ancestors have much at stake in the continuance of the community, so 'it must be God'); secondly, condolence in the case of death of an infant or young child, where ordinary malevolence could not be in operation so the purpose must be outside man's knowledge; thirdly, in the case of hapless, non-normal people - God's concern has a wider arena than the minds of men can encompass; and fourthly, God is seen as the provider of the bark used in the poison ordeal (see p. 57), which is an occasion when God speaks to man directly.

Young's interest in names extends to the various words for God used in northern Malawi. The name *Chiuta* predominates among the Tumbuka; this refers to a rainbow, provision of rain being a special province of the deity's activities. Among the Chewa, the name *Mulungu* is the usual word; it is also used among the Tumbuka, though less frequently. This refers to creation, coming from the verb meaning 'to put together'. He notes that all these conceptions are remote from the Christian idea of God the Father. At the same time, he suggests that for Africans there is a feeling of real evidence for the power of God: existence of God is not something that needs to be demonstrated.

Returning to *Notes on Customs and Folklore*, discussion of religious ideas can be seen to lead logically to consideration of the question of burial. The work of the spirits comes to the fore here, since, if the dead person is not sent away in comfort with a friendly farewell, the spirit can return. Hence the compulsion to attend funerals is very strong for the Tumbuka; if there is a death in the village a person who is away must return as soon as possible. When a death is announced, a fowl is carried, indicating friendship; kin must be fully informed before burial. If a married woman has died, and has not been taken to the man's home, then heavy compensation is due; but there is no case if she has been taken to her husband's village. The body is prepared, washed and clothed by the *bazukuru* (grandchildren or their classificatory equivalents). These also have the right to take what they wish from the possessions of the dead person; a relative who attempted to refuse them this would be stricken by the spirits. The *bazukuru* also have the responsibility of bringing the body to the grave; the grave itself is dug by functionaries known as *bachimbwe* (hyenas). Elder brothers or relatives of similar responsibility on either side (known as *bankhoswe*) remain seated. If the grave is difficult to dig, this indicates possible anger by the spirits, and the *ng'anga* then has to be consulted.

The *ng'anga* will in any case normally have been called to establish the cause of death; death is something that should not occur, though this belief is modified in the case of very old people and immature children.

The *bachimbwe* are also responsible for filling the grave. The personal possessions and the clothes of the dead person will be buried together with the body; indeed, in the Balowoka period, when a great chief died, serfs, wives and older friends would have to be buried too. Some would be buried alive while others would be killed; this fate could be avoided by sneezing, which indicated disapproval by the spirits. The logic behind this is that a senior person such as a chief would continue his occupation after death, and thus his household had to go with him.

Those who take part in the burial have to wash afterwards so that death does not come repeatedly to the village. On return from washing, they leap over a fire on which the *ng'anga* has thrown some medicine, and themselves consume medicine mixed with cold gruel. Afterwards the *bazukuru* and the *bachimbwe* and the bereaved family sleep at the door of the house where the death took place. Latecomers would approach the house of the death, and the women would receive them with wailing, the men explaining how the death occurred. Beer is prepared when people leave the house, and there is dancing at night when the beer is ready. Those taking part in the dance praise the dead person, and receive presents. This is followed by worship at the grave, where a libation of beer is poured.

Friends of the dead are debarred from marriage or from having marital relations for a year, and the penalty for breach of this prohibition is heavy. They must also refrain from shaving their hair for a year. When the hair is eventually cut, there is brewing of beer for the whole of the village; there would be dancing for up to three days, then praise for the deeds of the dead person followed by worship at the graveside. Gifts of beer and flour will be seen to be taken by the spirit if the beer froths or if the flour is disturbed by mice. The one who shaves a widow's head becomes her next husband. At the time of shaving of the hair, the spirit is brought back intentionally, and the person responsible for the death has to be found

through the poison ordeal. When all customs have been observed
during the year, the spirit will have no more resentment and can be
welcomed back.

Burial practices show clearly the interdependence of the living and
the dead. This can be a form of social control, since the spirits
continue to take an active interest in the affairs of the living. They are
specially concerned with funerals; a departed spirit knows if anyone
has neglected the funeral, and is able to punish the offender. It
remains to consider Young's discussion of more terrestial forms of
social control, namely Tumbuka conceptions of justice. Continuing
the theme of the 'good village', he shows that four destructive
agencies are recognised; these are quarrelsomeness (including
wounding and killing), falsehood, laziness, and theft (which can
include adultery). The system is seen by Young as quite effective in
circumstances where all offences are between neighbours, but less so
with rapid social change and the presence of recent innovations.
Justice for the Tumbuka relates not only to the individual, but extends
to his group. Recourse is usually made to a court of elders. These are
of the clan (*mphara*) in cases where this is the same for both plaintiff
and defendant. Appeal can be made to the elders of another *mphara*
if either party is dissatisfied with the outcome. If plaintiff and
defendant belong each to a different *mphara*, then a neutral *mphara*
is chosen, and appeal can be made from this to yet another. In theory
there is no limit to this process.

Quarrelsomeness is an offence, since contentious individuals cause
trouble; individual quarrels can be patched up by the elders, but
matters are much more difficult in cases where a curse has been
uttered. Thus in ordinary cases the elders will settle the matter by
imposition of a fine, but for a curse to be lifted the party to the quarrel
who wishes to resume relations must call on the services of the
ng'anga. The *ng'anga* will bring a powder from the bark of the
mpamba tree, and mix it with water. The two parties to the quarrel
will now drink from it, the one who uttered the curse drinking first.
Each ejects then drinks a mouthful, and calls upon the ancestors to
witness the reconciliation. It is also possible to use flour for this
ritual. A constantly troublesome person, unforgiving and
unforgetting, can be sanctioned in various ways. Initially he is
taunted as a warning, but if all else fails, elders can meet and drive
him away. He can be received and accepted by another group if he

learns his lesson, but if not he can be put to death.

The severity of the offence of homicide depends on the circumstances. Compensation can be accepted by the aggrieved clan, but if the killer cannot pay compensation he can be sent bound to the clan of the victim; it is in this way that the class of serfs originated. If an inadequate payment of compensation is offered, a vendetta can begin; when one or two deaths have resulted, the dispute can be settled, by transfer of serfs if necessary to equalise the losses. Falsehood and theft are also dealt with by the elders, and laziness too is a serious offence within the village context. This again can be dealt with by rebuke and taunting. Here Young is critical of the stereotype of the 'lazy African', to which he had subscribed himself in his early days at Livingstonia. He suggests that the stereotype occurs because the same incentives that prevail in the village context do not apply in the case of work for Europeans.

If various procedures for appeals fail, the ultimate appeal is to supernatural sanction, through the use of the ordeal, usually the poison ordeal, *mwavi*. This is seen as a god-given device, which ensures that if a person has done wrong he will die of poison. Refusal to cooperate in *mwavi* ordeals is an indication of guilt. The bark containing the poison is collected by the parties themselves and their friends; anyone can be chosen to administer the poison, which is mixed with water. Vomiting of the poison is an indication of truthfulness, death an indication of deceit. But it is not necessary for humans to take the poison themselves, and this is not normal if both are members of the same community. The ordeal can be administered by proxy, to a fowl or to a dog or for that matter to a serf, who is seen as barely human. Another kind of ordeal involves the use of boiling water, into which each party puts his hand and forearm. Blisters indicate guilt, lack of them indicates innocence.

A person can insist on his right to do the test, but in all cases group interest is paramount. Moreover, medicine cannot be legitimately obtained for private use: thus medicine can be used for improving gardens generally, but not for improving one's own particular garden. The charge of using private medicine can be rebutted only by resort to *mwavi*. An incorrigible offender can be described as *mfwiti*, a word which translates etymologically as 'death-dealer'. Such a person's activities might be tolerated through fear, but the ultimate sanction is death; this is administered through burning, the *mfwiti* being responsible for building his own funeral pyre.

Young saw the Tumbuka system of social control as perfectly logical; it suffered only from the fact that it depended on relations between neighbours, and could thus not adapt easily to a changing situation. The system shows how justice is administered in relation to the closeness of the contending parties and how, if all else fails, ritual sanctions can be resorted to. Young notes that the Tumbuka frequently see European-type imported methods of litigation as less satisfactory than the old; in particular, compensation to the victim is an important part of traditional justice, while in the British system the court retains the fine. This theme is also followed by Young in his work *African Dilemma*, written jointly with Melland. Young and Melland point out that acquittals on legal technicalities, such as are found in Western law, are meaningless in African tradition.[15]

In summary, it may be said with confidence that Young was concerned to portray the characteristic *values* of Tumbuka society and culture. He wished to demonstrate that the Tumbuka had their own values, in contradistinction to the attitude of some other writers who could view African society only with contempt. By highlighting the idea of a 'good village' he portrays the Tumbuka as a moral community. The social structure is supported by the ancestors, whose intervention secures good conduct. The ideal of a 'good village' is not, he realises, always in accordance with reality. The founding of a new village is a potentially hazardous undertaking, and it is necessary to call the *ng'anga* to safeguard it. Anti-social behaviour can 'spoil' a village, and offenders are dealt with in such cases by swift retribution (though the most severe punishments are used only as a last resort). Self-restraint and hard work are important values within the village context.

It is particularly important for Young to stress that the *ng'anga*, the safety-doctor, is a crucial functionary. Here Young departed from Donald Fraser's (though not David Livingstone's) censure of the practices of the traditional doctor. Young also stresses that, since the *ng'anga*'s activities are beneficial, the distinction must be sharply drawn between him and the *mfwiti*, the death-dealer. He notes that some administrators and legislators had failed to see the important difference between them. He also suggests that many of the *ng'anga*'s preparations are effective, as they are based on years of trial and error. In his contribution to *African Ideas of God*, he describes the *ng'anga* as the 'liaison officer' in the sphere of ancestral dominance, working side-by-side with his chief or community leader. In his article in *Man* (1932) he examines the equipment of three traditional doctors in some detail; here he shows how their preparations are adapted to new situations, and that their work is not ousted by education. He is, however, critical of certain aspects of Tumbuka tradition. He sees belief in taboo as 'twisted thinking' and 'opposing itself to penetration by the message of Jesus'.[16]

Generally speaking, Young writes with sympathy on Tumbuka tradition, but he is wary of possible changes. He notes at several points that the system works successfully within limited horizons; he does not disapprove of outside contact as such but at times fears its unintended consequences. He has great praise for the wisdom of the elders, referring to 'the not infrequent flashes of light into surprisingly thoughtful minds that have come to us as we talk with the older people in the village'.[17] He fears that their wisdom will be elbowed out in the eagerness of youth, and is concerned that European influence can only accelerate such dangers. Again, while not commenting unfavourably upon traditional dancing in the villages, he maintains that some dances are debased by those returning from the mines, and describes such dances as 'disgusting'. It appears, however, that he hoped that reintegration could be achieved through Christianity.

Young makes a number of explicit references to authors and events which influenced his analysis. He likens the magical safeguarding of a village by the *ng'anga* to the Riding of the Bounds in Berwick, and to similar Borders customs. He quotes Ruskin with approval on the matter of refusing to draw a rigid distinction between 'religion' and 'superstition'. In his early days at the mission, he remarks, he was strongly influenced by a work by Dudley Kidd, with the uninviting title of *Kafir Socialism*.[18] This work contains numerous remarks of a prejudiced nature, but is more sympathetic to African traditions than some similar studies. Kidd particularly argues that for the African, there is an emphasis on collectivism (called by him 'socialism') rather than individualism. He goes on to elaborate this theme in discussion of conceptions of justice. He notes that justice involves collective rather than individual responsibility, and that guilt rather than innocence is presumed. The severest punishments, Kidd notes, are reserved for anti-social activities such as witchcraft. He goes on to suggest that commerce, education and missionaries have all encouraged individualism and that, while progress could be possible, the danger existed of lack of new restraints. Kidd also draws attention to ancestor worship in religion, and to the distinction between the witch-doctor and the sorcerer. He urges the importance of ethnographic investigations, so as to trace previous mistakes and to improve matters in the future. As well as anthropology, this exercise is seen to include study of folklore and history.

Young also mentions the work of Edwin Smith, particularly his article 'Indigenous Education in Africa', contributed by Smith to the Seligman *Festschrift*.[19] This was not published till 1934, and could not be referred to directly in *Notes on Customs and Folklore*; though Smith's ideas could well have influenced Young earlier, as they were well known in missionary circles. In that particular article, Smith urges that when Europeans try to do things for Africans, they should first examine the African conceptions. He considers the case of education, criticising the Phelps-Stokes Commission for disregarding the indigenous methods adopted. He demonstrates that education is not to be equated with schooling, but that it is rather the whole process by which one generation transmits its culture to its successors. He goes on to discuss initiations, also riddles and folktales; he suggests that the latter constitute the 'literary education' of Africans. He quotes approvingly Rattray's comment that the stories are the African's 'Old Testament';[20] such a notion had a strong influence on Young. Smith concludes that African education is genuine, and that it is European 'civilisation' which causes demoralisation, through factors such as labour migration and urbanisation, leading in turn to disturbance of the family. These matters were also the concern of Cullen Young.

Young refers to a number of other writers on relatively minor details. Torday [21] is mentioned in support of the ideal of pre-marital chastity in traditional Africa. Hobley[22] is referred to in connection with taboo and conceptions of the deity. Young's colleague Donald Fraser is mentioned for providing material about omens.[23] Willoughby[24] is referred to in relation to safeguarding of villages. William Murray of the Dutch Reformed Church Mission at Nkhoma is quoted in relation to marriage,[25] and Archdeacon Johnson of the UMCA is referred to regarding social control.[26] Fred Moir of the African Lakes Company is referred to in connection with the poison ordeal.[27] There is also mention of D.R. Mackenzie, author of *The Spirit-Ridden Konde*.[28] Mackenzie had previously been a colleague of Young, and shared his linguistic and ethnographic interests.[29] In spite of its sensational title, his book on the Ngonde is a serious study which avoids value-judgements. Young had cause to express regret that Mackenzie had been transferred to a non-Tumbuka-speaking area of mission activity.[30] Young's debt to some writers is clear but unacknowledged. Thus his discussion of burial practices owes much to MacAlpine, and there is evidence of more general influence from the periodicals the *Aurora* and the *Livingstonia News*. It is not clear how much professional anthropology had been absorbed by Young by the time he wrote his *Notes on Customs and Folklore*. Some of Malinowski's[31] work became known to Young, and Young would no doubt have been sympathetic to Malinowskian functionalism. Young had a good command of Tumbuka, believed in living close to Africans, and was constantly concerned to check and recheck information; yet he did not do anything that would constitute 'pure fieldwork'. He was remarkably observant, and supplemented his investigations by the use of material provided by key informants. It is likely that they presented an idealised view, especially of the past, in the way that Malinowski had warned against. This should be borne in mind in conjunction with Young's comments about the old and the young; though it needs also to be noted that he *was* interested in the generation gap, and he returned to the theme in his broader discussions. The impact of French thought, such as Durkheim's work, was probably minimal or non-existent, except indirectly through Malinowski. Young seems not to have been especially interested in French culture, and his command of French was limited, at a time when much of Durkheim's work had no English translation.[32] Sir James Frazer's approach was however rejected by Young, despite its popularity among many amateur anthropologists.[33] Young was aware of the criticisms of Frazer's unsophisticated use of the comparative method which were made by Malinowski and his successors.

Before leaving Young's Tumbuka studies, it remains to consider his selection of material: his choice of subjects to include and exclude. If *Notes on Customs and Folklore* appears to be incomplete, leaving many questions unanswered for the modern anthropologist, it must not be forgotten that 'modern anthropology' had only just begun

to exist at the time of its publication; and little systematic study of
Africa by anthropologists had been attempted. If the theme of the
moral community is taken to be a legitimate one, then it is followed
through fairly consistently and successfully. Yet some criticisms must
be made. To be fair to Young, he made many of his value-judgements
clear, as already noted. He indicated that he was concerned with
ideals, and that these did not always accord with reality. He accepted
that breaches of the Tumbuka moral code were frequent, hence the
necessity for ultimate sanctions coming from the spiritual world. He
suggested particularly that unchastity and adultery could be quite
frequent deviations from the ideal; but he thought that the existence of
an ideal of pre-marital chastity and fidelity within marriage was an
indication that self-restraint was possible. He thought that African
marriage had more to commend it than many commentators
suspected. He admired the undisturbed state of Tumbuka existence:

> It is hardly an exaggeration to say that primitive African
> life was, essentially, a finer thing than that which
> succeeded it, since its finer qualities were community
> qualities, whereas under the succeeding regimes such
> qualities as, say, consideration for others could only be
> maintained in individuals against a terrific weight of
> unsympathetic general tendency. The Christian view
> aims at restoring the situation .... Africa's contribution to
> the problems of human progress may therefor (sic) be
> expected along the lines of loyalty to the early ideal of
> the 'good village' with the boundaries of the village
> extended to match the extended interests and concerns of
> men in the modern world.[34]

He tended to assume that the ideal of the 'good village' had been
at least partly realised by the indigenous Tumbuka; this accords with
his preference for the Tumbuka as against the Ngoni conquerors. He
suggests that first the Arabs, by dealing in slaves, and then the Ngoni,
by their militarism, had undermined the foundation of traditional
society. His view of the situation here was no doubt biased by his use
of elderly informants. Without written records, it is true, there is no
way of totally refuting the suggestion that the ideal of the 'good
village' had been realised before the intrusions. But his informants

will have had a natural tendency to idealise the past, and had obvious reasons for blaming unhealthy features of their own situation on the arrival of the Ngoni.

This does not seem to have been realised by Young, and as in his historical works he shows a general tendency to be uncritical of his informants' reports.

On more specific questions, too, there is a constant tendency to present a *defence* rather than merely an exposition of Tumbuka culture. Thus he avoids mention of certain matters which might have caused others, especially those in the church, to view the Tumbuka with disfavour. This is particularly noteworthy in the lack of any discussion of polygamy, in spite of the importance this could have for supporting the Tumbuka value of *increase*. Missionary organisations had become more liberal on many issues after Le Zoute, but had remained strict on polygamy.

A further matter which is not discussed by Young is that of the use of beer as a reward for agricultural labour. He recognises that beer is important, even centrally important, to collectivism, generosity and hospitality. He also shows its importance for ritual. But the economic importance of the provision of beer as a way of recruiting a work group is completely disregarded. This practice will almost certainly have been known to Young, since in the later 1920s he took an interest in the study of agricultural activities.[35] Yet the association of beer-drinking with hard work would have been anathema to those Scottish Presbyterians who would have been among the readers of the text.

Some missionary commentators have themselves noted that Young's studies might present an over-idealised picture of village life. J.G. Steytler,[36] who was Principal of the Normal School at the Dutch Reformed Church Mission at Nkhoma, was one of these. He saw Young's presentation of the ideal of the 'good village' as attractive, but warned that village life had its darker side too. Particularly he argued that hazards such as war, epidemic and famine produced a life ridden with fear; superstition bred on this, and the witch-doctor helped to keep such belief alive. However, in periods of calm he saw the ideal presented as having more validity. G.W. Broomfield of the UMCA also felt that Cullen Young's picture was over-idealised. He makes this observation on the general work *Contemporary Ancestors*, but the orientation criticised prevails also in the Tumbuka studies. He comments 'The major criticism which I would like to make of the book is that it gives a rather one-sided picture of African life. There are darker sides which are hardly mentioned. Anyone going to Africa with so little information about the latter would have some unpleasant shocks'.[37]

Such criticisms have a familiar ring now that functionalism has been dethroned as the paradigm for anthropological investigation. But there has unfortunately been little systematic testing of the accuracy of Young's ethnographic accounts using recent fieldwork. One exception, however, is the study by Gregson, in the thesis 'Work, Exchange and Leadership: The Mobilization of Agricultural Labor among the Tumbuka of the Henga Valley' (1969).[38] Gregson refers to Young's work, but concentrates mainly upon his historical studies. He does however draw special attention to the use of beer to attract agricultural labour, the topic neglected by Young. He comments also on the question of movement from matriliny to patriliny, which *was* one of Young's themes. In the case of the Henga valley, he argues that the situation had become fairly flexible. A patrilineal ideology existed, but other claims could be accepted if supported by authentically patrilineal members of the descent group. Following Schneider he argues that the Henga are a patrilineal people with some matrilineal characteristics. He notes, particularly, that lines of authority and descent can occasionally be through women; that descent groups try to control some of their female members; that adult brothers and sisters have relatively frequent interaction; that some children are brought up in situations where statuses of father-husband are lacking; and finally, that marital solidarity is not intense.[39]

In examining the structure of one village (called Chimwemwe) he notes that as many as 38 per cent of extant marriages are polygynous, but that only one case could be found of a man with more than two wives. He notes the special sleeping facilities for the unmarried. The girls' house transmits a peer-group culture which does not necessarily relate to kinship; but the girl usually still eats with her mother. The boys' house is more directly organised around patrilineal kinship, and groups are smaller and more diffuse. Virilocal residence is seen as the norm, but matrilateral ties are still of importance and matrikin can be neighbours. Like Cullen Young, Gregson describes the gift-giving leading up to eventual agreement on marriage, in some detail. Young does not however discuss elopement in his direct studies of the

Tumbuka (though this is mentioned in the more general work, *Our African Way of Life*); but Gregson suggests that this occurs in a significant number of cases. The marriage is later regularised after such an event by the payment of a fine. The overall impression obtained by Gregson is that Tumbuka-Henga society involves a choice between alternatives rather than a formal structure; here he follows directly Van Velsen's analysis of the neighbouring Tonga.[40]

Much of the rest of Gregson's analysis is concerned with the use of beer as a reward for agricultural labour; he notes that labour groups are recruited also for the Presbyterian church and for the Malawi Congress Party, and that in such cases there is no reward in the form of beer. He concludes in a way which would be unpalatable for the advocate of abstinence, arguing that beer-labour is more efficient than agricultural labour involving no such reward. Gregson recognises in this connection that the anthropological study of work is a relatively recent specialism.

A very useful doctoral thesis in religious studies is that by S.S. Ncosana, 'Spirit Possession and Tumbuka Christians' (1985).[41] This contains a valuable account of pre-Christian Tumbuka religious conceptions, and the reaction of the missionaries to them. Ncosana does not directly contradict Young on any important question, but the discussion is considerably more sophisticated, and some original material has been collected from informants. Ncosana, like Young, stresses the reality of the spirit world in African culture; his concern is particularly with the work of the ancestral spirits, though he does present a general discussion of Tumbuka cosmology. He stresses that the ancestors are generally seen as benevolent; punishment by the ancestors is only to remind the living of their obligations. His particular interest is in the question of spirit possession, and he eventually goes on to consider the theological implications of its continued presence among Tumbuka Christians. He shows that the Scottish missionaries had originally been very suspicious of possession. This had stemmed from the challenge in 1827 to the Church of Scotland by Edward Irving, on the question of the church's lack of teaching about the Spirit. Irving was disciplined and eventually formed the Catholic Apostolic Church. When the memory of this event remained fairly recent, Scottish missionaries were concerned to avoid any kind of emotionalism or emphasis on the work of the Spirit, or spiritual gifts; they preferred in-depth teaching

of the Christian faith, and hence delayed baptism. But younger
missionaries, such as Donald Fraser, had been influenced by
subsequent revivals in Britain.[42] Thus though initially there had been
a feeling that possession was the work of the Devil, eventually there
was some accommodation to it. The younger missionaries and the
indigenous ministry were better able to see possession as the work of
the Holy Spirit, though eventually this outlook was discouraged.
Young would have counted as one among the younger missionaries;
he had been influenced when studying to be an accountant by the
'Student Volunteer' movement, which had a strong evangelical
flavour: though his own outlook soon became much too broad to be
encompassed by the rubric of 'evangelical Christianity'. He was
concerned to defend many indigenous Tumbuka religious conceptions
as steps on the road to Christianity, while still wishing to stress the
uniqueness of Jesus. However, few theological conclusions are drawn
by Young in *Notes on Customs and Folklore*. Young does mention
spirit possession, in the context of his theme of the relationship
between the living and the dead.

Ncosana presents a more sophisticated account of Tumbuka
cosmology than that of Young. In particular, he draws upon new
information collected from elderly informants, and adopts a more
historical perspective. He suggests that territorial spirits are important
in addition to God and the spirits of the ancestors. Spirits of chiefs
are included among territorial spirits, and stand in an intermediate
position between God and the ancestors. Ncosana examines
particularly the regional cult of Chikang'ombe (mentioned only in
passing by Young), recognising that with the arrival of the Balowoka
there was an expansion of the importance of the deity, *Chiuta*. The
cult of Chikang'ombe was present at Nkhamanga, the centre of the
new authority structure; but the first Chikulamayembe was only
partially successful in bringing worship there under his control. The
priesthood of this cult was left untouched, and in places far removed
from Nkhamanga, worship took place through other localised spirits.
However, with the Ngoni incursion, the cult centre of Chikang'ombe
was disrupted; it was the foundation of the authority of
Chikulamayembe, who was deposed by the invaders. Moreover, the
Ngoni Paramount Chief became sole ruler, and did not tolerate
gatherings, whether religious or otherwise, which were not concerned
with his praise. Spirit possession generally was however less

affected; there was much intermarriage, and the conquerors were subject as a consequence to Tumbuka spirits. *Mwavi* had been taken over by the Chikulamayembe and was taken over again by the Ngoni.

It thus appears that Young had based his account upon inadequate information regarding the situation before the arrival of the Ngoni. This is somewhat surprising since elsewhere he is concerned to reconstruct the 'true' Tumbuka social and political institutions, following his own bias and that of his informants in favour of the pre-Ngoni period. He did not, however, always see Ngoni innovations as retrogressive: he seemed to support the form of marriage which involves payment of bridewealth, and this had been introduced by the Ngoni. One likely contributing factor to Young's neglect of territorial spirits is the fact that much of his information had been provided by Levi Mumba, who himself made no reference to them.

The Tumbuka are also referred to in Tew's (Mary Douglas's) contribution on 'North-West Nyasa' to the *Ethnographic Survey of Africa* (1950).[43] Young's reports are fairly closely adhered to here, though the analysis is now that of a professional anthropologist. Tew brings up the question of polygyny, and shows it to be very clearly recognised among the Tumbuka. She does, however, maintain that the Tumbuka have no initiation schools for girls, a statement which is contradicted by Young's evidence. Tew also pays attention to the question of the depletion of the population of adult males by labour migration. Young was interested in this subject, but did not deal with it in *Notes on Customs and Folklore*.

In conclusion about Young's Tumbuka studies, it can be said that, while they were in many ways amateurish, Young did clearly recognise this. It would be illogical and unjust to criticise him for ignorance of developments in anthropology that had not taken place at the time when he published his findings. Some subsequent comments on anthropological work are relevant to the understanding of Young's contributions. His interests in the ideal of the 'good village' are reminiscent of Redfield's discussion of the 'good life' in the small community. The question arises, Redfield goes on to suggest, as to how completely the anthropologist can absorb the 'inside view' without taking leave of his responsibilities to the community of anthropologists generally.[44] Insofar as this might be relevant to Young's case, certain factors are clearly significant. He arrived in the field when twenty-four years of age, and much of his stay was spent in work in the villages. He was able to absorb much of the 'inside view'; but he remained a missionary. His religious outlook became broader but was always present and significant to him. Thus his Christianity enabled him to keep a sufficient distance to avoid taking the inside view completely. Certain earlier experiences in Britain remained important to him, especially those arising from his Borders ancestry; this is evident occasionally in his anthropology.[45] It has been suggested by Scudder and Colson[46] that extended contact with a field situation can lead to recognition and respect for old friends, but also to a certain amount of scepticism regarding human nature. The first component is present in Young's work, but the second he seems to have kept to himself if he entertained it at all.

It is appropriate, with Redfield, to recognise the personal factor in anthropology, especially when no formal professional training has been followed. Thus Redfield asks: 'towards what understanding, and with what forms of thought, does this investigator study this community?'[47] It is hoped that this question is partly answered here in relation to Young's studies of the Tumbuka. It is perhaps also significant that parallels can be drawn (and not only by Redfield) between studies of communities and literary works such as novels. Thus it is eminently appropriate that Young was later to view the encouragement of African writing as one of his major concerns.

On his return to Britain in 1931, Young was able to pursue his anthropological studies in greater breadth and with greater rigour; but his subsequent writing on Africa remained heavily stamped by his Tumbuka experience. His broader concerns are well worth further study. His general pronouncements on the nature of 'Africanity' are perhaps better left till the political implications of his work are considered. For the moment it is worth examining his continued interest in anthropology in the light of his contacts with professionals in that field after 1931. Young was based in London between 1931 and 1946, and he was a frequent visitor to the School of Oriental and African Studies. He appears also to have had some contact with Malinowski at the London School of Economics. He admired Malinowski's work, and Malinowski for his part was welcoming to amateurs interested in anthropology.[48] Malinowski was also of the opinion that anthropology had practical applications, and Young shared this attitude. Malinowski was concerned to stress the essential function of beliefs such as magic, which to a westerner would seem illogical. Young, too, was concerned for African societies to be viewed on their own terms and not through Western eyes. He did not share all Malinowski's interests, such as in psychoanalysis. But the concern to *defend* as well as to explain an alien culture was nearer to Malinowski's interests than to those of many other contemporary anthropologists.

One matter is perfectly clear, namely that Young's interests were closer to Malinowski's than to those of his contemporary, Radcliffe-Brown.[49] Young's entry into anthropological interests had been through practical linguistic study, and the study of history. There is no evidence that Young showed much interest in natural sciences, even biology, apart from a certain amount of concern for evolutionary perspectives. Likewise the French positivist tradition and its successors had no attraction for him. Thus he would not have been able to accept a functionalist perspective which followed directly from an organic view of society. A different matter entirely was Malinowskian functionalism, based on the practical problem of making sense of field data: it was here that Young found his intellectual home.

Young's general interests in anthropology can be discerned to a certain extent from the numerous book reviews that were written by him, mainly in the *International Review of Missions* and *Man*.[50] A general overview of these again shows a correspondence between Young's and Malinowski's views. Young constantly praises in his reviews the value of direct contact and close fieldwork in anthropology rather than library research, though he does not deny the importance of the latter also. He stresses that the contribution of Africa to general culture is important, and that one should not assume that all advantages are on the European side. In a review of a work by Audrey Richards *(Hunger and Work in a Savage Tribe [1933])*,[51] he praises the anthropologist's concern with everyday activities rather than the unusual. His other reviews underline his interest in indigenous education, proverbs and folktales, and his respect for Edwin Smith. They show his concern to understand African justice, and to oppose the notion of 'ancestor worship'.

Finally, it is to be noted that Young participated in various debates in *Man*. This activity began while he was still in Malawi; his first letter, on the subject of iron 'tridents' found in Chikulamayembe's grave, has already been mentioned. As the correspondence developed, speculation arose as to the origin of these, Young believing that they (and for that matter the Balowoka) were probably of West African origin. Young was impressed by a contribution by Audrey Richards, who suggested that they were bow-stands rather than tridents. But nothing really constructive emerged from this debate.[52]

A more influential debate arose on the correct translation of the word *lobola*. Cullen Young, like the Tumbuka themselves, was concerned to show that this was not a matter of buying and selling. He did not therefore approve of the expression *bride-price*. Some contributors to this debate criticised this view; in particular Lord Raglan warned against a 'noble savage' concept and took a sympathetic view of the analogy with buying and selling. Young was also critical of certain changes affecting the payment of *lobola* among the Tumbuka - notably the inflation of the amount expected. But he saw the institution of bridewealth as basically sound. He suggested that since marriage among the Tumbuka involved transfer of a woman's child-bearing capacity from one kin-group to another (in a society where 'increase' was highly valued), *lobola* was a way of 'balancing the accounts'. This is a rare insight from Young's initial training as an accountant. He suggests *equilibrium guarantee* as an appropriate technical term for anthropologists to use, and he assures Lord Raglan that this *can* be translated into Tumbuka.[53] Young's only other letter to *Man* which is of more than ephemeral interest relates to a debate on the meaning of the word 'family'. Here he comments on the Tumbuka concepts of *fuku and mbumba* (sorority group), like the Roman *familia*.[54]

Thus Young can be said to have contributed first to the ethnography of the Tumbuka, and then to certain issues in general anthropology. At no time was he dogmatic. He spoke as an amateur, but amateur anthropologists were very common in the 1930s and the 1940s: indeed, the Association of Social Anthropologists of the British Commonwealth was set up in 1946 to distinguish the professionals from those with a more dilletantish interest in the subject.[55] Young's career was recognised in 1950 by the Edinburgh honorary degree. His anthropological works were however less influential than his historical studies, and it is to these that attention must now be turned.

III

The Historical Contribution

Cullen Young's writings on the history of northern Malawi have probably been more influential among scholars than have other aspects of his work. Much of the attention, especially recently, has been highly critical; but Young's works are a useful basis upon which the potential critic can build. His historical works have also had a much broader impact among the Tumbuka themselves. This is in itself an interesting phenomenon, since it throws light upon the way in which sociological knowledge becomes part of and influences society. Young's initial historical contribution appeared in 1923,[1] together with a study of the Tumbuka language. This generated considerable interest and debate among Livingstonia pupils and graduates, which in turn led to the issue of an updated and revised edition of the historical text in 1932.[2] Young's findings continued to be influential, and provided the basis for school instruction material on Tumbuka history which became widely used in northern Malawi.[3]

It is here proposed to examine the relationship of Young's historical work to such writings on the history of northern Malawi as already existed; a comparison will then be made between the old and the new versions of his direct contribution to Tumbuka history. The critical attention that has been given to his work will then be assessed; and, finally, an evaluation will be attempted of Young's work as a contribution based upon oral history.

Some travel writing on northern Malawi was already available to Young before he sailed to Africa; all of it was written by authors who were directly or indirectly concerned with missionary activity. It can be expected that Young was early acquainted with the works of Livingstone. Not only did these attract a wide readership in nineteenth-century Scotland; more particularly, his own father had taken a special interest in missionary biographies.[4] Especially significant will have been Livingstone's *Narrative of an Expedition to the Zambezi and its Tributaries* (1865); this contained several references to the Tumbuka.[5] By the time he was in a position to take serious interest in mission work, Young would have done some further reading on northern Malawi. He certainly possessed a copy of Elmslie's *Among the Wild Ngoni*, referred to in Chapter II.[6] This contains much detail of the northward movement of the Ngoni following the Zulu wars. Elmslie recorded much objective information, while praising the Ngoni for their strong, centralised government: but his overall concern was to depict them as bloodthirsty barbarians. Another source will have been *Adventures in Nyasaland* by Low Monteith Fotheringham of the African Lakes Company (1891).[7] This work depicts the situation in the far north of Malawi, at the dawn of British imperialism in the area. Here the Tumbuka and the Ngonde were living side by side, and the Arab presence was becoming more settled. Much of Fotheringham's concern is with military operations against the Arabs, the theme being that 'good' (i.e. British) imperialism was to succeed in driving out the 'bad' (i.e. Arab) - in the same way as had been expected with trading relationships. Fotheringham pays some attention to the history of population movement, and to the phenomenon of an ethnically mixed area. His assumption is broadly one of African innocence. There is no record of whether or not Cullen Young attended Donald Fraser's talk on 'The Zulu of Nyasaland', delivered before the Philosophical Society of Glasgow in 1901 and also published in that year.[8] This dealt with the march northwards to Malawi of the Ngoni, extolling their aristocratic and military virtues in contradistinction to the 'degradation' of the Tumbuka.

Once in the field, Young will have had access to the sporadic references to local history contained in the Livingstonia periodical *The Aurora*. One Livingstonia missionary, the Revd Dr George Steele, had shown a more sustained interest in history; Elmslie had praised his powers of close observation and his openness in dealing with African wisdom and experience.[9] Steele had died in 1895, but he had committed to print a short article in the *Nyasa News*, the periodical of the UMCA on Likoma Island.[10] This short contribution 'History of the Tambuka' (sic) consisted of an oral testimony from 'an intelligent Tambuka' in English translation. This stressed the decentralised nature of indigenous Tumbuka society, followed by the unifying influence of the immigrant chieftain named Chikulamayembe. The origin of this name is explained as referring to his wisdom and bounty, since he provided hoes (*mayembe*) to all who wanted them. The informant also mentioned the independent status of the neighbouring Phoka. Eventually, he points out, the Ngoni came to conquer the area and established their own chieftainships. At some point Young discovered a linguistic study by J. Rebman, of the Church Missionary Society, entitled *Dictionary of the Kiniassa Language*. This was published in 1877,[11] and was based on data provided by a single informant, who could also speak Swahili. This work contained certain historical details of the informant's place of origin, as well as the linguistic material.

The earliest records of the area in which the Tumbuka were found were Portuguese. This was a language which Young could not read, but by the time he became interested in Tumbuka history, some of it had been translated into English. A travel account by Lacerda, originally published in 1798, appeared in English in 1873 as *The Lands of Cazembe*.[12] The *Records of South Eastern Africa*, collected and translated by George McCall Theal, were also beginning to become available.[13] The latter collection contained reference to a journey made by a certain Gaspar Bocarro, in 1616, from the Zambezi to the coast at Kilwa.[14] Another source for details of this journey was available in R.N. Hall's work, *Prehistoric Rhodesia*: it was from this that Young took his list of stopping-places for Bocarro.[15]

Young notes the long gap between the Portuguese journeys and those made by Livingstone in 1859 and 1861. He also comments on the later circumnavigation of Lake Malawi (Nyasa) in 1875 by the first Scottish missionary party. His general impression is that of a sharp contrast between the Portuguese and the Scottish reports. He comments of Bocarro's account: 'Of importance to our present subject the main lesson to be drawn is that at the distant time there is no record of any habit of war or of tribal unsettlement; no proof of the

existence of any "warlike" or "marauding" tribes, or of any special
difficulties attending the journeys of white men through unknown
territory'.[16]

Apart from one reference to devastation by 'Zimbas', there is no
evidence presented by Bocarro of external invasions; nor were Arabs
or Portuguese present except along the Zambezi.

Young highlights the contrast between Bocarro's picture and that
presented by Livingstone 250 years later. Subsequent Portuguese
records collected by Theal showed relatively little change, and Young
therefore concluded that the devastation which Livingstone was to
report had been characteristic of relatively recent times. Young
continues:

> The more investigation is pushed it will the more
> probably be found that it is upon this period rather than
> upon any prehistoric African tendency to empire, rapine,
> and organised strife, that we must look as the origin of
> these ills that have been too loosely held to be natural in
> early human development. We may couple with this
> Arab period that of the great military despotisms in South
> Africa as being jointly responsible for the rise of fighting
> tribes and the lust of conquest; for the spread of the slave
> trade and the creation of that state of fear and suspicion
> as between man and man, tribe and tribe, which is so
> marked a characteristic of Central Africa even today.[17]

Thus Young puts the blame for devastation firstly upon Arab slave
traders and secondly upon Ngoni invaders. He tends therefore to
suggest that indigenous Tumbuka society was basically ordered and
peaceful when left to itself. The situation had been changed beyond
recognition, however, by the arrival of the slave traders. It was the
subsequent devastation which would justify missionary and imperial
intervention: Tumbuka society was not degraded in itself. It is also
worth remembering that Young tended to take the side of the
indigenous Tumbuka rather than that of the Ngoni conquerors, as he
also did in his ethnographic works. Here he differed from both
Elmslie and Fraser.

Young's early historical excursions reveal his abiding interest in
the meaning of personal and place names. He noted that Rebman had

mentioned a people, the Wakamanga, who can be identified as those of the area which became the seat of Chikulamayembe; but that the other names mentioned by Rebman (apart from the Yao) had not been encountered by other pioneers of the Lake. Moreover the missionary party of 1875 did not record the name Nkhamanga. Young attributes this to the Ngoni incursion; this was commented upon by Livingstone, the invaders being given the name *Mazitu*.[18] The Ngoni were a warrior and not a trading people, and their domination brought about a decline in the power of Nkhamanga, which had previously been a centre for trade with the coast. Even in Rebman's time, Nkhamanga had already been broken up, though its prosperity was still remembered.

Young also comments on references to the Tumbuka in both Lacerda and Livingstone. The Tumbuka, he notes, are not referred to by Bocarro. The peoples known then as the Mang'anja and the Nguru are mentioned by him, in the same geographical situation as they were found in Young's time. Bocarro also said nothing about the Yao, who were still scattered at this time - a fact confirmed in a written account by Abdallah,[19] a UMCA convert who became ordained and who wrote a history of his own people in 1919. Young regards the continued existence of peoples of the same name in the same geographical area over a long period as indicative of the stability of the situation in the recent past.

Having cleared the ground by assessment of printed materials, Young continues by examining the history of the Tumbuka on the basis of oral sources. He observes that a consensus existed to the effect that the original Tumbuka were an ancient race, over whom a new chieftainship had been established by incoming traders, in a peaceful manner. The ancient race had dug in the ground, and remains could be identified. The original Tumbuka had occupied Nkhamanga and as far west as the Hewe valley. Even these people, it was argued, were immigrants to the area; origins in West Africa or elsewhere in Central Africa were suggested. Till about 1780, they had not developed any organised tribal form. Young describes the situation prior to that date as 'the closing scene in that hidden period of human history in Africa where the country still received the slow migrations of increasing population without much more strife than is natural within growing families'.[20]

Existence remained simple and peaceful, according to this account;

a common speech did however enable intermarriage over a wide area. Lack of pressure of movement and migration had meant that no need had been felt for a centralised government, a strong chief, or a military organisation. A common ancestor could be a rallying point but there was no authority on a larger scale. Young noted that certain original Tumbuka names could be identified. Some of these related to a particular locality, others to ancestry.

Around 1780, however, an important change took place as a consequence of the peaceful invasion which led to establishment of the Chikulamayembe dynasty. For the significance of this event Young drew heavily on material from a key informant. This was Saulos Nyirenda, who as already mentioned chose Young as the recipient of his unsolicited written history, in 1909.[21] Nyirenda's influence on Young was considerable, and his account is worthy of detailed examination. The periods before and after the Ngoni incursion will be considered separately.

Saulos Nyirenda's account (pre-Ngoni times)[22]

Nyirenda's account is both pro-Chikulamayembe and pro-British, and this is hardly surprising. The manuscript was delivered to Young in 1909, while the British had restored the Chikulamayembe dynasty in 1907. The text was anonymous, and it is not clear when Young learnt of the authorship. Nyirenda had been a teacher, but had left such work for commercial employment, with the African Trans-Continental Telegraph Company. This was not an uncommon development as commercial salaries were higher.

Nyirenda is concerned to praise the British; he remarks 'Look at today, the land is being put straight and the proper owners are being seen'.[23] He makes only brief reference to the pre-Chikulamayembe period; he maintains that during that time there was undisturbed land with only one clan, *Mwachanda*. He also mentions the names of the principal original occupiers of Malawi, before the arrival of the Ngoni. He then goes on to develop his main theme, the tale of the Balowoka, or those who crossed the Lake. Their leader was Mlowoka (singular of Balowoka), and they came with a plentiful supply of goods. Mlowoka founded the Chikulamayembe dynasty. He came 'as an Arab' in appearance: that is to say he wore some Arab

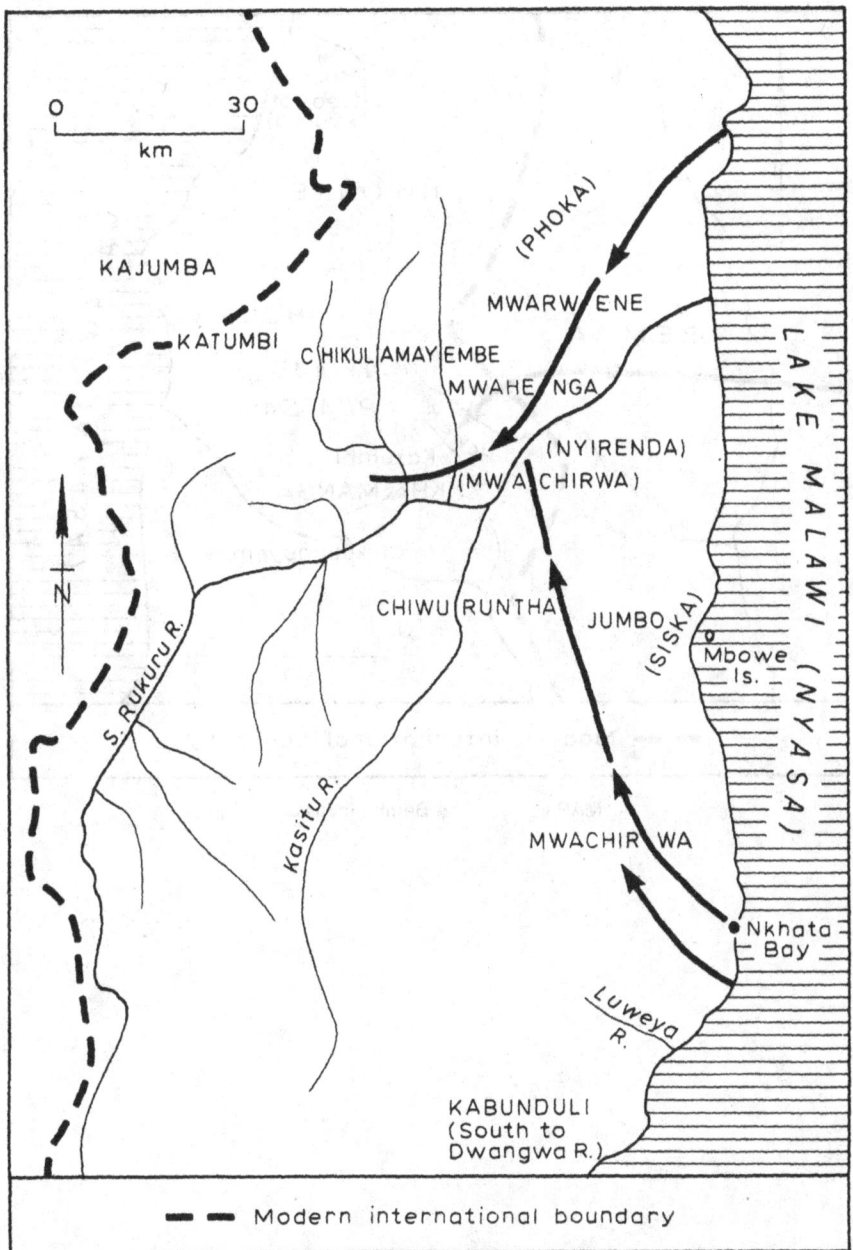

MAP 3 : The arrival of the Balowoka, and Kawunga, showing subsequent
distribution of territory.

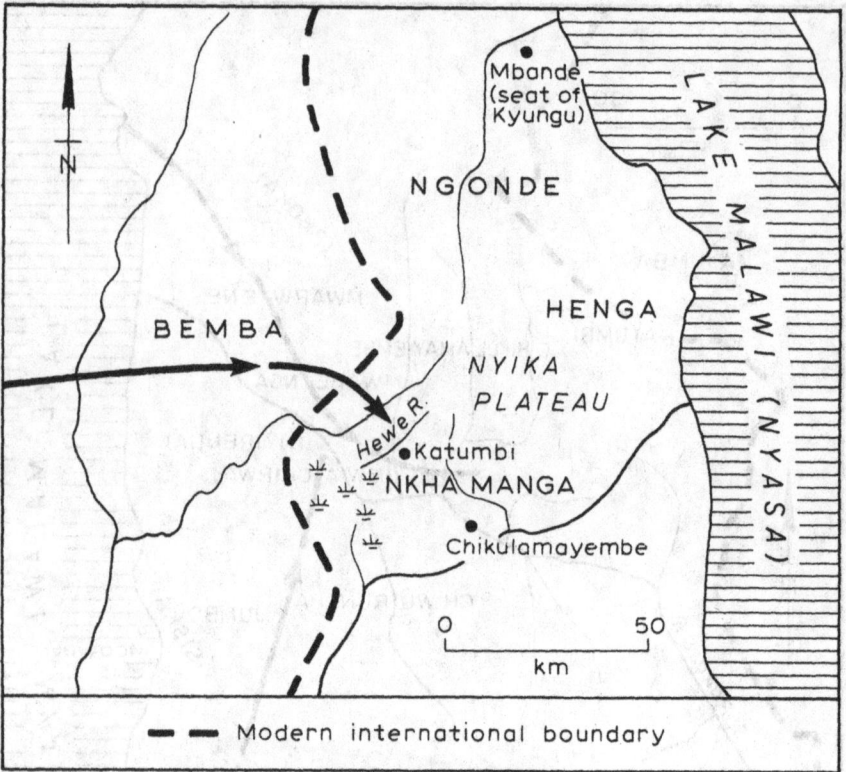

MAP 4 :   The Bemba invasion.

garments but was not an Arab himself. Nyirenda relates that he arrived 'on a plank', and Young assumed that this meant a dhow. The account mentions that Mlowoka came with several companions: Katumbi, Chiwuruntha, Kajumba, Mwahenga, Mwalwene, Jumbo, Mwamlowe and Kabunduli. The party had come in search of ivory. The value of this was not appreciated at the time by the Tumbuka, and Mlowoka introduced the Tumbuka to trading relationships with the outside. They were very impressed by Mlowoka's economic sophistication; previously the Tumbuka had killed elephant for meat, and the ivory had been used only for everyday household purposes. Mlowoka's commercial expertise soon led to the assumption of political authority. He became recognised as Paramount Chief among the Tumbuka, and nominated various headmen as chiefs by putting a cloth turban round their heads. He was able to divide the various districts of Tumbuka territory among the followers who had accompanied him (see map 3). One companion, Chiwuruntha, was allocated an area which included the upper reaches of Tumbuka country; he found there already a certain headman, Mwachirwa, and recognised him. The Phoka territory remained independent of the new arrivals, as Steele's informant had noted earlier.

Mlowoka was followed by another dressed as an Arab, named Kawunga. He also came in search of ivory. On his arrival, Mlowoka allocated him land around Mt. Nthwezuru and the Siska area southeast of it. Kawunga was an ancestor of Saulos Nyirenda; the name *Nyirenda* derives from the name of a caterpillar with a high reproductive capacity. It was felt appropriate for Kawunga because of his tendency to marry many wives and hence to beget many children. Saulos Nyirenda stressed that the successors of this clan, who settled in the Henga plain at Mzokoto, did not do homage to Chikulamayembe (though Young comments in a footnote that the earlier allocation of land contradicted this assertion). The Nyirenda chieftainship had its own turban; no daughter of the chief was given as a wife to Mlowoka, whereas in other parts of the territory that he came to control Mlowoka made strategic marriages. On one occasion the independence of Nyirenda was challenged by the Chikulamayembe, who attempted to assert his authority by force of arms. But the Nyirenda fought fiercely against the army that Chikulamayembe had sent, and chief Chiwuruntha was killed in the battle. The defeat was decisive, and there were subsequently no further quarrels between the Chikulamayembe and the Nyirenda.

Saulos Nyirenda examines the question of succession after Mlowoka. He subscribes to the view that the dynastic name *Chikulamayembe* is an indication of generosity, meaning 'carry hoes'. The new dynasty was characterised by a patrilineal form of succession except on one occasion. Mlowoka was succeeded patrilineally by Gonapamuhanya, who lived to a very old age. But he was succeeded by his sister's son Kamphungu, a member of the Nkhonjera clan. Kamphungu was fierce and authoritarian; he expelled the sons of Gonapamuhanya, and provoked boundary disputes with the Chewa. The dispossessed sons eventually took steps to recapture their rightful heritage. They sought and obtained the help of the Nyirendas to this end, and launched an attack on Kamphungu using bows and arrows and also incendiary tactics. Kamphungu was killed, and the patrilineal succession was restored. It was subsequently declared that 'sister's sons do not ascend the throne', and Young comments that this was the end of a temporary and unsuccessful return to matriliny.

During this period there was also an invasion by the Bemba (see map 4), whose aim was the annexation of Chikulamayembe's country.[24] The Bemba leader on this occasion (Kyepere) succeeded in taking the territory of Katumbi and also that of Uyombe, whose chiefdom was under Ngonde domination. This brought about an alliance between the Chikulamayembe and the Kyungu (the Ngonde king). The combined forces of the Tumbuka and the Ngonde were able to drive out the Bemba by the burning of huts and stockades. It is on the question of the Tumbuka-Ngonde alliance that Nyirenda makes what is probably his most contentious point. He maintains that the Kyungu respected the Chikulamayembe as an elder brother, and that he came from the same stock. He goes on to argue that the Kyungu initially visited the Chikulamayembe to discuss the allocation of territory, and maintains that boundaries were amicably agreed upon.

Nyirenda's account of pre-Ngoni times also refers to two incidents where chiefs lost their position. The first of these was Mkandawire, of Nkhamanga origin, who controlled the Fulirwa area. He lost his chieftainship to Mwafulirwa, who also came from across the Lake, after Mkandawire failed in a rainmaking competition which the Chikulamayembe had organised. A subsequent attempt to dislodge

Mwafulirwa failed; the Kyungu had agreed to assist in the exercise but Mwafulirwa succeeded in placating him. The second chief to lose his position was Kabunduli. Some of his territory was invaded by the Chewa, but he did not succeed in driving them out. The Chikulamayembe therefore looked for a substitute chief. Mankhaka was chosen, and he succeeded in dislodging the Chewa. He then became recognised as chief, with Kabunduli demoted to his subordinate; the alliance was forged in the customary fashion for Chikulamayembe, by the taking of Mankhaka's sister as a wife.

Finally, Saulos Nyirenda's discussion of pre-Ngoni times relates the events which led to warning of confusion because of the forthcoming invasion. The Ngoni first moved northwards through Tumbuka territory, before moving south. Bwati, the Chikulamayembe of that period, prophesied that confusion would reign after his death; but that eventually a young child would be installed to restore the situation. Bwati was succeeded by Mkuwayira; his reign was short-lived because the Tumbuka fell to Ngoni subjugation. But a young child of the ruling house, named Chirongozi Gondwe, fled with his mother to Ngondeland. With support from the British he eventually succeeded to the restored Chikulamayembeship.

Cullen Young on pre-Ngoni times.

Cullen Young's account of these events[25] was considerably indebted to Nyirenda. He was the key source for the *Notes on the Origins and History* (the second part of *Notes on Speech and History*). But Young also relied on other informants, whose names were not mentioned. One influence will certainly have been Andrew Nkhonjera. He was a Livingstonia graduate who produced an account, published in 1911-12, which like Nyirenda's stressed the supreme importance of the Chikulamayembe dynasty.[26] The apparent intention was to influence British policy towards it. Nkhonjera makes many similar points to Nyirenda's about the wide expanse of the authority of the Chikulamayembes. He provides more details of the process of succession in the dynasty, and there are some differences from Nyirenda's account.

Young took many oral testimonies from other informants who are

mostly not named. He will also have been influenced by Donald
Fraser. Fraser collected and eventually published some historical
material, though in a less systematic fashion than Young's.[27] As
already noted, Fraser was more interested in and supportive of the
viewpoint of the Ngoni.

In Cullen Young's account, Nyirenda is not contradicted on any
important matter. There is a fuller discussion of the territorial
expanse of the chieftaincies authorised by Mlowoka; and there is a
detailed examination of the names of the aboriginal inhabitants of the
various chiefdoms. Young indicates clearly the importance of
strategic marriages in securing the domination of Mlowoka. He also
highlights the idea of a *succession* of people who crossed the Lake.
Nyirenda refers to Mlowoka and his party, also Kawunga and
Mwafulirwa, as separate arrivals; even the Chewa paramountcy was
apparently of translacustrine origin. Some of Young's information
came directly from Mwafulirwa, and this is acknowledged.
Mwafulirwa was old but still mentally active at the time of Young's
investigations. He maintained that the quarrel between the Fulirwa
people and the Mkandawire had been of much longer standing.

The most significant addition made by Young to Nyirenda's
account is that of an even greater territorial expanse for the authority
of the Chikulamayembe. Young maintains that such authority existed
over the Ngonde and their Kyungu. This is implied by Nyirenda only
to the extent that the Kyungu had come to discuss the question of land
allocation with the Chikulamayembe. Nyirenda also mentions
military assistance provided by the Ngonde. Young, however, goes
further and argues that the Ngonde first sought agreement of the
Chikulamayembe before occupying territory. He claims support for
this view from both Tumbuka and Ngonde informants. This is an
important political point. By the time of publication of Young's
account, Henga were present in the far north of Malawi in territory
also settled by the Ngonde. They had arrived as fugitives from the
Ngoni. These would be interlopers if the Ngonde Kyungu had sole
jurisdiction in that territory, but not if the Chikulamayembe were in
overall charge.

In support of the contention regarding Chikulamayembe's
overlordship in the far north, Young suggests a possible common
origin of Mlowoka and Chawara, the first Kyungu. This was also
suggested by Nyirenda, though Young did not see the matter as

conclusively proved. One difficulty, he suggests, is presented by the difference between Henga and Ngonde speech. He speculates as to a possible Yao origin for both of them. More generally, he sees the arrival of the Ngonde in Malawi as part of a wider movement from east to west, of which the Balowoka were also a part. He examines the journeying of Chawara, who had been forced to seek new territory following a quarrel with his brother. Chawara is reported as having moved south across the Songwe river. He was attracted by the territory of chief Simbowe near Mwambira, in the neighbourhood of Mpande hill. Young maintains that he sought the advice of Mlowoka at this point, on the question of how to capture the territory successfully. The advice was that he should capture the village by following Simbowe's men along the elephant route; as an expert elephant hunter, Mlowoka would have been well informed on this subject. Chawara, according to Young's account, took this advice and captured the territory. He became the first Kyungu, and established his capital at Mpande. Young goes on to argue that, though it was impossible to dogmatise, it appeared that Mlowoka and Chawara 'already knew each other'. He states that this assertion was frequently made by his older Henga informants; also he suggests that such help and advice would not have been given to a mere stranger. Eventually, Young argues, the dealings between the two leaders were finally consolidated, apparently around 1790, by a treaty on boundaries. Without indicating the source he suggests that the boundary used to begin at Chiwondo, then climbed the Phoka mountains, and eventually dipped down northwards. There was a subsequent revision southwards, and this was apparently done amicably. The arrangements were sealed when Chawara slew an ox and Mlowoka slew a man. Young argues that this indicated the higher authority of Mlowoka, since an ox was the more valuable.

Young's final observation on the Ngonde of this period is to the effect that present-day appearances could be misleading. The Ngoni invasion had led to a break-up of the power of Chikulamayembe, whereas although the Ngonde had suffered some disruption the ruling house was left relatively untouched. He saw this as giving the erroneous impression that the Kyungu was a superior authority to the Chikulamayembe whereas he maintained that the opposite was in fact the case. The fact that the Kyungu was entrusted to wreak revenge against Mwafulirwa is also quoted by Young in support of the idea of the overall supremacy of Chikulamayembe.

The main part of Young's discussion of the pre-Ngoni period deals with the history of the Chikulamayembe dynasty. Here he builds on Nyirenda but also takes account of oral testimony from various sources; some of this contradicts Nyirenda. Young indicates the various successors to the Chikulamayembeship. This information is too detailed to be suitable for close examination here, though the main developments are presented in Figure 1. There were certain ambiguities in the method of succession, and these have been noted. A particularly interesting assertion by Young is that a form of adelphic succession prevailed. As he puts it: 'It will be found that what is involved is "succession through males" and that on the death of a Chikulamayembe his son will only succeed him if there are no brothers of the deceased available in whose "house" the chieftainship has not yet been held or its perquisites "eaten"'.[28]

In spite of this, it is evident from Figure 1 that adelphic succession was not automatic; the issue is however complicated by the fact that no information is provided as to matrilateral links of the various incumbents of the Chikulamayembeship.

Young clearly admired Mlowoka. He saw him as showing in his personal qualities the 'African beau ideal'. He is reported to have been kindly, skilful in hunting, and generous at all times. He was in no way connected with slaving, but he built up Nkhamanga as a trading centre so successfully that 'Nkhamanga' became the accepted name for the whole area between the Dwangwa river and the Rukuru valley, for over a century. Young appears to have seen in Mlowoka a synthesis of the Tumbuka virtue of open-handedness and the idea of 'legitimate commerce' which Livingstone had advocated.

Young's interest in the origin of names surfaces again in his discussion of the name 'Chikulamayembe'. He states that this was first used for Gonapamuhanya, Mlowoka's immediate successor. Steele's informant, mentioned earlier, seems to have thought that the name referred to generosity, and Nyirenda also took this view. But Young suggested that it was rather the opposite, since it referred to a tribute in hoes that was expected. He argues: 'The verb "kukura" denotes the action of loosening and pulling out the hoe from its wooden handle and thus the imperative "kukuramayembe" besides meaning "pull out your hoe" could come to mean "pay your tax"'.[29]

Young does consider another possible explanation suggested by

THE CHIKULAMAYEMBE DYNASTY
(one possible version)

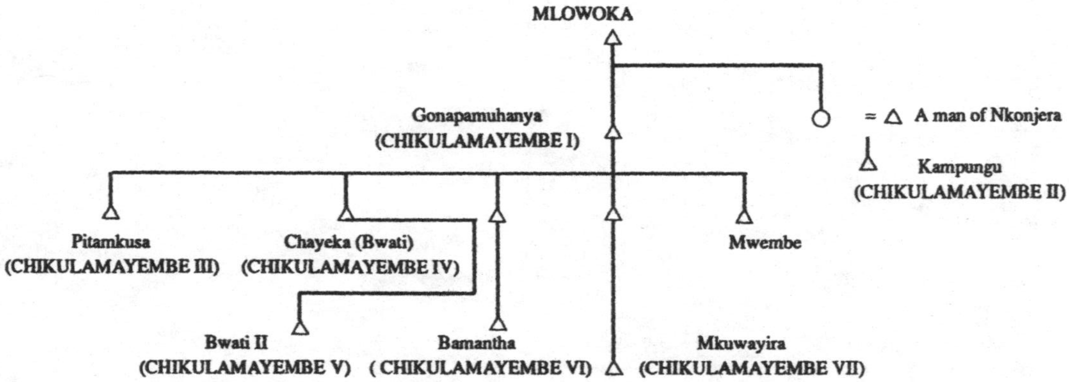

MLOWOKA

= △ A man of Nkonjera

Kampungu
(CHIKULAMAYEMBE II)

Gonapamuhanya
(CHIKULAMAYEMBE I)

Mwembe

Pitamkusa
(CHIKULAMAYEMBE III)

Chayeka (Bwati)
(CHIKULAMAYEMBE IV)

Mkuwayira
(CHIKULAMAYEMBE VII)

Bwati II
(CHIKULAMAYEMBE V)

Bamantha
(CHIKULAMAYEMBE VI)

Ambiguities

1. Uncertainties as to exact matrilateral filiation in most cases. The father/son link is fairly clear, but not the house to which each brother belonged: yet much evidence is cited in the text for plural marriages.

2. A lack of clarity as to when the rule of adelphic succession applied.

3. Conflicting traditions as to whether there were one or two Bwatis.

4. An alternative tradition which maintains that another Chikulamayembe, *Mujumba* intervened between Bwati and Mkuwayira. According to this, he was was a member of the house of Bwati I. (This Mujuma is not to be confused with the name of the restored Chikulamayembe mentioned on p.85).

Figure 1

informants; this was that the name derived from *chukwajembe* in Swahili, meaning "carry hoes" (i.e. as barter); but he considers that the reference to tribute is the more probable. Another matter of the origin of names is mentioned by Young in relation to the incumbency of Gonapamuhanya. His concern here is with the origin of the clan name, *Gondwe*. Apparently one (unnamed) son of Gonapamuhanya had developed a stiff leg, and left a furrow behind when walking. This resembled the track left by a large iguana (*gondwe*), and thus the name of the reptile became associated with the clan.

He goes on to relate the story of the unsuccessful attempt to bring Kawunga's territory in Mzokoto under Nkhamanga jurisdiction, and the consequent death of Chiwuruntha. He points out, however, that the matter did not end there. Rather there were two further pitched battles, at least, between Mwahenga's people from Muhuju and the Nyirendas from Mzokoto, before peaceful coexistence was finally established. Young confirms that the end-product of this conflict was the recognition of the independence, or semi-independence at least, of the Mzokoto area; attempts to bring the area under Mwahenga's jurisdiction had failed. He is at pains to stress that skirmishes of this kind were scarcely to be seen as having historic significance, and were not on a par with post-Ngoni disturbances. He suggests that 'they were, if ancient tales regarding communal strife are true, much more of the nature of public tests of strength than what we would understand as battles. The death of one or more invariably brought the proceedings to an end and the following day usually saw some sort of payments made to square losses'.[30]

Saulos Nyirenda's account: post-Ngoni times.[31]

Nyirenda depicts the Ngoni not as a people with a heroic past, but rather as imperialist intruders. He shows his own people, the Henga, as having displayed spirited resistance to their domination. He admits that the Henga were eventually put to flight northwards; but he points out that the Ngoni were able to succeed in doing this only through an alliance with the Chewa chief Mwase Kasungu, whose position was bolstered by having acquired firearms from Arab sources. Nyirenda tells of the initial encounter with the Ngoni, who marched northwards through Nkhamanga and then to Tanzania, before returning southwards and settling in Malawi and Zambia (see map 5). He comments on their propensity to seize cattle in the course of their journey; their departure was therefore viewed with relief, and it was not expected that they would return. But some Ngoni reappeared in Malawi as a consequence of the dispersal which took place on the death of their leader, Zwangendaba.

On their march through Nkhamanga the Ngoni had captured a child, Mafechura. He was prodigious in learning military skills, and awakened curiosity about the area from which he originated. The Ngoni had generally been favourably impressed by the terrain in Nkhamanga. Thus after the death of Zwangendaba, two of his children, M'mbelwa and Mtwalo, decided to go back to where Mafechura had been captured. A third son, Mperembe, joined them later. The Ngoni met with resistance and lack of cooperation from the Tumbuka, and their effective control was often limited; but they did succeed in conquering the Tumbuka political authorities and in installing their own chiefs. They were now confronted with an unfamiliar situation, since they were no longer transients but had come to settle permanently. The Ngoni had a long tradition of assimilating foreigners while on the move, but the question arose as to whether this policy should be pursued in a stable situation. It was decided that it would be possible to absorb the younger men and to teach them Ngoni methods of warfare, while the older men were viewed with deep suspicion. The policy of assimilating the young was successful to the extent that some fierce fighters from their subjects became highly competent in Ngoni military methods. What was not anticipated was that these skills would eventually be used against the Ngoni instructors. Nyirenda makes particular mention of Kanyoli and Mwendera Wadokota in this connection. Both were of the house of Chikulamayembe, but had been brought up among Ngoni warriors. Kanyoli had lived in close association with Mtwalo, and became warlike even by Ngoni standards. There was a third fierce warrior, Kambondoma, brought up with the Ngoni aristocracy; he appears later in Nyirenda's account.

The Ngoni were largely successful in maintaining their domination by the seizure of cattle, but in due course they met with organised resistance. The first to stage an open rebellion were the Lakeside Tonga. In about 1874, the Henga were called upon to take the Ngoni side in quelling a rebellious element among the Tonga; but in the event some Henga took the Tonga side and the rebellion proved successful. The matter was decided at the Battle of Chinteche in 1875. Cullen Young comments in a footnote that this would have been only a temporary setback to the Ngoni had it not been for the arrival of the British.

Nyirenda goes on to show that rebellious tendencies of this nature led some Ngoni councillors to express concern about the wisdom of the assimilation policy. But the principle that the young could be trusted but not the old was reaffirmed, and the aim now became to massacre the old people. The plan was summed up in the saying 'we will root out the potatoes and let the cassava remain'. Potatoes, with widespread roots in the soil, represented the old; while cassava, with a single main root, represented the young. It was intended that the massacre should take place at a meeting at Mtwalo's kraal, to which the Henga were summoned. Ostensibly the aim was to administer war-medicine, but a surprise attack was to be launched. But the plan was leaked by a sympathetic Ngoni, and the Henga were prepared for the attack and defended themselves successfully.

This incident led to further distrust of the Ngoni by the Henga. Kanyoli now openly distanced himself from his captors. He challenged the Ngoni to attack his own Henga people, but they did not respond. Many Henga now called their children away from the Ngoni; Kambondoma was one of those who responded to this invitation. Henga elders and headmen now debated political and military matters. Defence was an important question, but so too was the objective of restoring the Chikulamayembe line. The majority took the view that defence was the first priority. They supported Kanyoli as the obvious leader, since he understood Ngoni military methods and war magic. All but the Nkhamanga people concurred with this position. The Nkhamanga persisted in their wish to enthrone Chikulamayembe immediately, and Mujuma was chosen. The other chiefs did not resist this move. There was thus established a division in the area between different styles of government. The upper reaches of the Henga valley were under military rule, led by Kanyoli who in turn was helped by Kambondoma. The lower reaches were under the civilian rule of the reestablished Chikulamayembe.

Two successful attacks were launched against the Ngoni. Fighting was fierce but the Henga were victorious and Kanyoli was honoured.

But in 1879, resistance against a Ngoni attack proved much less successful. M'mbelwa and Mtwalo now enlisted the support of Mwase Kasungu, who as already noted had access to firearms. Nyirenda attributes the Ngoni recourse to reinforcements of this nature to their weakness if they were left unaided. Nyirenda further maintains that the Ngoni were nearly defeated in spite of such assistance. Mwendera Wadokota was attacked, but now he also had guns, and he resisted successfully. But the Ngoni suddenly noticed that the Henga had no food in their stockade, and the Henga were successfully starved out, Mwendera Wadokota being killed. On a subsequent occasion, the Henga were victorious when an invasion by Mperembe's son Waso took place near Nkhamanga. Kanyoli led the resistance, with Kambondoma turning the battle in favour of the Henga by producing surprise reinforcements.

But by 1889, faced again with an alliance between the Ngoni and Mwase Kasungu, the Henga were forced to accept that their position was hopeless. The combined forces of their opponents were strong and the weapons were powerful, and it was conceded that the only course of action was flight. They were not pursued by the Ngoni, who feared Kanyoli; rather the Ngoni diverted their attention eastwards and raided Siska country. Initially the Henga stayed in the Chiweta area, by the Lakeshore, though there were various other settlements as far as the boundary of the Kyungu's territory. But further military ventures were to come, this time of an offensive rather than defensive nature. Kanyoli was approached by a Nyakyusa named Mwasewa, who had quarrelled with his own people. Mwasewa treated Kanyoli with deference, and urged him to lead his soldiers northwards on a raiding expedition. He agreed to do this and was very successful, bringing back numerous cattle. Kambondoma, whose soldiers had initially been reluctant to raid northwards, now became enthusiastic because of Kanyoli's success. But it was now the rainy season, and much marshland was impassable. However Kambondoma persisted and this time met with fierce resistance from the Nyakyusa; this time the Henga army was defeated and Kambondoma was killed. Kanyoli had advised against wet-season raiding, but himself took part in engagements in the dry season in Nyakyusa country. In one of these, in 1885, he was killed.

The situation in the far north was now complicated by the presence of non-African elements. Already on his second expedition to the north Kanyoli had made an alliance with an Arab settler, who had taken the African name Chiparamoto. The Ngonde Kyungu had initially wanted to kill Kanyoli thinking him to be a Ngoni, and had sought Chiparamoto's assistance to this end. But Chiparamoto visited Kanyoli in secret, saying that he wanted peace since they were both strangers in the country. By 1885, Europeans were present in the situation, though were only six in number. They included Low Monteith Fotheringham, referred to in Nyirenda's account as 'Bwana Monteith'. Fighting subsequently occurred between the Ngonde and the Arabs. The Ngonde resisted the Arab attacks, but were initially restrained by the Europeans. But subsequently the Europeans joined battle on the Ngonde side. The Nyakyusa also came in against the Arabs, and eventually the Arabs were forced to return to their stockades. After an interval, the Europeans decided to advance against Mlozi, the leader among the Arab traders. They were assisted by Ngonde and Nyakyusa, but found the Henga blocking their path. The combined forces fought against the Henga and inflicted heavy casualties. Many Henga who survived went over to the Arabs; there were, however, some Henga levies, of whom Nyirenda appears to have been one. A further two years passed before the conflict with the Arabs came to an end. In the meantime, a force had been recruited from all locally-available African groups: Nyakyusa, Tonga and Tumbuka were all represented. Eventually peaceful terms were agreed to, and all rejoiced and danced. This happened in 1889, after the arrival of Sir Harry Johnston as Governor.

Thus was brought the *Pax Britannica*, and serious warfare ceased at this juncture. Nyirenda argues that this proves that the Europeans came with good intent, and he sees their influence as beneficial since law and order returned. The breakdown of law and order is laid firmly at the door of the Ngoni:

> .... before the Ngoni came while our chiefs were still
> [over] the land here, Chungu (sic), Chikuramayembe,
> Kanyenda and his father Karonga, we do not hear that
> people fought together at random. There were the poison
> ordeals and small village quarrels; in the morning they
> would be friendly in the very place where they had
> wounded each other, there was no carrying the matter
> on.[32]

Although tax now had to be paid, Nyirenda saw this as acceptable in return for securing peace; and above all, the Europeans were now setting about restoring Chikulamayembe to his former glory. Thus Nyirenda concluded: 'Salute, we thank you Europeans greatly; you have settled us well and we also have the words of God; in the old days we wandered far astray'.[33]

Cullen Young on post-Ngoni times.

Young was less dependent on Nyirenda for his account of the post-Ngoni situation.[34] The Ngoni had previously been written about by Europeans, sometimes with admiration. Elmslie[35] contributed to Ngoni historiography, and they were referred to by Archdeacon Johnston[36] of the UMCA. They had been discussed also in the writings of Sir Harry Johnston, Frederick (later Lord) Lugard, Low Monteith Fotheringham, and Fred Moir.[37] Also, and particularly important, the Ngoni period was sufficiently recent for Young to be able to draw on eye-witness accounts. But Young's general perspective follows that of Nyirenda, and he portrays the Ngoni as having interfered with a stable, viable and on the whole peaceful polity. A different view had been expressed by Donald Fraser, as already noted. Fraser admired Ngoni discipline and centralisation, and seemed to see their incursion as progressive.[38] Even Nkhonjera, well-connected with regard to the Chikulamayembe, admitted that the Ngoni invasion had been facilitated by the lawlessness prevailing in Nkhamanga, and by the weakness of the Nkhamanga chiefs.[39]

Cullen Young did however fill in much background information about Ngoni history. He recounts the movement north from South Africa, led by Zwangendaba after the defeat of Zwide by Shaka. He shows that the Ngoni assimilated many alien elements on their march northwards. He dates the crossing of the Zambezi as 1825, this being ascertained because it coincided with an eclipse of the sun. He shows the route of the march through Malawi (see map 5). He examines in detail the succession dispute following the death of Zwangendaba in Tanzania, and the subsequent division of the Ngoni into five different sections. He outlines the places of eventual Ngoni settlement in Malawi, and confirms that there were difficulties in pursuing a settled

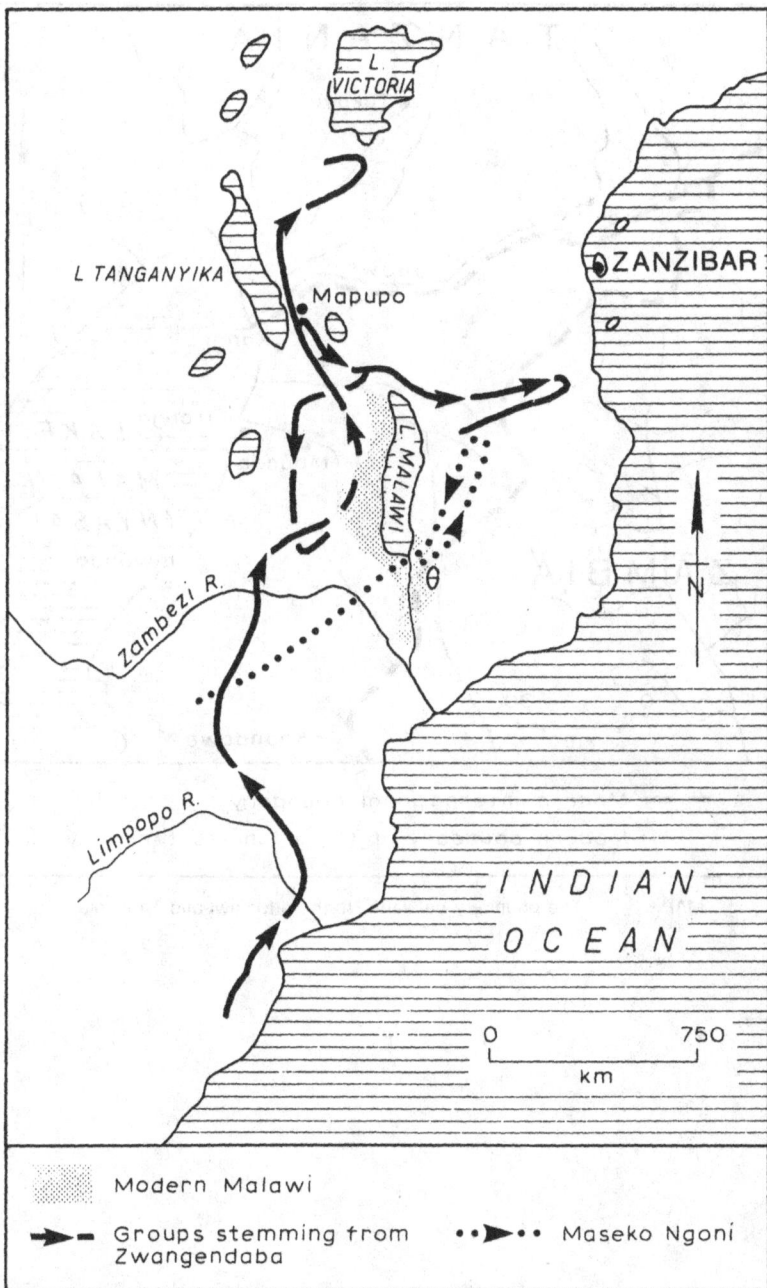

MAP 5 :   Ngoni migrations.

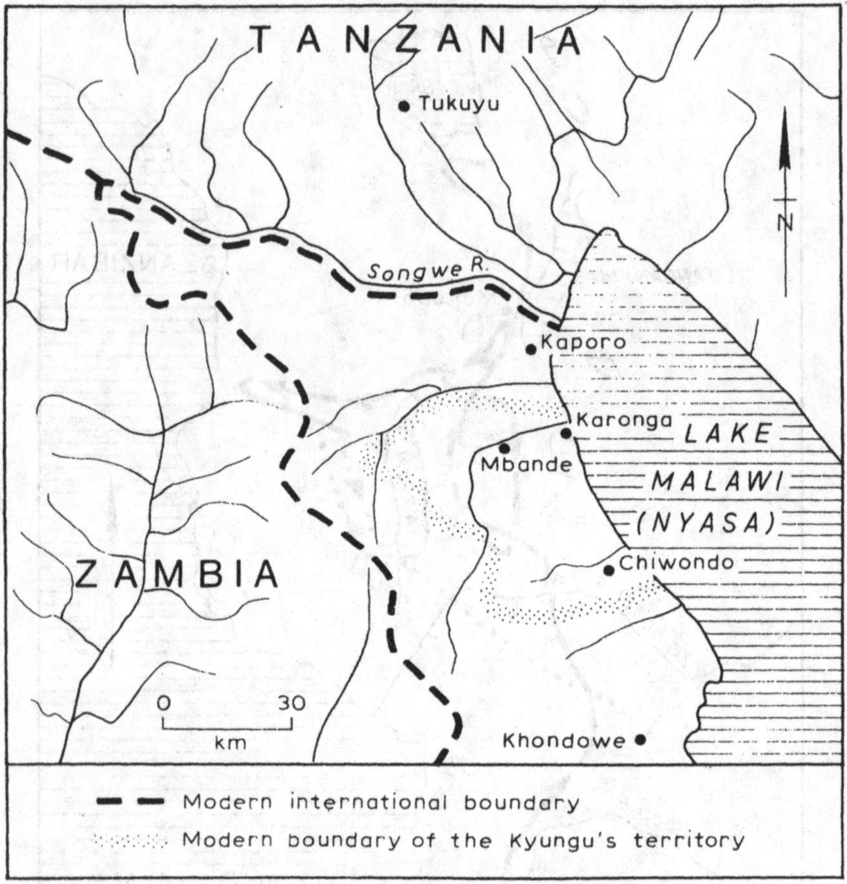

TANZANIA

• Tukuyu

Songwe R.

• Kaporo

Karonga
Mbande •   LAKE

MALAWI
(NYASA)

• Chiwondo

ZAMBIA

0   30
km

Khondowe •

- - - Modern international boundary
∴∴∴∴ Modern boundary of the Kyungu's territory

MAP 6 .   The boundary between Northern Malawi and Tanzania.

existence. He does not however repeat Nyirenda's account of the capture of Mafechura.

Young goes on to relate how M'mbelwa tried to restrain his regiments from killing too many of his new subjects; he had asked 'can I get milk when the cow is dead?'. He shows how expansion southwards in Malawi was necessitated by a combination of enslavement, stock increase, new arrivals, and unfamiliarity with settled agricultural methods. He suggests that the young men who were assimilated were less restrained than the original Ngoni. This created particular problems in conditions of stable settlement, where slaughter was local and not a matter of distant forays.

Nyirenda's account is fairly closely followed with regard to the Tonga rebellion; Young again argues that the arrival of missionaries altered the balance of power, to the disadvantage of the Ngoni. Most subsequent events in the Henga rebellion are related in the form of direct quotations from Nyirenda's account. Young stresses that it was Mtwalo, not M'mbelwa, who advocated a massacre of the old; he suggests that M'mbelwa had preferred a strategy of dispersal, since the old were important as a source of supplies. Young also mentions the direct intervention of M'mbelwa, who was greatly concerned about Henga military successes and about the crowning of a new Chikulamayembe. It was to ensure future military success that the alliance with Mwase Kasungu was forged. Young points out that the civil government of Nkhamanga fell first, with the death of Mujuma. The military government of Kanyoli and Kambondoma was not dislodged until the Mwase-Ngoni alliance in 1879-90. The flight of the Henga is reported by Young, with the comment that the Ngoni lack of interest in pursuit was due to the presence of the missionaries, who were by this time just beginning to make contacts with the Ngoni that eventually led to cessation of their military activities altogether.

Young also mentions a further, unsuccessful rebellion, which had not been reported by Nyirenda. Some of the information on this was derived from Baza Mdokowe, the surviving rebel leader. He was headman of an area near Mt Hora. When he saw the advance of Ngoni regiments, he led his people to the top of the mountain. This strategy proved foolhardy since the Ngoni easily surrounded them; eventually hunger and thirst drove the rebels down to be massacred. Baza Mdokowe and one follower were the only ones to escape; they miraculously succeeded in descending a spur which was so dangerous that the Ngoni had left it unguarded.

Young's account of the northward move of the Henga is less detailed than that of Nyirenda, though sometimes Young adds information of his own. He shows how on the move various settlements were left, retaining some Henga inhabitants. He confirms from his own military experience during 1915-16[40] that Kambondoma's incursion was unwise in the wet season because of the high water level. Most of the details are as Nyirenda reports them, but Young had more eye-witnesses to draw upon. A further comment that he made on Kambondoma's raid was as follows: 'It is their last bit of history before the coming of the white man was to lay bare to the world all their doings, and they colour in the picture of Kambondoma's great fight and solitary death - the last to fall among countless slain - with a wealth of picturesque and vivid incident.[41]

He suggests that after the death of Kanyoli, the Henga missed his leadership and as a consequence played a neutral and occasionally capricious role. He also comments that those Tumbuka who had taken the Arab side were, after punishment by the British, the first to be responsive to their influence. He suggests that this marks a landmark in voluntary partnership. A further consequence of the British presence that he notes was an interest in moving southwards; some Tumbuka who had fled the Ngoni were now cautiously inspecting their ancestral sites. Seeing them now pacified, some chose to return and this became a continuing process. On the other hand, the *Pax Britannica* also enabled the Ngoni leaders to settle new areas peacefully, and some of their Tumbuka subjects went with them. Young notes that this is what had led to much confusion regarding clan-names.

The 1932 revised edition

Those Tumbuka who were literate in English found the historical section of *Notes on Speech and History* very interesting and often controversial. Young was fascinated by the debates that he had provoked and as a consequence he produced a revised edition which eventually appeared in 1932. In its preface he remarks:

It contains much that was not available when I wrote, in

> 1923, the earlier book. Since then an interest in their
> own past has sprung up among the people concerned
> which has led to my being inundated with contributions
> from enthusiastic, and in the majority of cases, far from
> impartial clansmen who desire that the story of their
> fathers may not be under-estimated.[42]

These matters were of political as well as personal significance to their authors. Indirect Rule was now being implemented by the British in Malawi, and the time was evidently ripe to press such claims. Whatever account was accepted by the British administration, even erroneous, was likely to become the norm as far as policy was concerned. A new appendix[43] on clan histories appeared in Young's revised version. The ones that appeared in print were those that Young considered to be the most important. Most of them are not unfortunately acknowledged individually, though a list of Malawian collaborators is contained at the beginning of the revised volume.[44] A further major change is the inclusion of three totally new chapters.[45] The first of these is by three Ngonde collaborators, who take issue with the claim of Nkhamanga sovereignty over the Ngonde. There are also two chapters on the Tonga viewpoint, and again the intention is to dispute Nkhamanga pretensions.

One interesting feature of the chapter on the Ngonde claim is that one of its signatories had previously helped Young to collect data for his earlier account of Ngonde-Nkhamanga relations; but in the new contribution the previous claims for Nkhamanga sovereignty in Ngondeland are now rejected. Young was aware of the discrepancy, but merely suggested that it was indicative of the difficulty of collecting reliable historical data in African villages. He does not resolve the controversy, stressing rather that the findings were only tentative. The Ngonde informants take issue particularly with the earlier suggestion that Mlowoka had arrived before Chawara. They maintain that Chawara could not possibly have travelled south to interview Mlowoka, since Mlowoka had not appeared on the scene at this point. In support of their standpoint they maintain that Saulos Nyirenda had been unable to say where the supposed interview took place when asked to do this by Ngonde headmen. They also deny that the Kyungu dynasty had been founded by a Mlowoka, and they dispute the view that Mlowoka made a journey northwards. Young, however, continues to maintain that both Ngonde and Nkhamanga tradition support his own earlier version of events.

The Ngonde contributors also take issue with the account of the incidents concerning the Fulirwa area. They maintain that the Kyungu annexed the territory from Mwafulirwa and proceeded to divide it among his own children and his sub-chiefs. He would not have been able to do this on his own initiative if he had been subordinate to Nkhamanga. Rather the Kyungu took the territory from Chikulamayembe, since Mwafulirwa was one of his subordinates.

The Ngonde authors also reject the claim that the fighting against Kyepere was on the basis of an alliance between the Chikulamayembe and the Kyungu. They argue rather that the Kyungu joined battle on his own initiative and that the two never met during the fighting. They also raise questions about the ordering of the incidents with Mwafulirwa and with Kyepere. They observe that the incident with Kyepere was a generation earlier than that with Mwafulirwa; many who fought against Mwafulirwa were still alive when the Ngonde version was written. The stories about boundary-fixing between the Chikulamayembe and the Kyungu are also rejected, and there are numerous criticisms of particular details. The Ngonde critics' main concern is to expose the bias in the earlier account. They argue that Cullen Young admits his bias by stating that beliefs as to the relative position of the Kyungu and the Chikulamayembe were 'erroneous', and in need of correction. As a consequence, they maintain, the claims of Nkhamanga are magnified and exalted. Indeed, they suggest that the details concerning the Ngonde were all so misleading that they ought to have been left out.

In his own comments on the Ngonde critics, Cullen Young merely states that the contribution was most welcome; he views with satisfaction the fact that the debate was now in the hands of the principals themselves. He does not come down personally on either side; he republishes the old account almost word-for-word, followed by the Ngonde criticisms. He comments that some of the material that he had collected on the Mkandawires contradicted the Ngonde account. He does however, show special interest in one point made in the Ngonde version, to the effect that the Kyungu had crossed a river Kyari on the journey to Malawi. This suggested to Young an original home in the area of Lake Chad, and strengthened his interest in the idea of a West African origin for the incomers in Malawi.

The next set of critical material comes from a Tonga viewpoint. This is signed by Yuraya C. Chirwa, a Tonga schoolmaster who later became senior assistant at the Overtoun Institute.[46] Chirwa suggests that Kabunduli was not one of the Balowoka, but that he was a sister's son of Kalonga Mazizi, the original Chewa paramount. Young seems to have been influenced by this comment, for he now merely states that Kabunduli was a *possible* companion of Mlowoka. Young also now maintains that the land between the Henga and the Lake remained with its original Tonga occupiers, with the newcomers coming to claim the debatable areas. Chirwa also points out that Tonga history contains no recollection of fighting between Kanyenda and Mankhaka.

On the post-Ngoni situation, Chirwa stresses the extent to which the incursion occurred. He suggests that the Ngoni subjugated all territory in Malawi into which they penetrated, except for Nkhotakota and Kasungu. He attributes the proposal to kill off the old to the bad advice of Mperembe; while he argues that the leaking of the plan was the work of Tonga armour-bearers. He suggests that the Tumbuka felt safe and did not assist the Tonga, some in fact helping the Ngoni; also he maintains that the Tumbuka did not know of the plan to massacre the old. The Tonga relationship to the Ngoni, therefore, was in many respects different from that of the Tumbuka.

Cullen Young comments on the Tonga claim. He maintains that it can be demonstrated that Chikulamayembe was paramount over the Siska country in the Lakeshore; he had placed a kinsman near the Ruzi stream in Henga territory, to enable messages to be passed between the Siska chief, Mbwana, and Nkhamanga. But he accepts that south of Siska territory Nkhamanga sovereignty was not recognised.

Apart from the particular viewpoints of the Tonga and the Ngonde, there are in the revised account numerous corrections of details. Much of the corrected information relies on the clan histories which were presented in the revised edition for the first time. They are important as sources of new information regarding the pre-Balowoka situation, and also for details of the Balowoka themselves. The history of the Mkandawire clan is referred to frequently in Young's new text. The contributor (Revd Y.M. Mkandawire)[47] is indicated, unfortunately the only time when this is done. Young uses the material on the Mkandawires mostly to reply to Ngonde claims.

Of particular interest in the clan histories is the new material on the Balowoka. This time it is indicated quite clearly that the leader of those who crossed the Lake was Katumbi: Mlowoka's supremacy is recorded as having come later. It is suggested that Mlowoka was a nephew (no indication as to which side of the family); a younger nephew, Chipofya, is reported as having also been a member of the original party. This is an important change from the 1923 version, in which Katumbi had been assigned a more junior position and Chipofya had not been mentioned at all. It is suggested in the clan histories that Chipofya originally settled in the Rumphi area, near Njakwa; he then moved to Hewe, but after two generations his family moved to Mwazisi. But although one of the Balowoka, Chipofya never took a chieftainship. The suggestion is also made in the new version that although Mlowoka himself was generous and open-handed, the same was not true of some of his companions; indeed it is maintained that some of them took advantage of the ignorance of the indigenous population. There are also numerous changes in detail in the 1932 text. The matter of the 'tridents' in the graves of the Chikulamayembes is noted, as referred to in Chapter II. Doubt is now expressed as to the arrival of Chiwuruntha with the first party. One member of the party who appeared in the earlier version - Kajumba - no longer appears in the list.

There is some more detailed information included on the post-Ngoni period, and the account is more accurate in the later version. Young was now in a position to consult better documentation on the move northwards. There is an important correction of the date of crossing of the Zambezi. The eclipse of the sun that coincided with this is now set at 1835, not 1825, as a result of information from Cape Town Observatory. This change necessitated adjustments of some other dates which had been fixed in relation to the Zambezi crossing.

In summary it can be said that new information led Young to change his account in a number of important particulars. The Ngonde and the Tonga viewpoints were especially important though characteristically Young refused to commit himself to a particular version. Rather he recorded all points of view, seeing them as a contribution to an ongoing debate. But conspicuous in its absence is any representation of the Ngoni viewpoint. The 1932 account relies on some better documentation, but there is no evidence of collection of oral testimony or written statements from Ngoni informants. The Ngoni could no doubt have taken issue with a number of claims made by Young, but his pro-Tumbuka stance remained. He even closes the main text in the new version with the following words: 'It is to be hoped that the mistaken policy of the old Tumbuka families, who hid their true race in the foolish dress of being taken for "Ngoni", may not long delay the appearance among them of a reliable historian'.[48] This was not the only occasion on which Young complained about 'Ngoni-isation' of the Tumbuka.[49] But as will be seen shortly, Young did assist in preparing an account of the Ngoni version after he had left the mission field.

Before leaving the presentation of Young's historical contributions, it is worth examining the reasons for the change of name from 'Tumbuka-Henga' to 'Tumbuka-Kamanga', between the original and the revised texts. Again, this topic was of great interest to Young because of his concern for the origin of names, and he discusses the matter in various places. His earliest reference to the topic appears in an article published in 1923,[50] in response to a previous contribution by Meredith Sanderson on the subject of Henga marriage customs.[51] Young comments here that *Henga* was really one of three possible names (the other two being Tumbuka and Kamanga), and that dispersal caused by the arrival of the Ngoni had added to the confusion. Europeans popularised the term Henga, he continues, because those who first encountered the British (in Karonga) referred to themselves by that name. He shows that the Henga were the first to free themselves from Ngoni domination; they became identified with the claims of Chikulamayembe since they were the first to press them. But he notes that the name *Tumbuka* was recorded by Lacerda, Livingstone and Rebman. It could be seen that those who called themselves Henga did not reject the name Tumbuka, but there were many Tumbuka who would not describe themselves as Henga. Initially Young preferred the name *Tumbuka-Henga*, on the grounds that there were certain dialect differences and that Tumbuka ancient sites paralleled each other rather than overlapped. In 1923 he did not see the name *Tumbuka-Kamanga* as acceptable for the people as a whole; he thought this inappropriate because Nkhamanga gained prominence only during a short period of dynastic rule.

But by 1932 Young's position had shifted. He acknowledges this explicitly in his *linguistic* work.[52] He now argues that Nkhamanga was important as a seat of power. He points out that this was temporarily obliterated by the Ngoni, and that the Europeans first made contact with the Henga section. He now comments of the Henga 'Neither themselves nor their speech have the slightest claim for separate recognition once the nature and scope of the authority of the Chikulamayembe in Nkamanga is recognised'.

The name *Tumbuka-Kamanga* therefore serves to underline the postulated authority of the Chikulamayembe from the Dwangwa northwards as far as Ngonde country. Young seems, therefore, determined to make a political point about the importance of the Chikulamayembe dynasty. Though aware of the Ngonde and Tonga criticisms, he again makes the maximum territorial claims for it. This is especially significant because of its implications for Indirect Rule.

Responses, critical and otherwise

Cullen Young's historical work has exercised more influence upon academic writers than any of the rest of his publications. Some responses have been highly critical, especially in recent years; while others have at least wished to press certain claims which Young had appeared to overlook. The historian Leroy Vail, already mentioned in Chapter II, has been particularly sceptical of Young's claims. Kalinga, another historian, has been critical of claims in respect of the Ngonde. The anthropologist Van Velsen has objected to many of Young's observations on the Lakeside Tonga; while the Ngoni minister, the Revd Yesaya Chibambo, has pressed his own people's claims. These and others will be examined individually before an overall review is attempted.

Vail has been the foremost critic of Cullen Young. He has shown particular concern about the tendency in many circles to see Young's work as the authentic, definitive account of historical events in northern Malawi. Vail has identified many inaccuracies and biases, and has obtained new data by both archival and field research. His most strongly-worded criticisms appeared in 1971, in a review in *African Studies* of the 1970 reissue of the revised *History*. He describes this book, especially its section on clan histories, as 'next to useless to the specialist and incomprehensible to the general reader'.[54] He identifies the chief fault as being the absence of information regarding the full background of informants. Moreover, Vail maintains here that Young's lack of appreciation of the complexity of Tumbuka history, and his uncritical acceptance of traditions, made the reprinting of the book 'a positive menace to an accurate knowledge of northern Malawi's history'.[56] Vail clearly sees the account as so misleading that it would have been better left out of print.

Furthermore, in his contribution to *The Early History of Malawi*,[56] Vail cites evidence for the widespread influence of Young's account. He points to ethnographic surveys by Tew and Wilson, and to historical accounts by Pike and Omer-Cooper.[57] It is therefore appropriate to examine in detail the criticisms made by Vail, together with the alternative version which he puts forward. Vail takes issue with Young on two main counts. Firstly he objects to the notion of a unified Tumbuka people before the arrival of the Balowoka. He maintains that Young exaggerated such unity, and suggests rather that the traditional structure was very loose. In particular he points to important differences between the northern and southern parts of the country, in respect of culture and religion. These topics have already been examined in Chapter II. Secondly, Vail argues that Young exaggerates the power and extent of the leadership of the Chikulamayembes. He sees their power as economic rather than political, and of much more limited geographical extent than Cullen Young claims. He considers this to be the case even if the disputed claims over Tonga and Ngonde territory are discounted. Vail also goes on to show how it came about that Young was convinced of exaggerated claims for the authority of the Chikulamayembes. He notes the eventual trading ascendancy of the Tumbuka over the Ngoni, and also shows how both Europeans and Africans saw the utility of producing a myth of unity under a powerful chief. He also points to the way in which Cullen Young was in close contact with spokesmen for the Chikulamayembe.

With regard to the origin of the Balowoka, Vail does not rule out the possibility of a Yao origin, as Young had also tentatively suggested. But his main concern is to stress their role as traders rather than as political functionaries. He questions the assertion that the incomers established any real power over the area postulated by Young, and most of his criticism is based upon information provided by Young himself. Vail suggests that the status of some of the lieutenants of Mlowoka was highly dubious. Whereas, he argues, Katumbi, Mwahenga and Mwalwene do seem to have been Mlowoka's followers, the claims for Kajumba, Mwamlowe and Jumbo appear much less convincing. The loyalty of Chiwuruntha and Kabunduli he sees as extremely doubtful, and in any case Chiwuruntha's authority seems to have been restricted to at most the northern fringe of Mzimba district. For Tongaland he sees that there might have been trade feelers put out by the Chikulamayembe; while evidence is totally lacking for sovereignty in Ngonde territory - a conclusion which is supported by Wilson's study of the Ngonde polity.[58]

Vail does however see that a better claim might be made out for effective political control over a more restricted area. He sees a legitimate claim as being possible for the territory between eastern Zambia and the Lakeshore. This crosses Nkhamanga, Henga and Phoka territory, and thereby forms a natural trade route. It might be suggested that Mlowoka himself, when making strategic marriages, secured economic rather than political interests. Vail shows how Mlowoka married into the clan of the Luhanga chief, Mubila. Mubila appeared to have preeminence among the other chiefs in Nkhamanga's central area - an unusual situation in circumstances where chieftainship tends to be purely localised. Mubila continued to rule after the marriage took place. In the next generation, Gonapamuhanya became the first Chikulamayembe. His father was Mlowoka, while his mother was Mubila's daughter. Gonapamuhanya succeeded to both an economic and a political office, while Mubila's direct patrilineal descendants were reduced to the level of village headmen. This succession was irregular by traditional standards, therefore some political power has to be acknowledged for the incomers.

Government, however, remained elementary. Vail points to the absence of a centralised bureaucracy, or army, or legal system worth speaking of. There was no external threat, so little government was required. There was, he suggests, no hierarchical relationship between the Chikulamayembe and the other Balowoka. Beyond the centre, the power of Chikulamayembe was recognised but weak. Mwahenga set up sub-chiefs without consulting the Chikulamayembe. Katumbi set himself somewhat apart, by having a more ritualised, institutionalised chieftainship. However, religious activities retained some independence from the political officers. The existing priestly guardians of shrines were not displaced, but the newcomers cooperated with them. But some control of religion appeared, since new shrines were established which were directly under the Chikulamayembe, while some old shrines were subservient. An attempt was made to unite certain shrines, but this proved unsuccessful. There was also a bid to control *mwavi*.

The military weakness of Nkhamanga is a further indication of lack of centralisation, according to Vail's account. The Nyirendas were incomers who succeeded not only in settling an area, but also subsequently in asserting their independence. Saulos Nyirenda and Cullen Young both report the way in which they defended themselves successfully against Chiwuruntha's army, and the death of Chiwuruntha himself in this operation. Vail also shows how the growth of the slave trade was another factor which weakened Nkhamanga. The Balowoka traders showed no interest in this new activity, and thus Arab (Swahili) traders such as Mlozi were able to insinuate themselves. This led to economic as well as military weakness, and the Tumbuka thus proved easy prey to the well-organised warriors who invaded the territory, namely the Ngoni. The Chikulamayembeship, already weakened, was easily conquered; and the reigning Chikulamayembe (Mkuwayira) was captured and later died.

This was not, however, the end of the story. It has already been seen that the Ngoni were unaccustomed to a settled existence. Their administrative policy was to segregate themselves while working through traditional rulers, a set-up not unlike the British system of Indirect Rule. The Ngoni also rejected the slave trade. Their view of wealth lay in traditional terms, i.e. people and cattle, and the sale of slaves would have led to depletion of the population which they controlled.

Even when the British arrived, the centralised chieftainship and military organisation were not totally ineffective. In particular, Europeans admired their authoritarian form of government. But whereas the Ngoni economic traditionalism led to a rejection of new trading opportunities, the Tumbuka had replied positively to these ever since the arrival of the Balowoka. The Tumbuka participation in new methods of obtaining wealth such as the trading of ivory eventually led to the demise of Ngoni hegemony. When by the 1880s the Scottish missionaries found the Ngoni leaders more cooperative, this was more out of desperation than anything else; the Ngoni traditional way of life was on the wane in any case.

The British recognised the validity of Ngoni sovereignty in Mzimba district (under M'mbelwa), and it was not till 1904 that British over-rule was accepted there. But the problem remained as to how to deal with the 'no-man's-land' between here and Ngondeland. It was at this juncture that the myths surrounding the Chikulamayembes became a relevant consideration. Vail examines the question of why they gained so much currency, and why Cullen Young believed them.

Vail suggests that there were strong pressures on all sides to accept the myth of a powerful empire controlled by a Chikulamayembe paramountcy. Both missionary and administrative interests could respond favourably to such a structure of authority. This was already seen to be so with the Ngoni, and it would be to the advantage of the Tumbuka to be able to produce something similar. The Tumbuka saw the British as allies against the Ngoni, and the educated Tumbuka from the mission wished to have a say in the new situation. Among the latter were Nyirenda and Nkhonjera. Cullen Young was also teaching John Gondwe;[59] he was the son of a Chikulamayembe, whose claims had received limited recognition by the British in 1907. Young arrived in Malawi in 1904; his work was not primarily in Ngoni territory, and it is logical to assume that the claims made for the revival of the Chikulamayembeship made a deep impression on a young missionary who was determined to give a fair hearing to indigenous culture.

Vail[60] also comments that by 1907 educational standards were being taken into account in deciding upon a suitable successor to the Chikulamayembeship. The new incumbent was Chirongozi Gondwe, brought up in Karonga and therefore something of an outsider. He had attended school in Livingstonia and had subsequently joined the police. His appointment was very popular, and he soon set about creating a new tradition around the Chikulamayembeship. He died in 1931, and John Gondwe succeeded. His claim was supported by the mission and especially by Edward Bote Manda, a Tonga minister and teacher who had strong nationalist aspirations. Manda maintained that it was essential to have a leader who supported the aims of the educated classes, and therefore saw John Gondwe as eminently suitable. The colonial government was now introducing Indirect Rule, with the consequence that chiefs would now have enhanced powers and their own treasuries, rather than being mere tax-collectors and labour mobilisers. Manda had also hoped that John Gondwe would take vows to support Christianity and to oppose intoxicating drinks, but was not successful on this matter. But after appointment, John Gondwe tried to invoke Cullen Young's claims regarding the extent of his territory. He attempted to secure a position for himself in Mwafulirwa's country, and later in some Ngoni territory near Hora. The attempt to 'invade' Mwafulirwa's territory was suppressed by the DC, but even after this there were some attempts to infiltrate parts of Ngoni territory. The British district administrators now recognised the importance of examining the authenticity of the claims made by Young, upon which such incursions were based. One such administrator was J.C. O'Brien, DC for Karonga. Vail eventually found that O'Brien's views concurred with his own.[61] None the less, Young's historical studies frequently *were* quoted by colonial officials when information was needed upon which to base Indirect Rule.[62] A wider influence for them was secured by the distribution of summaries of Young's version of Tumbuka history in schools run by the Livingstonia mission. This practice continued until the Tumbuka language ceased to be used officially in Malawian schools, in 1968. Thus, despite numerous shortcomings, Young's historical studies have formed the basis of an 'invented tradition'[63] for the supporters of Chikulamayembe.

Van Velsen also provides some criticisms of Young's account, in so far as it affects the Lakeside Tonga.[64] As with Vail, the findings are based upon field investigation; and Van Velsen eventually published a monograph on the Tonga. The main critical point that Van Velsen makes is to the effect that Kabunduli was not one of the Balowoka, but that rather he came with his own party, including Kanyenda. Kabunduli initially settled in Tongaland, but he later moved southwards, although some of his sister's descendants remained in the north. Kabunduli and Kanyenda both opposed the treaty between Mankhaka and Chikulamayembe. Moreover Mankhaka was the leader of the Kapunda Banda clan, who were rivals of the Phiri clan of which Kabunduli and his followers were members. The rivalry between the Phiri and the Kapunda Banda is central to Van Velsen's analysis, but is barely touched upon by Young.

Van Velsen, like Vail, is sceptical of the claims made by Young for overlordship in a very wide area. Van Velsen also makes some general observations on oral history. As an anthropologist, he stresses the importance of considering such traditions in the light of present-day knowledge of the society in question; and following Malinowski, he sees myths as charters for existing social relationships. He shows that legends can explain and validate present social and political relations in terms of the past: thus caution is needed in treating them as historical evidence. It has already been seen that versions of oral tradition were used to validate claims to positions for the benefit of the British government; Cullen Young was aware of this. But Van Velsen points to a further dimension, that of the tendency of Europeans' theories to feed back into popular legend. This clearly happened with Young's works, in both its original and its revised editions.

Kalinga has commented upon various aspects of Young's work in his study *A History of the Ngonde Kingdom*.[65] This is based on oral tradition. He takes issue with any suggestion that the Chikulamayembe's jurisdiction extended over Ngondeland. He argues that Young arrived at certain historical conclusions without strong evidence: such as the inferences that he drew from the mention of a river named *Kyari*. He also notes that even in the exposition of the Ngonde viewpoint, there is no discussion of the political, economic and social set-up before the arrival of the Kyungus. Kalinga attributes the biased account to the fact that Young's Tumbuka informants aimed to show that the whole of northern Malawi was under Chikulamayembe. At most, Kalinga suggests, it could be argued that there was a boundary disagreement. One Chikulamayembe in particular - Pitamkusa - was concerned to subdue some weaker rules, and Fulirwa could have been the next on the list. Kalinga suggests that the Ngonde, for their part, overplay in their tradition the conciliatory role of the Kyungu so as to exaggerate the extent of their own territory. He sees it as beyond dispute that the Kyungus were established two centuries before the Balowoka arrived. Some Ngonde tradition, he notes, does accept that the first Kyungu made a southward journey, but this was of a general exploratory nature and had nothing to do with Mlowoka. Kalinga does however recognise the value of the contribution of the Ngonde spokesmen in Young's historical work, and also praises Young's classification of all clans in the main Tumbuka-speaking zone according to their area of origin.

Gregson's study 'Work, Exchange and Leadership'[66] has already been mentioned in Chapter II. This contains a number of comments on Young's historical studies, and relates them to recent events. Gregson sees the political structure and especially the Chikulamayembeship as insecure, and as a consequence easily vulnerable to Ngoni invasion. He sees the looseness of structure as something which has been perpetuated, and prefers to analyse Tumbuka society in terms of choice between alternatives rather than of social structure; here he follows closely Van Velsen's perception of the Tonga.[67] Gregson sees Young's historical studies as interesting, but describes them as 'speculative reconstructions'.

S.Y. Ntara was mentioned in Chapter I, and can be considered again here in his capacity as a historian. Ntara published a work *Mbiri ya Achewa* (The History of the Chewa) at Nkhoma in 1944-5. A revised edition was published in 1949, and has been subsequently translated into English (appearing in 1973). Ntara's work is of interest here partly because of Cullen Young's reaction to it, and partly because Ntara refers to incidents also recorded by Young. The 1973 edition also has some useful comments by the editor (H.W. Langworthy).[68]

Certain incidents are reported by Ntara without much departure from Young's description, such as Baza Mdokowe's unsuccessful rebellion on Mt Hora. There is however some interesting new information, on the subject of a northward move by Kalonga, the Chewa paramount. This account states that he and his followers moved northwards, with many dropping out on the way. His party included the mother of Kanyenda (one of Kalonga's wives), and Kanyenda himself. They went through Nkhamanga, to Karonga and eventually to north-eastern Zambia. Here they found Kamphungu, who did not allow them to pass through his country; but in the end Kalonga's followers defeated him, and they intermarried with women of that area. They had been established there for some years, before Mlowoka arrived. Mlowoka found that, like the Tumbuka, the Chewa did not appreciate the value of ivory and were using it for ordinary domestic purposes. He offered Kalonga a trading relationship, promising riches in return; and Kalonga accepted. Mlowoka kept his word, and Kalonga gave one of his daughters as a wife to Mlowoka in appreciation of his consideration. This friendly relationship persisted until the death of Kalonga; then the Chewa began to be hated and were plundered by their neighbours. Eventually Kabunduli, the nephew of Kalonga, and Kalonga's son Kanyenda returned south, asking the Chikulamayembe to look after the land which they had been occupying.

Much of this story is questioned by the editor, Langworthy. He sees no reason why Kalonga should have wanted to make such a journey, and does not consider it likely that he would have been allowed to pass unimpeded till he reached Kamphungu's territory. Langworthy suggests that the story is necessary simply to explain the origins of some of the chiefs, especially that of Kanyenda. If the trip were made at all, he argues, it would hardly have been made as late as the second half of the eighteenth century, as is implied by the appearance of Mlowoka in the account. By this time Kalonga had little power in his own area. Langworthy also argues that it would have been highly unlikely that Kalonga was unaware of the value of ivory, since the Portuguese had been present on the edge of Kalonga's territory by 1600 at the latest.

A further critical point can be noted. Mlowoka is reported as having told Kalonga of the value of ivory; as having established a trading relationship; and as having received a wife from Kalonga. Yet although Cullen Young and some of his informants make exaggerated claims for the authority of Chikulamayembe, the suggestion is not made that he had any political power in Chewa territory; reference is made only to a border dispute. Thus the relationship established by Mlowoka can be seen as commercial rather than political, and as Vail has suggested, this is probably also true where claims to political authority *were* made by Young and his supporters.

Kanyenda is also mentioned as having succeeded to Kalonga's paramountcy, rather than Kabunduli (who would have been the normal matrilineal heir). Ntara explains that this form of succession occurred because of Kabunduli's carelessness. There is further discussion of subsequent succession, and Langworthy suggests that this account could usefully be compared with that of Cullen Young; Yuraya Chirwa had contributed some material on this question in Chapter IX of the 1932 revised edition of Young's historical study. Young and Ntara do not contradict one another on any important matter of Chewa history, though Langworthy is somewhat sceptical of the version that they both adopt.

One commentator referred to by Ntara at various points is Rangeley. W.H.J. Rangeley (1909-58) was well-informed on the history of Malawi and published extensively, though he did not live to complete a book-length study on the subject. He joined the Nyasaland administrative service in 1934, and rose to the position of Provincial Commissioner. He had an Oxford Diploma in Anthropology, and published ethnographic as well as historical material.[69] A correspondence between Rangeley and Young has been preserved in the Society of Malawi Library[70], and much of this deals with evaluation of Ntara's historical text. Young supported Rangeley's historical endeavours, but he had special praise for Ntara since he liked to see African authors succeed. Ntara himself was conscious of the importance of the 'inside view'; he commented as follows:

> Some Europeans who have been to this country have attempted to write something about the history of our people in their way of thinking. Although they have done so, it is important that such a story be retold and written down by one of us, with a hope of preserving the story as it has been handed down by us from parents to their children in succession.[71]

Rangeley, however, was much less enthusiastic about Ntara than was Young and indeed he was somewhat paternalistic. In 1952 he wrote of *Mbiri ya Achewa*: 'It is regrettably what one unfortunately expects from Africans at their present stage of development. It is quite non-critical and is little more than individual non-analysed quotations of the stories of various chiefdoms'[72]

Young was enthusiastic about Ntara in the way that he had been previously about Nyirenda. Like the Tumbuka, the Chewa now had their 'father of history'. He even suggested that Ntara be nominated for an award of the M.B.E., but Rangeley was much less keen. He was also sceptical of the story of Kalonga's journey northwards, as Langworthy was later. But Young found this idea exciting and as being in accord with Yuraya Chirwa's comments.

The overall impression of Young's correspondence with Rangeley is that the relationship was reasonably cordial; but Rangeley was sometimes irritated by Young's tendency to accept things uncritically. Rangeley was also more aware of the fact that oral testimonies vary from one generation to the next. Their evaluative standards were different in any case. Both were interested in Malawian history and culture: but whereas Rangeley remained paternalistic, Young seems to have been so concerned in the last few years of his life to defend Africans' literary abilities that at times he tended to be somewhat uncritical. Rangeley was, incidentally, also critical of some of the details of Young's interpretation of Bocarro's journey.[73]

It remains to assess Young's account of the post-Ngoni period, in the light of further material contributed both by indigenous historiographers and by Western anthropologists. In view of the total absence of presentation of the Ngoni viewpoint in any of Young's own studies, it is particularly interesting to consider the work of the Revd Yesaya Mloneyi Chibambo, which appeared in translated form in 1942. By this time Young was in no way concerned to play down the Ngoni viewpoint; indeed the English text of Chibambo's account entitled *My Ngoni of Nyasaland*,[74] was published by the USCL with some footnotes by Cullen Young.

Chibambo was the son of one of the original Ngoni families who had travelled north. His father had held the position of mouthpiece for the view of big chiefs; and his father's elder brothers had been famous warriors. Chibambo's impeccable aristocratic connections were combined with a modernising outlook. He thus became a Christian and entered mission employment. In 1920 he received the Honours Diploma for Schoolteachers, awarded by Livingstonia, and in 1929 he was ordained. He worked for many years at Ekwendeni with the Revd Charles Stuart, who translated the text of his History. Chibambo developed a very strong historical consciousness, and was very systematic in his investigations. He wrote on both customs and history, and his Tumbuka-language account *Midauko* became recognised as authoritative throughout Ngoniland.[75] Only the historical part of this appeared in Stuart's translation. Vail maintains that just as Young was responsible for systematising Tumbuka history, Chibambo performed the same task for the Ngoni. But the Ngoni had the advantage that their exploits were more immediate in living memory: and it was easier to draw a picture of a glorious tradition from the events in Ngoni history than was the case with the Tumbuka.[76]

Chibambo was systematic but far from impartial. His concern was to *defend* the value-system of the Ngoni, against potential critics both African and European. He realised that some Europeans would deny any value in Ngoni tradition, simply because it was African. Chibambo was rather concerned to expound the view that a certain amount of eclecticism would be appropriate in European attitudes to African culture. He resented the tendency of some Europeans to lump all Africans together as savages. He himself was conscious of a feeling of Ngoni superiority, and as has already been seen, it was possible to convince some Europeans of the rightness of this view. The Ngoni had shown themselves to be relatively resistant to absorption of European values, especially with regard to material culture. At the same time, they had welcomed the religious and educational insights which had been provided by the mission. It is significant that the Mombera Native Association, founded in 1919 by the new education Ngoni elite, made one of its first tasks the restoration of the old powerful Ngoni chieftainship.[77] It has been shown in Chapter I that Chibambo himself had been concerned to articulate resentment of unequal treatment of European and African mission employees at Livingstonia. There was no successful outcome to the complaint that he made in 1921, but Chibambo remained in the mission, and did not (like some of his contemporaries) transfer to a church of African origin.

Chibambo's historical account advocates the Ngoni view of events in northern Malawi. He rejects Saulos Nyirenda's argument, which Young had accepted, that the Ngoni had 'spoiled the land'. He also provided much more detail on many events than that made available by Young. In some cases the interpretation is different and more favourable to the Ngoni. But more often Chibambo provides information on matters which Young hardly touched upon. He writes of the quarrels in South Africa, the subsequent move north, and the Zambezi crossing. He shows that one split had already occurred before that crossing was made, the fissiparous group eventually settling in the Dedza area of Malawi. But much of the information about the early stages of the journey was by now already widely known from other accounts. There is a useful discussion of the journey further northward: of the problems surrounding the paramountcy, and of the dynastic disputes which followed the death of Zwangendaba. Chibambo tells of the eventual settlement in northern Malawi, with its attendant rebellions: he also considers the impact of Arabs and Europeans (especially missionaries). The wealth of detail about the journey and the succession adds considerably to Young's account. Chibambo was far better informed and, though there are a few differences on points of fact, on the whole Chibambo amplifies rather than contradicts Young's account. In the discussion of settlement and conquest, the main differences reflect which side the author took; thus Young supports the Tumbuka, Chibambo the Ngoni. Chibambo argues that the tribes into which the Ngoni penetrated were subdued with very little difficulty. He supports the contention that such tribes were scattered and lacking in centralised authority. His version takes the view that claims made for the authority of the Chikulamayembes were exaggerated; though Chibambo himself exaggerates Ngoni authority by maintaining that the Ngoni conquered the Ngonde.

Chibambo draws the explicit comparison between Ngoni methods of government of their subjects and the British policy of Indirect Rule. He also discusses the question of Ngoni assimilation of young people from among their subjects. He maintains that one effect of this policy was that some of those so assimilated began to perceive the limits of Ngoni power. He reports the Battle of Chinteche as an event remembered by the Tonga with great pride; he suggests that subsequently many of the young Nkhamanga men began to get out of hand and to belittle the Ngoni. Chibambo maintains that it was in accordance with this development that a review of fighting men took place at Ekwendeni; but he denies that there was any intention to massacre the old, since large numbers of women were also present in the village and the cattle kraal. Rather he insists that the sole purpose of the exercise was to administer war medicine. He goes on to report the breakaway of the Tumbuka subjects, which was completed by 1879, making the comment that not all chose to leave. He shows that the Chewa under Mwase gave important military assistance to the Ngoni. Most of the remaining rebellious activities, such as that of Baza at Mt Hora, are reported in similar terms to those of Young. Chibambo also notes the continuation of operations in Siska country after the Henga had fled, leading to eventual Siska surrender. However, he maintains, with the end of the risings there was peace; and this had all taken place *before* the arrival of the missionaries, who were only just beginning to build, at Bandawe. The clear suggestion is that the Ngoni rather than the missionaries had secured the pacification of the area.

Arabs as well as Europeans were encountered by the Ngoni, but Chibambo argues that there were very few dealings in slaves with the Ngoni; rather, ivory was the main commodity. By contrast, he maintains, the chiefs of the Tonga, Siska, Nkhamanga and Chewa all engaged in extensive slave trading. Since the Ngoni did not support the Arabs, he maintains that the cause of the Europeans and that of the Ngoni were the same; it was merely unfortunate that they knew little about one another. This leads Chibambo to his main propaganda piece on behalf of his own people. He notes that there had been the prophets of Israel; he sees God as having been slowly revealing himself in every nation, even among the backward and despised. He states that Ngoniland also had its seers (*izanuzi*) who foretold of something great coming from the water, and who advised that the new foreigners be received courteously. He suggests that this prepared the way for the reception of missionaries, and that the chiefs in particular showed themselves to be friendly. At first, he admits, the Ngoni wanted the Tonga to be left alone by the missionaries so that they could be raided; but eventually schools were permitted after Christian prayer appeared to be successful in producing rainfall. He also comments that though the Gospel eventually succeeded in shaking the power of the Ngoni, this did not take place immediately, and that raiding did not cease completely until 1893. He notes that M'mbelwa's children did not attend school, but Mtwalo's did so; also that British annexation of Ngoniland in 1904 took place without bloodshed.

Chibambo's contention, then, is that there was another side to the story that the Ngoni brought no good by settling in northern Malawi. In the first place, he sees the Ngoni as having unconsciously prepared the way for the Gospel. In the second place he argues that the Ngoni showed better ways of government, law and discipline (he deplores the few instances where Ngoni adopted customs of their subjects). He argues further that the missions had been a civilising influence: Mtwalo died in 1890, and M'Mbelwa a year later, but there was no dynastic strife since people knew the Gospel. He suggests that the missions also helped the Ngoni and the British government to come together in friendship.

It is difficult to speculate as to how Cullen Young evaluated this account. He had always taken a pro-Tumbuka stand, and had not given the Ngoni viewpoint a hearing in the revised edition of his *History*. But he was often concerned to have all points of view properly represented, and he may well have seen Chibambo's account as a useful corrective to any bias which he might have perpetrated. He would certainly have approved of Chibambo's comments about the activities of the Ngoni seers in preparing the way for the Gospel, and of the comparison with ancient Israel.

The impact of Chibambo was considerable. The Tumbuka-language version of his account was widely used in schools. He also had a less direct but significant impact through the work of the anthropologist and educationist Margaret Read; Chibambo served as her guide in Ngoniland during her field studies,[78] and on the basis of her research Read produced two books and several articles.[79] Read is concerned to show how the Ngoni maintained their aristocratic distinctiveness; this was done through methods of socialisation, which included transmission of a strong historical consciousness through folktales, historical accounts, and songs.

It appears that Cullen Young wished Ngoni claims to be heard through Chibambo and subsequently through Read; but that privately he continued to display some scepticism. He seems to have regarded Read as having been over-influenced by key informants. There is evidence of direct contact between Young and Read on the subject of Ngoni claims. In the course of this Young seems to have felt that he was being treated in a patronising fashion; in correspondence with Rangeley he remarks on Read's 'Malinowski' smile of superiority when referring to such controversy.[80] Rangeley himself had occasion in 1952 to write on the subject of Mtwalo, especially concerning succession disputes, and the subsequent dispersal and settlement pattern of the Ngoni.[81] He suggests here that his own analysis does not depart from that of Young to any marked degree, though he provided much more information; some of this was based on direct contact with Mtwalo II, who had succeeded in 1944.

Rangeley also notes that his conclusions do not depart significantly from the findings of Lane Poole. E.H. Lane Poole, sometime Commissioner for the Eastern Province of Northern Rhodesia (Zambia) wrote a book on the peoples of his province, which first appeared in 1934, but which went through two further editions.[82] Most of his information came from oral tradition, though he was indebted to Cullen Young in some important respects. It is unfortunate that he did not consult Young's revised *History*, but relied on the earlier *Speech and History*. He thereby failed to note amendments such as that regarding the date of the Ngoni crossing of the Zambezi. On the whole, Lane Poole sees Young as the best authority on the northward movement of the Ngoni, though he takes issue with some matters of detail.

Thompson, a recent commentator on the Ngoni,[83] needs also to be mentioned. He is opposed to a number of widely-accepted viewpoints upon various aspects of the Ngoni. He notes the different accounts put forward by Nyirenda and Chibambo. He is concerned to defend the Ngoni against various criticisms: especially the one which has frequently been voiced by European writers, to the effect that the Ngoni were merely bloodthirsty savages. He supports the contention that a massacre of food-producers would make no sense, and comments that even Nyirenda admitted that raiding ceased once the Ngoni had succeeded in imposing their authority. Thompson also argues that the movement northwards from South Africa was a gradual process, which did not only take place as a response to defeat in war; population growth and inadequate resources are suggested by him as other factors. He rejects the suggestion of Cullen Young and others that the Ngoni were ignorant of good agricultural practice. Rather he maintains that they practised shifting cultivation, a common method in Africa, and perfectly efficient as long as land is plentiful. He suggests also that it is misleading and ambiguous to speak of a decline in Ngoni power. Drawing partly on the analysis of another observer, Rennie,[84] he maintains that the only real decline was in military terms; and that this occurred because the neighbours of the Ngoni were beginning to improve their own defences at the time of the arrival of the Europeans. On the question of the succession struggle following Zwangendaba's death, Thompson sees the various alternative versions as little more than attempts to justify the claims of the various disputants. He sees segmentation and eventual fragmentation as endemic to the dynamics of the Ngoni political structure. Here he draws upon the analysis of another investigator of Ngoni history, the anthropologist Barnes.

Barnes did fieldwork among the Ngoni, but also relied extensively upon historical material;[85] this included Cullen Young's, and that of all the other authors mentioned here whose work was published before 1954. He notes many differences in detail between his predecessors, and uses his fieldwork to throw light on issues concerning succession disputes. He notes that the different versions of events following the death of Zwangendaba reflect the place from which they have been collected - a point which Read also noticed.

Barnes's specific points are to be found in his monograph *Politics in a Changing Society*. But a great advance in general understanding of subjects of this nature is made in his article 'History in a Changing Society' (1951).[86] This is a broader comment on historiography, in which Barnes articulates some of the problems relating to the handling of tradition. The issues that he raises are ones of which his predecessors were not always fully aware. He notes particularly that the tales told by the Ngoni of his acquaintance always relate to 'good' aspects of the Ngoni past. All tales are of victory except when it comes to the British. Barbarities are minimised, and the beneficial aspects of discipline are emphasised. The defeat by the British in 1898 is seen by them as the cause of subsequent failure and departure from tradition. Barnes notes that only legend would have been available for the Ngoni, since until recently their society was non-literate. But for a literate society, by contrast, good documentation might be available: yet it might still not be easy to distinguish between legend and history. He shows how legends which deal with the relations between different Ngoni groups such as villages *do* have some impact on the present, since past relationships are often maintained. Inter-group relations among the Ngoni were only slightly controlled by the Administration; thus he suggests that the legends continued to have an important function. A final aspect of tradition which Barnes notes is the effect of literacy. He suggests that, though some accounts of Ngoni history by Europeans and South Africans had become available, their impact seems to have been minimal. He notes, however, that vernacular historical accounts were used in schools, though their effect outside the classroom was uncertain.

A historiographical assessment

As with the anthropological works, it is unfair to criticise Young for lack of sophistication in his analysis and methods of data collection, when this sophistication came even to the professionals only some time after Young had published. Thus systematic investigation of the techniques of doing oral history came only in the nineteen-fifties, too late even for some of Young's critics. Moreover, the methods of the 'critical historian' were still being developed throughout the twentieth century, and Collingwood, writing on this subject in 1946, fully recognises this.[87] However, it is worthwhile to apply some critical apparatus to Young's work. In the first place this assists in showing how far his historical writings are of value today; and secondly, even if some are found to be of little or no value, it is still important to recognise their influence. Moreover where distortion can be recognised, it is useful to suggest ways in which it might have come about.

Some historiographical generalities are contained in the observations of critics who have already been mentioned. Thus both Barnes and Van Velsen are seen to draw attention to the problem of 'legend'. A wider range of general issues is dealt with by Cunnison, in his study of the Luapula peoples of Zambia.[88] Here he distinguishes between *personal* and *universal* history. Personal history is concerned with particular kin-groups, based upon memories of direct experience passed down within them. In these the person who tells the story can state his relationship to the characters involved. Such history does touch upon the details of the past of neighbouring tribes, but lacks critical comparison of alternative accounts. The broader perspective is contained only in the second type, universal history. This is present for the Luapula peoples largely for natural history and for the early stages only of human history. A distinction of this kind could usefully have been applied in Cullen Young's work; had he been aware of it, he could have developed a more sceptical attitude to the claims and counter-claims of the various clans.

The most systematic prescriptions for the work of the oral historian are contained in the work of Vansina.[89] He notes that particular difficulties can arise when tradition is intentionally conveyed by an informant. He shows, too, that there is a great need to examine the purpose of a tradition. He argues against the use of school pupils as informants, and suggests that it is better to go to those who were the original sources of the pupils' information. He sees the testimony of those who have left their environment as particularly likely to be distorted; such informants, he maintains, may no longer be familiar with the material, and their outsider status may be a further source of bias. For Vansina, the worst kind of informant is one who has derived his information from several sources: this is likely to lead to the obliteration of contradictions, and to the addition of the informant's own interpretations Vansina's 'good' informant, by contrast, is one who lives a customary life and who repeats the material without hesitation.

The situation in Livingstonia was one in which the tendency was to use informants of a different kind. Only in the early stages was there antagonism between the mission and traditional authorities (in contrast to the situation with many other African missions). Chiefs frequently worked in full cooperation with the mission, and both Chikulamayembes and Kyungus were trained there.[90] Traditional aristocrats who had become mission converts appeared to be the authoritative sources of information on their respective claims.

Saulos Nyirenda, in particular, broke all the rules that Vansina outlines. He was educated, he lived outside his own environment, and he had produced his own synthesis. He also had a fairly obvious axe to grind; Young recognised this, but supported rather than substantially corrected it. Moreover, the 1932 *History* lists twenty-eight collaborators. Of these five are identifiable as Malawian ministers of religion. Others are known to have passed through the mission, and the same could probably be said of most, perhaps all of the remainder. It appears that nearly all the informants used for the revised *History* had a partisan purpose. Thus the record is one of claims and counter-claims, rather than a scholar's evaluation of the evidence followed by presentation of his own conclusions. Young found contact with ordinary villagers easy and rewarding, but misleadingly he saw his key informants as the experts. Much of this is excusable if one bears in mind the lack of development of techniques for collecting oral testimony, at the time of Young's investigations. Less excusable is the fact that, as Vail points out, he failed to indicate the source of his information on clan histories, thus severely impairing its utility.

A final problem is that Young showed little overt awareness of the way in which tradition could be created and manipulated within the colonial context. He was not ignorant of such matters, but he lacked an overall perspective on them. But it has recently been shown clearly by Ranger[91] that the British colonialists frequently set about inventing traditions for Africans; and that such codification transformed flexible custom into hard prescription. The distortions of one generation could become the realities of the next. It is shown by Ranger that the 1920s and the 1930s were a great period for invented tradition. The rise of Chirongozi Gondwe can be placed in this context and is an example mentioned explicitly by Ranger. Indirect Rule enabled educated 'inventors of tradition' to make their mark. Thus after 1931 the Tumbuka paramountcy began to assume the characteristics of a progressive Christian monarchy; it was a 'traditional' institution, supported by the mission-educated and by a missionary such as Young. In this way was institutionalised a form of 'progressive traditionalism' which only later gave way to a full-scale nationalist movement. In Chapter V the question will be examined as to whether some such progressive traditionalism has become part of state ideology in modern Malawi - since Malawians are now expected to show loyalty to the 'wise and dynamic leadership of His Excellency the Life President'.

As with his anthropological works, it must incidentally be noted that Young saw the processes which he described within a Christian framework. Again the veneer was very light, but it was perceptible. The Scottish Enlightenment tradition had succeeded in reconciling the claims of reason and religion with no total victory to the former. What remains in this view of history is a notion of a historical process which involves the working out of God's purposes. Men are historical agents and are vehicles of the divine purpose. All peoples are involved in this process, which is not confined to any race or class. Young does not mention such matters directly in his detailed historical studies (though Chibambo expressed himself in such terms). But in his general works on education and African culture Young is concerned to show how God has revealed himself 'at sundry times and in divers manners'; thus historical events among the Tumbuka could be seen as steps in this evolutionary process. The supporters of Chikulamayembe were also the supporters of European rule, and at least initially Young saw this as a progressive, Christianising force. Chibambo, interestingly, made parallel claims for his own Ngoni people.

IV
Educational and Literary Concerns

It needs to be remembered that for most of his career Cullen Young served as either a schoolteacher or as a publisher. Though teaching was not initially to be Young's main function at Livingstonia, he soon found himself devoting most attention to this side of the mission's work, either directly or as an inspector. He had no formal training as a teacher, but all missionaries were expected to be educationalists of a sort, and versatility was at a premium. Young was also exposed to the educational philosophy and practice of different missionaries. He will have been made aware of the presence of both strict and liberal tendencies among his colleagues, on matters such as the acceptability of African tradition, and the possibilities for African advancement. Laws and Elmslie typified the strict tradition. They were able to accept the idea that Africans could succeed in reaching high positions, such as the ordained ministry; but this would come only after a long period of probation, with no short cuts being acceptable. However another tradition, associated with Fraser, was much more accommodating to African culture. Fraser's influence was considerable at a relatively early stage in Young's missionary career; they served together at Loudon between 1910 and 1913. Fraser had encouraged the Ngoni to compose their own hymn tunes, building upon indigenous tradition. He was also less concerned than some of his colleagues to train a small elite to Scottish standards, and was more sympathetic to the expansion of primary education.[1]

Young's early training at schools and colleges will have influenced

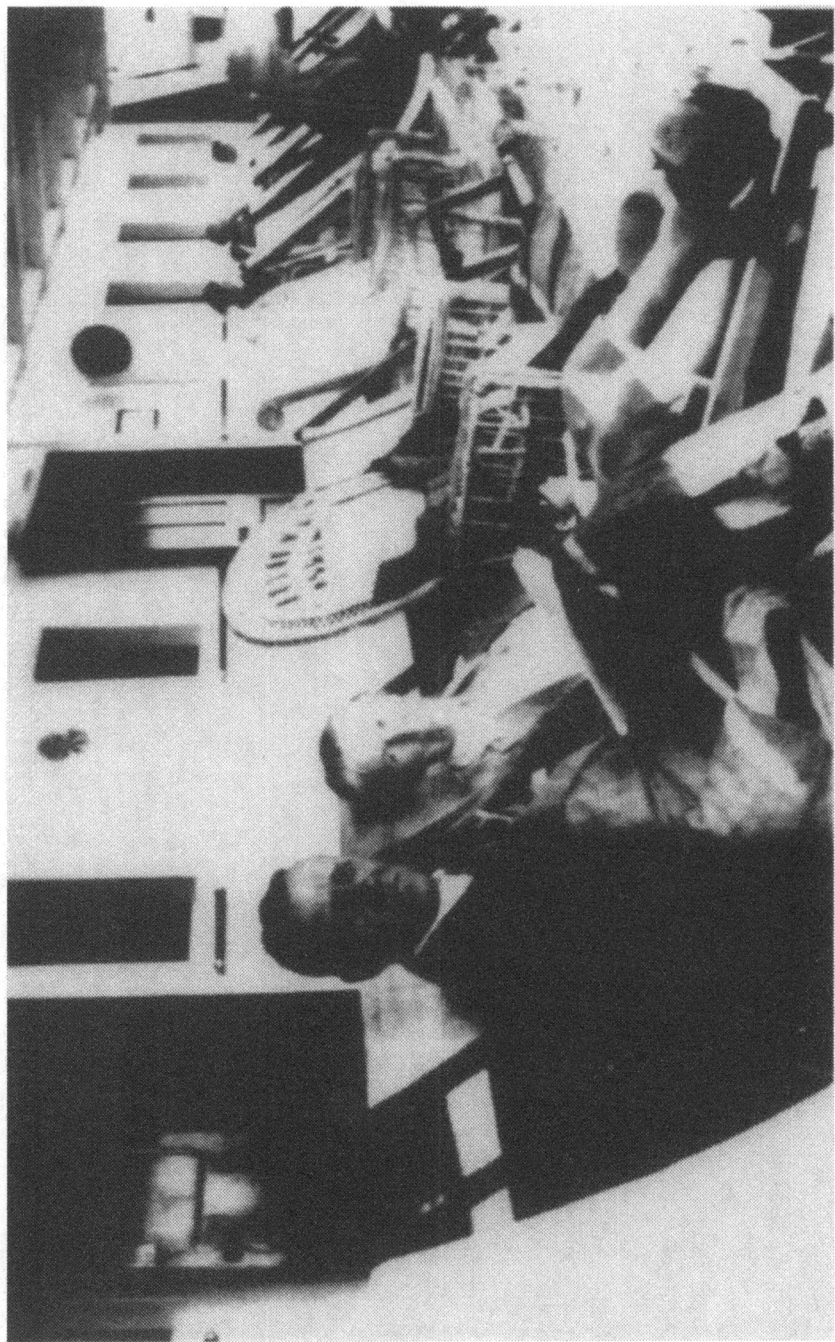

Cullen and Jessie Young, on their final journey from Africa in 1931

his ideas to a certain extent, though it is difficult to pinpoint this. He absorbed the elements of a classical education at the Glasgow Academy, and sometimes he vaguely recalled this in his later writings.[2] He was an enthusiastic participant in sporting activities at school, and continued these through his old school association, while an accountancy student. His sporting interests continued till later in life, and he encouraged physical education at Livingstonia. He remained proud of his old school connection; he kept in touch with the Academy and, on one occasion, contributed an article to the *Glasgow Academy Chronicle* on the subject of his hunting experiences in Malawi.[3] He did not attend a university; his accountancy training did however give him an understanding of economics and commerce, which is occasionally reflected in his writings.[4] He seems to have acquired a sound grasp of the subjects taught at New College, Edinburgh; but his work is not full of biblical or theological references. Informal education will also have contributed to Young's outlook. The Enlightenment tradition in Scotland saw no conflict between science and religion. Young's family background was one in which missionary activities were widely discussed, and Dr John Young had some personal links with missionaries. Young acquired from his home background an interest in reading as a leisure activity, and this continued to influence him throughout his life.

Between 1904 and 1907, Young was mainly concerned with the business side of the mission. His first steps in teaching were an offshoot from this, since he was given the responsibility of running classes in commercial subjects. This work was concentrated at the Overtoun Institute, the centre of Livingstonia's educational activities. Young commented on his experiences with his initial class of eight pupils for the commercial course, in his communications to the Livingstonia Mission Reports. Already he was stressing the theme of the importance of 'character' in education, and was viewing with concern the apparent lack of interest in this shown by many white employers.[5] Young was in due course to have doubts about the consequences of commercial education, since it did not respond to village needs. After furlough during 1907-8, he returned to the mission to engage in work which he found more congenial. He was now responsible for general educational work in Karonga, involving the supervision of village schools. He moved to Loudon in 1910, and there he began his close association with Donald Fraser. Furlough came again in 1913-14, and in 1915 he returned first to Tamanda and then to Loudon. The war interrupted his educational activities at this juncture; when he was released from war service, he proceeded to Kasungu, where he remained till furlough in 1919-20. On his return he was posted to the Overtoun Institute. He was by now an experienced supervisor of village teachers, and his services were called upon as Headmaster of the teaching school. He remained there till 1925, but evidently found such work much less congenial. He seemed more at home with ordinary villagers than with the more educated element, and he missed the direct contact with the village people while working at Khondowe. When in 1925 he left for extended furlough, he gave a clear indication to the mission authorities that he would prefer district work on his return. His motives for extending his furlough so as to work for the RTS were mainly related to his family; though a contributory factor could well have been relative dissatisfaction with the kind of work he was now expected to do. When in 1928 he returned to Malawi, he again succeeded in obtaining district work, at Loudon. He remained there till his final departure in 1931.

His comments upon various aspects of mission work show certain characteristic themes. He supported the fee-paying principle, seeing self-help as the only real road to African advancement. He was optimistic, expecting that advancement would be slow but steady; and the longer he stayed in Africa the more he became impressed with his pupils' work. But while seeing his optimism as being more and more justified, he still believed in taking a stern hand, especially in the early stages. He also had occasion to be wary of the consequences of formal education, in cases where it was seen as overriding the importance of maturity. He saw 'moral character' as important in both teacher and taught. He also saw physical education as being of value, partly as an appropriate form of sublimation of sexual drives.[6] He carried out and apparently accepted the ready recourse to expulsion as an instrument of discipline. He saw women's education as comparable in importance to that of men.[7]

It was in 1909 that Cullen Young gained sufficient confidence to express himself in print at any length upon an aspect of mission educational policy. This was in response to an article in *The East and the West* by A.G. Fraser.[8] The Revd Alexander Fraser was Principal of Trinity College, Kandy (Srilanka), and had previously worked for the Church Missionary Society in Uganda. He was eventually to become (in 1924) Principal of Achimota College in Ghana, and he published extensively on aspects of the educational policies of missions. He was the son of Sir Andrew Fraser, who at one time was Lieutenant-Governor of Bengal. Andrew Fraser and Cullen Young's father had been students together at Edinburgh University[9], and it is possible that there was some personal connection. Alexander Fraser's article was on the theme of 'Education in India and Ceylon in View of the National Movement'. It struck a responsive note in Cullen Young, who perceived it as foreshadowing developments that would inevitably occur eventually in the African context. Fraser's article began by developing a systematic critique of British educational policies in India, which had followed Macaulay's suggestion that an anglicised Indian middle class should be created. Fraser was critical of a system where 'the Indian pupil is treated as if he were an Englishman, in that his own environment is largely ignored, and all that is truly oriental in his life is left uninterpreted and undeveloped'.[10]

In Srilanka (Ceylon), Fraser continued, the policy of anglicisation had been carried out to even greater extremes. He deplored the effect of such policies of 'denationalisation' (a term used by Donald Fraser, who was probably not related). He maintained that a vernacular-based education would have enabled the educated class to mediate between the masses and the culture of the colonisers; whereas the English-medium school simply meant that the educated became divorced from their own people. Fraser saw a further danger as being that when nationalists eventually began to oppose such a policy, they would also oppose Christianity. He noted that in Japan it had become possible to provide an Eastern-type education which had also absorbed some Western elements, and he saw this as an example for the Indian sub-continent to follow. In Christian missionary work, too, he urged that Christianity be related to Eastern religions somewhat as it could be related to Judaism; he stressed the message of 'completion'. He also emphasised the importance of competent teaching of Indian history. Finally, he urged that more serious attention be paid to teacher training, so that Indians and Europeans could eventually serve as colleagues together.

Cullen Young was evidently very impressed by Fraser's article,

and he commented on it enthusiastically in the *Livingstonia News*.[11]
He maintained that Indian experience could teach useful lessons for
those working in Africa. He did not accept Fraser's position
uncritically; and he noted with disapproval Warren Hastings's policy
of using *only* the national language and excluding English. He
suggested that the most appropriate solution would probably lie
somewhere between the two extremes. Throughout his career as an
educationist, Young continued to grapple with the problem of the
correct mix between the indigenous language and English.

Another theme which Young continued to wrestle with was that of
the relative importance of primary and secondary schooling. He was
confronted with such questions when the inquiry into the Chilembwe
rising was set up, in 1915. He sent a written submission to the
investigators, in which he blamed such incidents not upon the
mission, but upon forces unleashed by other whites. He criticised the
demand for more advanced education, seeing the task of the mission
as being a more basic understanding of religion and the 'three Rs'.
using the vernacular. He also expressed concern that students who
had been disciplined might be taken on by non-mission white
employers, and regretted the lack of white cohesion on this subject.
He was not opposed to all advanced education, but he took the view
that it had been unnecessarily extended in response to demand from
outside the mission. He also deplored the policy of permitting labour
to go outside Malawi; he saw this as leading to a degrading,
cosmopolitan life, and to a lack of respect upon return.[12]

It appears, then, that in the earlier period of his service at
Livingstonia, Young did not hold a strong belief in education as a
contributor to African advancement. He preferred the villager of
limited education to those Africans who had wider horizons - a view
which most other whites in British colonies shared. He was by now
clearly uneasy at some of the consequences of commercial education,
an activity in which he had originally been involved himself. Soon he
was to be thrust into the wide-ranging debate as to the relative merits
of village-based and more advanced education. This was an ongoing
topic of controversy within the mission. The mounting opposition to
the broader objectives for education led eventually to Laws's forced
resignation in 1927.[13] The whole issue formed part of a wider debate
which also involved discussion of educational policies regarding
American Negroes.[14]

An obvious criticism of much of the content of more advanced education at Livingstonia was that the skills and knowledge taught were not of use in the village context.[15] The effect, so it has been argued, was to initiate labour migration, and to create dependence upon white employers. On the other hand, more advanced education clearly had a liberating potential. There was an evident danger that, if African advanced education were stifled, political advancement would be stifled as well. Yet if education of Africans up to a high level were to be encouraged, the long period of training could present a problem. Those who had to wait in this way might resent the long probationary period, seeing it as a deliberate barrier to their own advancement. Such frustrations certainly occurred at Livingstonia; unduly long delays in accepting African ordination eventually gave rise to religious separatist movements.[16] Yet the issue is highly complex. The policy of insisting upon a long probation, if properly carried out, could ensure genuine colleagueship in the long run, between Europeans and Africans. The alternative policy, of accepting less demanding training for Africans, might reduce frustrations consequent upon the long waiting period; but it would make it more difficult for Europeans and Africans to serve as equal colleagues. There were of course some Europeans who expected a long probation but even when this had been served would still not accept African colleagues as equals. Cullen Young's opinion, if he had one, has not been recorded on such matters. He was able to support the Phelps-Stokes policy of 'adaptation', but the implications of this for the future of advanced education were unclear. His brother William was more forthright in his support for village-centred education and for the corresponding downgrading of the Overtoun Institute.[17]

On one aspect of educational policy Cullen Young adopted a clear stand. He was very concerned that the central position of religion in schools should remain. He was opposed to suggestions that there should be legislative restraints upon the activities of mission schools. Pressures for control of mission education arose following the Chilembwe uprising. Moreover, there was some evidence that, after Chilembwe, the colonial administration tended to display a preference for Anglican and Roman Catholic missionaries. In 1927 Young wrote to J.H. Oldham, expressing concern about the promulgation of the Nyasaland Education Ordinance. He feared that state involvement would jeopardise the religious component, and that funds would be diverted from African to European pupils. He also noted that there was no indication as to how the seats on the proposed Advisory Board for Education would be shared out among the missions.[18] In another matter, however, he was pleased with a government decision regarding education. This was the appointment of Major Alfred Travers Lacey to the post of Director of Education for Nyasaland, in 1930.[19] Lacey (1892-1966) served as an educationalist in East and Central Africa for the whole of his career following the First World War. He seems to have had a more sensitive awareness of African culture than some other administrators. In 1934 Lacey completed for the Cambridge Diploma in Anthropology a thesis with the title 'Notes on a recent Anti-Witchcraft Movement in Nyasaland'.[20] Lacey saw education as an important way of bridging the gap between black and white. Lacey differed from many Livingstonia missionaries in his advocacy of Chinyanja (Chichewa) as the vernacular for the whole of Malawi. Most Livingstonia missionaries favoured the retention of Tumbuka. However, Lacey did not press this policy to the point of refusing a grant to schools where Chinyanja was not used.[21]

On 15 March 1934, Lacey gave a talk to the Education Circle of the Royal Empire Society, on the subject of 'The Genius of the Bantu'. His lecture incorporated many themes which were among Cullen Young's favourites; he stressed the ideal of brotherhood, values expressed in proverbs and folklore, and the fact that Africans were not unintelligent, but had merely been cut off from the outside world. Young was present in the audience on this occasion. In the discussion, he praised Lacey's sense of mission, his eloquence which 'must come from the heart', and his contribution to the cause of education in Nyasaland.[22]

Finally it is worth mentioning Young's efforts in producing vernacular literature at Livingstonia. He helped to launch, and was first editor of, the periodical *Vyaro na Vyaro* (literally, 'countries and countries'). This was not the first Tumbuka-language periodical publication sponsored by Livingstonia Mission. In 1906 was begun *Makani* ('news'). However, this attracted little interest among African Christians. It was written mostly by Europeans, the few Africans who contributed doing so by invitation, and on a topic chosen by the editor. *Makani* survived only till 1908. However, Young was inspired to found a new periodical, one which would have the specific aim of encouraging Africans to air their views. Young continued to find attractive the serious discussions which occurred at the village talking-place; he felt that some substitute would be needed with the growth of urban living. The new periodical was begun in 1928, and had as its explicit policy the encouragement of African contributions upon topics of their own choice. Only a few took up the offer at first, and initially such contributions were mostly letters to the editor; but an interest in writing articles gradually developed. Young stressed that *Vyaro na Vyaro* was run on a democratic basis, with contributors seen as equal partners. He could not continue to edit the periodical after his departure from Livingstonia in 1931, but he continued to receive it regularly and to maintain an active interest in its contents. But his only personal contribution appeared in the issue for May, 1940, in a letter which commented upon the tenth anniversary of the periodical. Again, Young praised its importance as a forum for discussion.[23]

Young also contributed to Tumbuka literature in the form of a school textbook. In 1929 was published the first part of *Makuriro gha Mahara na Maluso Mukati mu Wanthu* (The Growth of Wisdom and Customs among Men). The second part appeared in 1931. There then followed several combined editions of this work, the last being published by the Hetherwick Press in Blantyre as late as 1965.[24] This textbook had a wide circulation in northern Malawi as long as the Tumbuka language remained officially recognised. It stresses the importance of the distinction between animals and man. It points to the collective nature of human existence and to the need for nations to learn from one another - this process to be led by the spirit of God.

Although Young's direct involvement in overseas mission service came to an end in 1931, he saw a clear continuity between this and his subsequent publishing work. This had been evident earlier, when he had taken extended furlough beginning in October 1925. Such had been agreed by the United Free Church Foreign Mission Committee with understanding in view of his family circumstances; but this acceptance involved suspension of the children's allowances during Young's 'absence from mission service'. The decision was duly communicated to Young in a letter dated 29 April 1926. Young's reaction was as follows:

> The letter is a very real disappointment and the
> disappointment lies in the fact that my going in for three

years for deputation work in the churches on behalf of vernacular literature - the side of missionary work that the committees are unable to finance - is treated as a severance from the committee: 'an absence from mission service' if I may quote from your letter. This hurts me pretty hard, I'm afraid ...

... I have received so much kindness from you and the committee that I do not write this as a grouse. Please don't think that. But I do want those responsible to know that their decision hurts me in a place that, perhaps, they had not thought of. I am not absent from mission service.[25]

This sums up very well Young's feelings on this matter. He saw his work for Christian literature as a logical continuation of his work in the field. He was appointed as Joint Secretary of the RTS for Scotland, dividing his duties on a geographical basis with his colleague, the Revd John Knox. He continued to do deputation work for Livingstonia, during his tenure of the publishing appointment. His stay in Europe also enabled him to attend the Le Zoute conference and to involve himself in the debates surrounding Phelps Stokes and the appropriate degree of 'adaptation' in missionary educational policies. Le Zoute also gave a great stimulus to the task of vernacular publishing. Young left the RTS earlier than expected, at the end of 1927, for motives which remain unclear. But he seems to have created a very favourable impression, especially with regard to his earnest and convincing advocacy of the importance of publishing work in Africa.[26] On his return to Livingstonia he soon immersed himself in literary production; as already noted, he began the editorship of *Vyaro na Vyaro* in 1928 and produced his own vernacular text (*Makuriro gha Mahara Mukati mu Wanthu*) in 1929. It seems that he was already earmarked for further work with the RTS.[27] When he eventually had to leave Livingstonia, he was fortunate in being able to embark on a new career which followed on logically from the old.

The RTS had been founded in 1799, and initially concentrated its efforts upon Britain. It aimed to promote a moral revolution, and saw inexpensive literature as a way of securing this. It contributed to the establishment of 'Victorian' moral standards. Throughout the

Nineteenth Century it expanded its work abroad, and in 1926, in the wake of the Le Zoute conference, it established its Africa Fund. Some works of an anthropological type were eventually published on Africa; and there was also a series of short books written by Africans for Africans, known as 'Africa's Own Library'.[28] Cullen Young began his employment with the RTS in 1931. He had a wide range of duties as 'Deputy Secretary and Home Superintendent', but was particularly involved with the supply of literature to Africa and the administration of the Africa Fund. Books published by the RTS were not only of a religious kind; but it was expected that a Christian tone be maintained throughout. It is of interest that the RTS also published the *Boy's Own Paper* and the *Girl's Own Paper*, and that to the former Cullen Young eventually made some minor contributions.

Cullen Young was a popular colleague and performed all his duties conscientiously, especially the meticulous care of financial arrangements. But the cause that was particularly dear to his heart was that of the sponsorship of African authors. The International African Institute, founded in 1926, had this as one of its major aims. In 1928 the Institute agreed to begin the award of annual prizes for works of imagination or general interest, written in African languages; one aim of this exercise was to encourage Africans to study their own languages seriously. Different languages were chosen each year, and the first competition was held in 1930.[29] In 1932, Chinyanja (Chichewa) was one of the languages approved; and as an authority on this language, Cullen Young was chosen as judge for the competition.[30] A prize-winning entry was that of Samuel Y. Ntara, whose historical contribution has already been referred to in Chapter III. The work submitted on this occasion was autobiographical, entitled *Nthondo*.

Ntara[31] was a teacher at a school in Lilongwe, run by the Dutch Reformed Church Mission. His ability had been noted by Lou Pretorius, one of the missionaries of that church. Young commented that when Ntara received the prize 'he purchased a cow for his mother, gave one-tenth of his income to the church, bought himself a bicycle, and went on with his teaching'.[32]

Shortly afterwards Ntara was transferred to the mission headquarters at Nkhoma, as the best place to pursue his talents further. The Dutch Reformed Church mission in Malawi had always encouraged African authorship, but for very different reasons from

Cullen Young's. The Dutch Reformed policy was always to concentrate upon village-based education and to play down any suggestion that Africans could attain the same standards as Europeans. Vernacular literature was an essential component of the segregationist policy which the mission pursued.[33] Cullen Young, by contrast, was supportive of African authorship as a way of stressing Africans' educational abilities. But a similar product can emerge from different policies, and Young maintained friendly relations with the Revd George Steytler of the Dutch Reformed Church, through this common concern.

Ntara's work was soon translated by Young, as *Man of Africa*, and was published by the RTS in 1934. The English edition appeared with a foreword by Sir Julian Huxley, with whom Young was personally acquainted. Huxley was a leading Humanist, but he retained some respect for religion. He commented that Ntara's work showed how Christianity could supersede local sanctions. Young's own introduction to the text stressed the importance of the interpretation of African ways and thought by Africans themselves. He also saw Ntara's work as illustrating the operation of matrilineal kinship. Young added some explanatory anthropological notes to the English translation.[34]

Young's direct involvement in judging African literature came again in 1942, when a second Chinyanja competition was sponsored by the International African Institute. By now he had the great advantage, where translation and related matters were concerned, of his renewed acquaintance with Hastings Kamuzu Banda. Ntara again won the first prize, for his historical study of the Chewa, mentioned in Chapter III. Young was impressed by this work but did not produce an English translation.[35] But the best of the runners-up were published in English in the collection *Our African Way of Life*, with its joint introduction by Young and Banda.[36] The significance of this will be considered in Chapter V.

The link with Ntara's work continued even after Young had retired from his publishing career, in 1946. In 1944 Ntara was working at a Dutch Reformed Mission school in Dowa. There his attention was drawn by the Revd J.J.D. Stegmann (superintendent of the Nkhoma mission at the time) to the historical importance of a certain village headman, named Msyamboza. He had lived between 1830 and 1926, and had witnessed the penetration of both Islam and Christianity, also the coming of the Ngoni and then the British colonialists. Ntara undertook the appropriate research, and in 1949 the biography *Msyamboza* was published by the Nkhoma Mission Press. The book contained abundant proverbial wisdom. Young was again approached to translate the work, which he did with considerable help from Banda. In 1949 it appeared in English with the title *Headman's Enterprise: An unexpected page in Central African History*.[37] Once again Young added some anthropological notes; he also drew attention to some other historical contributions, especially that of Rebman. Young also pointed out in his preface that the book showed that initiative was still possible in early communal groups.

Ntara continued to publish until after Young's death, but such material is not relevant to the present study. But another unrelated event is of interest. This concerns the relationship between Young and Jahnheinz Jahn (1918-73). Jahn was a crucial figure in the development of Western critical responses to African writing. In the early fifties he was compiling his anthology *Schwarzer Orpheus*, which was to be the first serious attempt to gather African poetry including some from the former British colonial possessions.[38] Jahn was in contact with Professor George Shepperson, of Edinburgh University. Poems by Shepperson which made allusions to Africa (written while Shepperson was serving with African soldiers during the Second World War) had appeared in the journal *Phylon*: Jahn had then made inquiries about the possibility of including them in an anthology of modern Negro poetry. Shepperson replied to Jahn's request pointing out that he was not himself an African or a Negro; but he suggested the names of a number of people who might assist, including Cullen Young.[39] Shepperson and Young were acquainted with one another, since Young had assisted Shepperson with translation work in conjunction with research on the Jumbe of Nkhotakhota, Malawi. Jahn was initially reluctant to approach Young; he disliked clergymen and also feared that religious poetry might be offered. But eventually he agreed to make contact, and received from Young a poem entitled 'The Ghoul'. This was written by Alfred David Mbeba, of Malawi (Tumbuka) origin but at that time serving as a teacher in Zambia. This poem was published by Jahn, in German translation, in his anthology. It portrayed the fate of a death-dealer (*mfwiti*) who himself died a lonely death, unmourned, like a wild animal. Jahn also included notes based on information supplied by Young, regarding the distinction between the *ng'anga* and the *mfwiti*.[40]

Young did not have much other direct involvement with the promotion of African authorship. He did, however, edit a collection of short stories written by African authors. This was published in 1947: Young is known to have prepared the collection for publication, though his name does not appear anywhere.[41] Young was also active behind the scenes in other aspects of editorial work; and he himself wrote some reviews of novels dealing with African subjects.[42] Young continued, however, to produce works of general educational interest throughout his career with the RTS/USCL; and he continued this activity after retirement. This material does not easily fit under any other heading, so it is appropriate to consider it here. Some of this dealt with theological questions, both in their own right and as an aid to religious instruction. Other publications contained advice about mission policy. Still others presented some statements about 'African culture', a matter which will be considered here but which will also be returned to in Chapter V. All of these themes do in any case overlap.

Much of the material of general interest is found in Young's *African Ways and Wisdom*. This was based on a course of lectures given by Young at a Church Missionary Society training school; it appeared in print in 1937, and was reissued in 1944. This work incorporated much material already presented in article form[43] but it constituted a coherent whole. Together with the Tumbuka trilogy, *African Ways and Wisdom* became required reading for new Livingstonia missionaries. Many of the themes were continued in his later work, *Contemporary Ancestors*, which appeared in 1940. The religious themes in the latter text were continued in a short book entitled *The Genesis Mosaic* (1941); while in 1944 appeared the pamphlet *Men, Women and Things*, based on the earlier Tumbuka-language text, with some additions.

The theological themes appeared mainly in the first part of *Contemporary Ancestors*. The main focus of interest is the question of reinterpretation and reassessment of Genesis. Young analyses parts of Genesis and suggests that they have parallels in the myths of origin which other peoples subscribe to. Here as elsewhere he argues that God, having revealed himself at sundry times and in divers manners left fragments of insight which became embedded in various traditions. He saw an evolutionary process whereby spirit, mind and matter moved from the more crude to the less crude, and argued that God was leading people to further knowledge. This applied in all traditions, in Africa and elsewhere. Such themes are continued in more detail in *The Genesis Mosaic*. Here Young examines parallels to the Old Testament in the traditions of various peoples including, naturally, the Tumbuka. He maintains that such an exercise could lead to a growing appreciation of the Old Testament. Previously, Young had urged concentration upon the New Testament in religious instruction in Africa; this was because he saw non-Jewish cultures as already being in possession of their own 'Old Testaments'.

Advice to missionaries appears mainly in *African Ways and Wisdom*; understandably so, since it was based on a missionary training programme. Here Young was particularly concerned to stress the importance for missionaries of correct understanding of African culture. The value of social anthropology is particularly strongly emphasised, and Young suggests that with such knowledge available there is no longer any excuse for ignorance. He also stresses here that rules of etiquette exist in African societies, and that these differ from those found in the West; hence he advocates that these be properly understood by missionaries. Young also criticises overemphasis on the metaphor of 'planting' of Christianity, saying that now it would be better to think in terms of 'rooting'. He urges the importance of respect for African susceptibilities, and sees the social anthropologist as the appropriate expert on 'soil analysis'. He repeats his discussion of the importance of the communal bond in Africa; and he also remarks again on the central importance of moral and spiritual matters in traditional African education - something which missionaries could usefully build on. His criticisms of the idea of incorporating African ceremonial into the Christian system are reiterated here.

The general observations on 'African culture' follow naturally from Young's advice to missionaries; he highlights the features of African life to which he thinks missionaries need to pay particularly close attention. It is immediately evident that *African Ways and Wisdom* is heavily stamped by Tumbuka material; missionaries who followed this course of instruction will have learnt about Africa from a Tumbuka vantage-point. Thus the same themes as are found in *Notes on Customs and Folklore* are apparent. Young begins with the notion of the 'Good Village'. He examines the communal bond, and

the extension of the world of the living into the world of the
ancestors. He shows the communal interest in marriage, essential for
the 'increase' which the community values so much. He explains the
function of bridewealth, again advocating the expression 'equilibrium
guarantee' as the best description of this institution. He shows the
various stages in the procedures for dealing with offenders; and the
importance of the ng'anga in safeguarding the community. Many
such themes are continued in Contemporary Ancestors, though here
there are a few more steps taken in a comparative direction. Taboos
are examined, also rites of passage. Young looks here at procedures
concerning death, and examines the relationship between Man, God
and the ancestors. He reiterates his critical comments concerning
'ancestor worship'. He looks at the significance of the mother in
Africa, her importance lying in the central community value of
increase. Young's discussion benefits here from his experience of
living on the Chewa/Tumbuka, matrilineal/patrilineal boundary; he
includes much material on the difference between these two kinds of
descent. Finally, he stresses how such a culture could be enriched by
Christianity.

Men, Women and Things, which appeared in 1944, is an expanded
version of the previous Tumbuka-language text. It deals with
human/animal distinctions, man's relationship to God, and similar
topics. It suggests that people in the past had suffered because of
being cut off, not because of lack of intelligence. It goes on to discuss
urbanisation, the division of labour, exchange, and types of money. It
concludes by talking of fulfilment, the carrying of what is good into
the future. There is an earlier work than this, written with Miss G.A.
Gollock, entitled God's Family in the World.[44] This was published in
1936, and consists of suggestions for Bible reading, with
commentaries. Most of the themes covered are those found elsewhere
in Young's work, here presented in simple language and juxtaposed
with biblical references. The main issues relate to changes in
religious and family life as a consequence of the impact of
Christianity.

This review of Young's didactic writings would not be complete
without reference to his four brief contributions to the Boy's Own
Paper.[45] These appeared in the rubric The Padre's Talk. This item
began to appear in the later 1930s; the paper had now begun to take a
milder tone, in place of the previous constant advice to take cold

baths that had normally been given to readers who wrote in with personal problems.[46] Cullen Young was only one of a number of contributors to this section. He did not write directly on African themes; but one column contains references to an African headman speaking of 'spoiling the village'.[47] His last contribution, published in 1940, discusses the problem of Christian duty in a period of compulsory military service.[48] Young had by now developed sympathies with Quakerism, and it is not clear what his own answer would have been. He merely expresses the view that it was a sign of progress that there were now two legitimate answers to this question: no doubt quite a controversial opinion at this particular juncture.

It is now appropriate to consider what turned out to be a major preoccupation for Cullen Young in the 1930s: the provision of literature for adult education centres on the Zambian Copperbelt. This work was administered by Young from London: his only visit to Zambia had been many years previously, when he relieved the Revd and Mrs James Henderson who were on furlough from the mission station at Tamanda during 1915-16. Young's abiding interest in literature was linked to his commitment to the study of problems of change in Africa, in addition to his interest in 'traditional society'. It was foreshadowed as early as 1927, in his article 'The New African'.[49] Development of mining began on the Copperbelt in the late 1920s, and production began, with some setbacks, in the 1930s. The social consequences of the attraction of a multi-tribal labour force to the area were recognised in the Merle Davis report *Modern Industry and the African*, which appeared in 1933.[50] This contained a section on 'The problem for missions'.[51] Particular attention was drawn here to the question of likely breakdown of traditional constraints; and to the implications of the attractiveness of the new material culture that was available on the Copperbelt. While the Report argued that the spiritual task of the missions should continue to be primary, it also saw opportunities for spare-time activities as a problem; accordingly, adult education was seen as an important task. A further factor was that, in 1935, disturbances occurred. In one town, Luanshya, the Mine Compound office was stormed by a mob; six Africans were killed, and many more were wounded.[52] This led to numerous conferences and discussions on the problem of ensuring a stable society on the Copperbelt; again, leisure-time facilities were sometimes indicated as a problematic issue.

In response, the missions concerned formed the United Missions in the Copperbelt (UMCB), in 1935. There were no resident missionaries on the Copperbelt at the time, and this made it easy for a more ecumenical outlook to prevail. Ecumenism did, however, stop short at the formation of a united church. This was because the UMCA was to participate in the venture, but as a High Anglican body did not feel able to participate jointly in the sacrament of Holy Communion. The Anglicans declared themselves not totally opposed to the idea of a united church, but preferred that any move in such a direction should be gradual. But the Anglicans were happy to participate in the UMCB, provided that it was not confused with more ambitious schemes for church unity. The RTS (now the USCL) gave every assistance to the new venture. Among the main aims were adult education and creative recreation; supervision of libraries and adult schools was undertaken.[53]

The USCL had hoped that support for the UMCB, especially financial, would be forthcoming from the mining companies. Contact with these was maintained partly by Cullen Young; some financial support came, but there was constant concern that funds made available were rather grudgingly given, and inadequate in amount. Young served as treasurer of the British committee of the UMCB till his retirement in 1946.

The reasons why the mining companies were suspicious, and Young's response to the situation, are worthy of close examination. They raise some general questions about the political implications of missionary work. The Merle Davis Report recommended activities such as those taken up by the UMCB as being a useful distraction from potentially disruptive political action; and it would have been expected that the mining companies would have welcomed palliatives of this nature. Even Young seemed not to dissent from this standpoint. In relation to the newspaper *Mutende* ('peace') published by the government as a way of avoiding labour disputes, he remarked:

> Mutende is a multi-lingual production, under European editorship, and occupies a place of great importance within the Copper Belt area, where the absence of any sort of provision for the intelligent use of leisure time was shown to have been a contributing cause of the unfortunate trouble in 1935 between government and

mine employees.[54]

Young was always concerned with problems that arose when people were taught to read, but then reading material was not provided, or was provided by inappropriate bodies. He saw this difficulty as particularly acute in the case of vernacular literature. He was concerned that material provided by Jehovah's Witnesses and Communists was gaining an important outlet on the Copperbelt. Thus the UMCB was expected to provide literature of the 'right' kind.[55] The overall aim of the exercise was presented in the 'Memorandum regarding the work of the literature superintendent of the inter-mission team in Northern Rhodesia', for 1936.[56] This clearly reflected Young's preoccupations. In particular, it stressed that bookshops established were not merely to be retail businesses, but that they would also serve as discussion centres:

> The full aim of the 'reading centre' will only be achieved if the book depots, at centre and branches, are used by the various members of the team as 'talking places'; whether in the open air under trees or in some hall attached to the welfare centre generally. Not 'talking places' in the sense of 'learning centres'; but places where the team and the Africans meet at leisure to chat, discuss, exchange minds, probe questions arising from current reading and so forth.[57]

Yet while such meeting places might be seen by some as having a palliative effect, others might see them as places where class-consciousness could develop. It is noteworthy that the more educated, white-collar employees were the earliest and most active trade unionists and nationalists on the Copperbelt. Such developments did not begin till the 1940s, but there is some clear evidence of a political dimension to the activities of the UMCB. For instance Epstein comments, 'The Luanshya African Welfare and Recreational Society developed out of a Library Committee which was run by a European, the Rev. G. Fraser of the United Mission to the Copperbelt'.[58]

A severe clash with the mining companies came in 1943. Various financial contributions were received by Cullen Young, but the representative of Roan Antelope and Mufulira mines, while sending a contribution of £200, did so with a cautionary memorandum enclosed. This expressed general concern about the participation by representatives of the UMCB in politically controversial matters. It noted, for instance, that one officer was showing interest in the formation of a trade union for African workers; while another had made criticisms in the *Bulawayo Chronicle* of the wage rates paid to Africans. The correspondent from the mine management maintained that such comments were outside the scope of a missionary organisation. In particular he urged that, before such statements were made, the representatives of the UMCB should first confer with the mine management.

After consultation, a reply was sent back by Miss B.D. Gibson, secretary of the British UMCB committee, to the effect that it was indeed appropriate that facts should be checked, before public criticism was made; but that if injustice was still seen to remain, it was the duty of the society's representatives, to the Africans whom they served, to speak out. The letter also defended the right to express views on race relations in the Empire generally, regarding situations that were not confined to the Copperbelt. The reply also suggested that it was expected that in most cases satisfactory results would be obtained when the mine management was consulted.[59] In public the conflict was smoothed over in this way, it but it clearly revealed the different assumptions from which the UMCB and the mine management were working.

The whole issue raises the classic question as to whether religion is necessarily a conservative force, or whether it can have more radical implications. Some commentators evidently felt that it could have a restraining impact on forces of disruption on the Copperbelt; and indeed such a function could be possible. The Book Centres proposed would be of a kind where every publication stocked would have been vetted by European missionaries.[60] Even the books by African authors would have been judged for their 'suitability' on the basis of the missionaries' criteria. Yet even reading of this nature could encourage a more independent development in Africans' thinking, and the 'talking-place' function of the Book Centres could foster the growth of a conscious African super-tribal identity, in opposition to European interests. The officers of the UMCB did not have such aims in view; rather such developments can be seen as unintended consequences. And even relatively conservative missionaries can be prepared to take a stand against racism and segregation, and can thus easily fall foul of European, especially settler interests. More problematic for Christians would be the kind of methods acceptable.

Cullen Young, like many of his missionary colleagues, was prepared to be forthright on the issue of racism. In 1941, together with other London members of the UMCB, he wrote to *The Times* criticising the assertion made by an earlier correspondent (Sir William McLean) that there was no colour bar in the British Empire. The letter pointed out that because of various job reservation regulations, imposed with the insistence of white trade unions (e.g. on the railways), such was not the case - although it was true that segregation was not enshrined by law. The authors expressed their fear that British policies would look like those that were being fought against in the war against Nazi Germany; a particular cause for concern, since numerous Africans were participating in the struggle.[61]

However, Young could be upset about the way in which nationalist movements might develop. His own preference was for slow, evolutionary change; he disliked the stridency of some nationalist literature, especially when it incorporated Marxist perspectives. As late as 1948, he was still maintaining that the missionaries' relative neglect of production of suitable literature had much to do with the undesirable turn which the nationalist movement was taking.[62]

None the less, UMCB's work did expand from the first depot at Mindolo to a chain of several others. Some missionary organisations even thought that the Copperbelt provided the opportunity to promote a genuinely Christian civilisation such as was no longer prevalent in Europe. Other problems arose, however, regarding the extent to which it was appropriate for the UMCB to be involved more directly in church life: and its relationship to the local European Christian population was never spelt out.[63] As already noted, the commemorative plaque for Cullen Young was installed in the bookshop that had been opened at Kitwe shortly before his death.

One aspect of social policy in the UMCB is worthy of mention, in view of comments made by Young. Debate developed in the British Committee in 1939 upon the practice that prevailed on the Copperbelt of sending children over 10 years old back to the villages. Concern had been expressed over the consequent separation of parents and children, but Young assured other committee members that such a procedure would be fully in accord with village custom. A comment was later received from the Revd A. Cross, the UMCB Team Leader on the Copperbelt. This pointed out that one should not neglect the fact that a stable urban population was now developing, and he maintained that the policy of encouraging family settlement was a good one. Cross pointed out, however, that as a consequence many children on the Copperbelt (around two-thirds) had never known their rural 'homes'.[64] In most other UMCB meetings Young made no distinctive contribution other than his comments on finances. He did not remain in touch with the UMCB after he had retired to Scotland in 1946. In 1954, the UMCB became the Copperbelt Christian Service Council.

The cooperation between missions which was in evidence in the UMCB was something which Young was equally concerned to foster at home. He frequently despaired of the fact that there was disunity in the effort to promote Christian literature - not just in Africa, but wherever else Christian missionaries had penetrated. He was active in negotiations which led to the formation of the USCL. This title was adopted in 1935, when the Christian Literature Society for India and Africa amalgamated with the RTS. The new title had the advantage of being able to sustain further acts of union without change of name. In 1941 the London Committee and in 1942 the Scottish Committee supporting Christian Literature for China were amalgamated with the USCL.[65] Young also stressed the theme of the importance of a united effort for Christian literature in his comments on the World Missionary Conference held in Tambaran, Madras, in 1938 (which he was not able to attend himself).[66]

After retirement, Young continued to be active in certain fields. He worked on the revision of the Tumbuka Old Testament,[67] and wrote a few articles for the *Nyasaland Journal*. He continued to provide editorial assistance to the USCL on African matters, and received payment for this. He joined the Scottish USCL Committee, though was not active on it because of his wife's illness. After his death, his literary contribution played a prominent part in tributes paid to him..

It remains to give an overall assessment of Young's contribution to the sphere of literature, which he himself considered so important. It is interesting that he did not pay a great deal of attention to the question of what should be published; his concern seemed merely to be that *more* should be published, urgently, and that distribution should be improved. He does not seem to have thought through the question of whether he was advocating a palliative, or whether he was paving the way for African nationalism. Like many other missionaries, it appears that his political awareness was limited by a feeling that much evil in the world could be resolved by an improvement in personal relations, rather than by major political upheaval.

A further problem stems from his particular concern with *vernacular* literature. He was not unmindful of the fact that literature in English could also have a relatively wide circulation among Africans; but he seems not to have anticipated the extent to which English was to become the main language of *written* communication for the majority of Central Africans. This development has led to a relative decline in the importance of publication in the vernacular. A corollary of the growth in the importance of English has been the importation of 'glossy' literature from Britain and the United States, also South Africa and Zimbabwe. Young's neglect of the English-language imported material led him to ignore the problem of an appropriate policy on the 'uses of literacy', such as interested Hoggart in Britain.[68] This was so even though it was popular literature of this nature at home that the RTS had been particularly concerned to supplant.

Finally, it is noteworthy that Young showed no interest in other kinds of mass media, namely radio and films, which appeared in Africa fairly soon after written communication. Radio, for instance, came to the Copperbelt in 1941, and soon established itself as an important medium of communication, especially for material in the vernacular. It is not however mentioned by Young at all.[69]

It remains to give a general assessment of the key features of Young's educational and literary activities. Their importance will be examined both for Young personally and for a general understanding of African culture. It can be seen that his educational and literary activities are related. Young retired from Livingstonia in 1931, and on his return he had occasion to teach missionaries who were destined for various parts of Africa. This led him to prepare material on some general aspects of 'Africanity' - although much of his apparently broadly-based material in fact contained a Tumbuka bias. He thus continued the process of incorporating a proper understanding of

African culture into missionary efforts, a task which had received its
initial impetus at the 1926 Le Zoute conference. His course material
subsequently appeared in book form.

A further aspect of the importance of his literary activities was that
they involved the committing to writing of records which had
previously formed only part of an *oral* tradition. He had begun this
process already in his Tumbuka studies. He had frequently been
made aware of the fact that cultures which had a written tradition
tended to be viewed with greater respect by Europeans than were
those which lacked writing.[70] He thus contributed to the formation of
a literary tradition in Africa, and to translating it for the benefit of
outsiders who wanted to know more. He did not of course do this
work unaided. Initially, he based his work upon his own
observations; but he welcomed it when Africans made their own
contributions, as was seen with his 1932 version of the text on
Tumbuka history. The stage where Africans were speaking for
themselves was one which Young clearly welcomed; hence his
constant encouragement of African authors.

Furthermore, while stressing the importance of such authorship,
and of literature generally, he did not wish to see this as a substitute
for maturity. Nor did he wish to see the previous lack of book-
learning in Africa as evidence of any lack of such maturity, in the way
that many colonialists tended to believe. On the contrary, he was
particularly concerned to stress the wisdom and thoughtfulness of the
elders.[71] He admired the quality of the response to Christianity that
came from old people, such as the remark from an old lady who said
'I always knew there was a God like that'.[72] He also appreciated the
observations of some old men, to the effect that the missionaries'
teaching completed what the elders had taught.[73] All this supported
his general feeling that the Franciscan missionary method, which
assumed that there was something of Jesus among those who did not
yet know him, was the appropriate one. Young saw this as far
superior to the Dominican method, which came with forms and
doctrines to be accepted.[74] The theme of the Christian message of
completion was of course one of Young's favourites.

Young's articulation of these perspectives is of considerable
interest. The attempt to systematise and preserve some notion of
'African culture' has been important in African nationalism. Many
nationalist movements have reacted against the disdain with which

African beliefs and customs had been viewed by Europeans in the colonial situation. A homogenised culture has had an important contribution to make to national integration in post-independence politics. The possibility that Young has made a major contribution to cultural nationalism of this kind, in an independent Malawi under Dr Banda, will be examined in Chapter V.

V

The Political Dimension

A Liberal political outlook prevailed in Cullen Young's family background. Both his father and his grandfather were very interested in politics. His grandfather had served for many years on the Council of the Borough of Berwick. Cullen Young's father had experience of political controversy from an early age; in 1832, when eight years old, he participated in, and voted at, a meeting to choose between a Whig and a Radical parliamentary candidate. At this meeting, Cullen Young's grandfather was taking an active part in support of the Radical. Incidents such as these made Cullen Young's father familiar with political matters, and led him to take a serious view of life.[1]

It is not clear exactly how Cullen Young's political attitudes were formed. He did, however, develop a clear preference for the Labour Party. He saw this as being in accordance with his work as a missionary, which involved solidarity with the poor. At no time did Cullen Young vote Conservative, and he looked upon that party with great suspicion. This standpoint was strengthened as he began to take a political interest in African affairs. Young also suggested on occasions that, having succeeded in eliminating slavery, the British Empire was in danger of encouraging wage-slavery. While at Livingstonia, he had found it easy to relate to ordinary villagers; and he disliked the more blatant aspects of social inequality that prevailed between missionaries and the indigenous population.[2]

This should not be taken to imply that Young was very left-wing. Like many other Christian socialists, he was middle-of-the-road, and in later life he leaned more towards the Centre. He opposed an over-deterministic view of the economy, and insisted that economic democracy was not the only kind on offer. He was very suspicious of atheistic communism, and even of some secularistic elements in the British Labour Party.

While at Livingstonia, and even more so on his return to Britain, Cullen Young was active as a commentator on African affairs. He was particularly interested in political and economic practices within the Empire, and in the question of transition to independent statehood. He was not unusual among missionaries in Malawi in having such interests. But whereas all missionaries declared a concern for the 'welfare' of their flock, some found it difficult to realise that the boundary between 'welfare' and politics could be difficult to draw. On the whole, however, Livingstonia missionaries were quite aware politically.[3] Robert Laws had lent his support to the formation of 'Native Associations',[4] and the first of these was founded in 1912. This was regional rather than tribal in character; its initial concern was with seeking a better deal from the colonialists, but such associations eventually turned out to be the germ of a nationalist movement. Laws was opposed to suggestions that there were innate racial differences in ability, maintaining rather that superiority and inferiority depended upon an individual's willingness to work. The Livingstonia mission was by no means innocent of racialist and segregationist policies, but it was more responsive to criticisms than were many other missions.

Initially, Cullen Young was reluctant to commit himself to print. But he had to report to the General Assembly on conditions in Malawi, and these comments were published. His address to the 1920 General Assembly described the people among whom missionaries were working in Africa as 'industrially enslaved'.[5] Young also decided, apparently on his own initiative, to send a written comment to the Committee of Inquiry into the Chilembwe Rising.[6] Considerably later, when in London, he was active in groups interested in African affairs, such as the East Africa Group of the Royal Empire Society; much of his contribution is reported in the periodical *East Africa* (in 1936 renamed *East Africa and Rhodesia*).[7] Two topics were of central concern to Young. The first was the general issue of the future of race relations in the Empire, especially the question of everyday social contact between the races. The second was the effect of labour migration, and of the taxation policies which tended to encourage it.

By the time Young left Livingstonia, he had made up his mind clearly on two issues. In the first place, he was convinced that there was no necessary limit to Africans' abilities; he felt that the views of educators who displayed optimism in their dealings with Africans had been vindicated. Secondly, he had recognised and had come to appreciate the value of comradeship in African culture; and he saw this as easily capable of extension to relationships between Africans and Europeans. But such a standpoint proved highly controversial as far as many readers of *East Africa* were concerned.

The periodical *East Africa/East Africa and Rhodesia* represented during the 1930s a wide range of commentary on conditions in Africa. Although the editorial line tended always to be that a form of white-dominated paternalism was beneficial to all concerned, a much wider range of opinion was reflected in the correspondence columns. It veered to the far Right only in the 1950s and 1960s, when colonialism in Africa was coming to an end. It ceased publication in 1967, when imposition of sanctions on Rhodesia under UDI meant that it lost its subscriptions from that country.

Cullen Young welcomed the debates in *East Africa*, and also praised it for publicising the various meetings on African topics that took place in London. He first contributed to a political debate in its columns in 1934, following a report of a speech by Godfrey Huggins (later Viscount Malvern), then Prime Minister of Southern Rhodesia. Huggins condemned white extremism, but at the same time maintained that without a change in human nature, white men would not accept Africans as social or political equals. He urged a definite race policy for British East Africa, and made favourable remarks on the idea of a Central African Federation. In the same issue of *East Africa* in which Huggins's views were reported (19 July 1934) the editor expressed support for such a position. He went on to argue that Africans preferred plain speaking to sentimentality, and that recognition of cultural differences was not to be mistaken for disparagement.[8]

Young wrote a long letter in reply to such comments, and this was published in *East Africa* for 6 September 1934.[9] Here he rejected the suggestion made by Huggins that equality between the races would never be admitted, and stated that he found such sentiments deeply disturbing. He went on to argue that, admittedly, it was difficult to foresee the future; but that Christianity was an important new force in the situation, which could make a significant contribution to reintegration. He urged that it was important to speak the language of comradeship, especially since Christianity was a component of education in British colonies but this was not the case with some other colonial countries.

The debate between Young and Huggins was commented upon by the editor (F.S. Joelson) in the issue of *East Africa* for 20 September 1934. He stressed that the matters raised were important; but he went on to maintain that perhaps there was less disagreement than appeared at first sight, since it was possible that different definitions of 'equality' were being employed. The Editor also drew attention, in a footnote to Young's letter of 6 September, to the forthcoming publication that he was to edit, entitled *East Africa Today and Tomorrow*.[10] This was to be published to celebrate the tenth birthday of *East Africa*; Cullen Young had been invited to contribute to the collection on the subject of East Africa in the future, especially concerning racial contacts.

Young's contribution duly appeared,[11] under the title 'Imperial Dilemma'. Here he reiterated the criticisms of Huggins that he had made already. He suggested that there was now much scientific evidence against the view that there were limited possibilities for high development by Africans. He pointed out that, while white domination was still normal in Africa, it was now beginning to be questioned. He praised the African virtue of comradeship, and saw this as a useful contribution to a future shared community life. This shared system, he continued, was not however to come about through the total Europeanisation of the Africans. Rather Young suggested that developments were taking place in the light of new knowledge:

> We are only now coming to realise that the African thinks habitually on a more lofty plane than we had imagined, and with this new knowledge we also realise that progress for the African towards any point at which equal intercourse with us is possible depends far less upon our moulding him into something new than upon our possessing a system within which what he has and is can find a place and have free chance of spontaneous life.[12]

The editor did not let Young's contribution pass without his own comment. He added a footnote containing a comment by Sir Harold MacMichael, former Civil Secretary to the Government of the Sudan, to the effect that Africans found abstract ideas like Liberty, Equality and Fraternity meaningless, but that a sense of homage came naturally to them. Such sentiments were repeated in a letter to *East Africa* for 1 November 1934. While admiring Cullen Young's ideals and earnestness, the correspondent advises him also to do some deep thinking.[13]

The debate between Young and Huggins is again mentioned at editorial level in *East Africa* for 8 November 1934. Here the editor comments on a speech by J.H. Oldham, which outlined a position which might serve as a bridge between the two protagonists. Oldham had expressed the view that it was likely, though not certain, that biological differences between the races did exist. But in any case, Oldham maintained, each race could maintain its individuality, but it would be possible to meet on the basis of common humanity.[14]

Young let this matter pass without comment, though he would not have approved of such sentiments. Oldham had shown himself to be liberal on many aspects of colonial policy, but his failure to show outright condemnation of racialism had been a cause for concern for some who might otherwise have supported him.[15] It seems however that Young was not willing to write to contradict the views of a missionary of Oldham's calibre, and he made no further contributions of his own to debates on racial issues in *East Africa*. In the issue of 22 March 1945, he was however one of twenty-five signatories (mostly missionaries) to a statement which supported the United Nations line for freedom and against discrimination. The statement also expressed opposition to the colour bar in Northern Rhodesia. It maintained that, while colonialism had brought benefits, colour prejudice was to be deplored.[16]

As noted in Chapter IV, Young wrote to *The Times* for 3 April 1941 on the question of the 'economic colour bar' on the Copperbelt. This was part of a debate which arose as a response to a leader in *The Times* for 18 February 1941, on the subject of the report on the 1940 disturbances on the Copperbelt. One commentator (Perham) had suggested that an economic colour bar was part of the problem, and Sir William McLean had written in denying its existence. Attention was drawn by another contributor (Moody) to the fact that a discrepancy existed between European and African wages, but McLean had maintained that this was due to differences in skill. Moody pointed out in a further letter that promotion prospects for Africans were better in the Belgian Congo, since an African driver would take over there from a European when the train crossed the border with Northern Rhodesia. The comment by Young and his UMCB colleagues on job reservation practices promoted by white trade unionists has already been mentioned.[17] The comparison drawn by Young with Nazism will be returned to when his contribution to the campaign against the Federation is discussed.

The other main issue which Cullen Young had occasion to comment upon was the question of labour migration, and especially its relationship to taxation policies. Labour migration had been a matter for concern for Livingstonia missionaries from quite an early stage. Initially they had not expressed total disapproval and their educational policies had the effect of encouraging it. This was because most of the skills taught at Livingstonia could not be used in the village context. The main stimulus to mass emigration for work was taxation imposed by the colonial government, but the flow had begun before tax was imposed (taxation began in 1897 in Tongaland and in 1906 among the Ngoni).[18] The phenomenon did however come under increased critical scrutiny by the missions, especially after the Phelps-Stokes philosophy had been popularised. There were arguments that labour migration was objectionable on moral grounds, in that it split families and opened African men's eyes to the seamier side of the white man's culture. Economic objections were also raised, because of the implications of depleting villages of large numbers of able-bodied males.[19]

Evidence from anthropological studies has subsequently suggested that the economic problems of adjustment to the absence of males may have been exaggerated.[20] However, at least in the short run, the experience of finding depleted villages was recognised as problematic by both missions and the colonial government. Concern for this issue led the Governor to appoint a 'Commission to inquire into Migrant Labour'. This was chaired by Major A. Travers Lacey, and William Young was one of its members. Its Report, which appeared in 1935, drew particular attention to the problems of taxation. It showed that tax bore no relationship to an individual's ability to pay; and that since, especially in the North, local earnings were not enough to enable payment of tax, the system led inevitably to mass emigration. It urged that the tax method should be changed to take account of ability to pay, and that locally-available opportunities for wage labour, such as cash cropping, should be encouraged.[21]

Cullen Young was in a good position to take a close interest in the findings òf the Commission, through his brother and through Lacey. In 1936 he took the opportunity to publicise its findings. In an article in *The Spectator*, Cullen Young urged that the conclusions should be taken notice of. He pointed out that the method of taxation led to hatred of white people by Africans, and that labour migration had undesirable social and economic consequences.[22] In the same year, he continued such themes in an article in the *Journal of the Royal African Society*. Here he spoke with approval of proposals to reform taxation in Kenya, which included a graduated tax system. He urged that such a scheme be adopted for Malawi. It would involve the same method of taxation for all races, i.e. according to income. He accepted that in the short run this would lead to a budget deficit, but he suggested that this would gradually be eliminated as the income of Africans increased, meaning that more would be paying tax. He also suggested that those with no cash income could be enlisted in voluntary public works.[23] He returned to the question of taxation once more in his comment on Lord Hailey's *African Survey*. He criticised this volume for its failure to give adequate consideration to the social consequences of taxation. Here and elsewhere he argued that existing fiscal practices contradicted the principle of trusteeship, involving as they did taxation without representation.[24]

But in no sense could Cullen Young be seen as a polemical anti-colonialist. Rather he thought that the ideals associated with the British Empire were noble ones. He favoured independence when 'ready'. He was prepared to make criticisms of particular aspects of colonial policy; and he saw the danger that ideals might not always be carried out in practice. In his dealings with both Africans and Europeans, he liked wherever possible to build bridges, rather than to support conflict. Thus he consistently found himself attracted to the idea of a relationship between trustee and ward in the colonial situation. Education and a supply of literature were seen by Young as important so as to ensure that the ward grew up. He was aware that problems could arise in perceiving the colonial relationship in this way. It might not be clear exactly when the ward had grown up, and there could be difficulties if trustee and ward had different views on the subject. He was generally unclear as to how such matters of controversy were to be resolved. He did however mention that the Church of Scotland had dealt with the problem by cooptation. In the mission church, there had been a gradual admission of Africans to the Eldership, until the point had been reached where there could be an African majority in a Kirk Session.[25] He was a forthright critic of anything that might impede the process of maturation. He forcefully criticised racism and any form of racial segregation in colonial policies. He feared, too, that racism could be couched in the language of paternalism.

This political line which Young took led inexorably to his forthright critique of the proposal of the Federation of Rhodesia and Nyasaland. He showed that what was involved was not true 'partnership'; rather, he suggested, the proposal displayed a *Herrenvolk* mentality. He reminded his fellow-countrymen, in a pamphlet published in 1944, that this was precisely what they were fighting against.[26] Young was eventually a little upset at the stridency of the tones used by some African nationalists, but none the less he thought it important to understand the reasons for such a development. He also noted the attitude that African nationalists displayed towards Field-Marshal Smuts. Young had shown an interest in Smuts since the German East African Campaign, and had admired his internationalist sentiments: but he recognised that Africans saw him in a different light, since he had done so little to alleviate discrimination in his own country.[27]

Young's overall philosophy approved of the idea of 'comradeship' or 'colleagueship'. He had perceived this in traditional African society, and he saw it as able to be extended to other races, for mutual benefit. He saw comradeship as existing in trade unions, except for those white organisations in Africa which were concerned to maintain differential rewards and to practise job reservation.[28] Moreover, at some point Cullen Young seems to have inspired Clements Kadalie, the pioneeer of black trade unionism in South Africa. Kadalie was a Livingstonia graduate, who made his way south in 1915. He saw the germ of some of his beliefs as having been the teaching at Livingstonia by 'good missionaries', that all men were equal and their lives valuable. Cullen Young clearly counted as a 'good missionary'

as far as Kadalie was concerned. In 1927 Kadalie toured Britain, and
Edinburgh was included in his trip. It was Cullen Young who met
him at the station and who took him sightseeing to places such as St
Giles's Cathedral.[29]

But with the exception of Kadalie, Young seems to have had little
connection with black African nationalists for a very long period; and
they were in any case very few in number. However, the situation
changed completely in 1939, for it was in that year that Young and
Banda became reacquainted with one another, following their
'chance' meeting outside Edinburgh University.

To appreciate the significance of this meeting, and of the
collaboration which it subsequently led to, it is necessary to be aware
of the events which took place after Young's expulsion of Banda from
the examination room.[30] The fact that Banda had succeeded in
travelling as far as Scotland suggests that he had acquired some
qualifications in spite of his departure from Livingstonia, and such
was indeed the case. The expulsion did not deter Banda from seeking
advancement; a few days afterwards he embarked upon a 400-mile
journey to South Africa. He knew that the Church of Scotland's
Lovedale College existed in that country, and he hoped to continue his
education there. The first thirty days of the journey were made on
foot, as far as Hartley in Zimbabwe. Here he obtained employment as
a sweeper in a hospital, and he remained till the end of 1916. He
became appalled at the conditions in which African patients were
treated, and was thus influenced in the direction of a medical career.
Towards the end of his stay he was joined by his uncle, Hanock
Msokera Phiri. Hanock Phiri was a teacher at a village school of the
Livingstonia mission, but he too thought he could find higher levels
of education by going south. Phiri and Banda travelled further south
together in January 1917; they obtained employment in a mine for a
brief period, but then continued south again. Their fare to
Johannesburg was paid by a Scotsman who heard them, and who was
intrigued that they spoke English with a Scottish accent. They both
obtained employment at the Witwatersrand Deep Mine (Boksburg);
Phiri left after one year but Banda remained. Banda seems to have
remained aloof from the seamy side of urban living; he concentrated
on serious matters, and attended night classes run by the Methodist
mission. He also became interested in politics, and became
acquainted with Clements Kadalie. During this period he transferred

his own religious allegiance to the African Methodist Episcopal Church, a black independent body. He was so impressed that he encouraged his uncle to come and join the church. Phiri accepted his nephew's invitation, and went further to become ordained as a minister of this church. He then returned to Malawi to start a mission there;[31] Banda for his part was to be sponsored by the church (which had American links) for studies in the United States, provided that he could pay his own fare.

Banda succeeded in reaching the United States, and initially he registered at the Wilberforce Institute, near Xenia, Ohio. He completed his diploma there, but could get no more church sponsorship. However, he was able to take a pre-medical course at the University of Indiana at Bloomington, financed by lecture fees and various labouring jobs. While there he met a Professor of Linguistics from Chicago University, who suggested that Banda could be a useful collaborator for Mark Hanna Watkins, who was doing research into Chichewa. Banda agreed and became fascinated by the project, the findings of which were published in 1937.[32] In return for this collaboration, Banda was offered a place at Chicago University. At this juncture he chose to study History and Politics. He now favoured a broadly-based education, since he was deeply suspicious of educational philosophies such as those endorsed by Phelps Stokes, which seemed to advocate only a narrow vocational education for black people. But on graduation in 1931 he returned to his medical interests, and after a short postgraduate course in chemistry he enrolled for a medical degree at Meharry College in Nashville, Tennessee. He graduated with a Doctorate of Medicine in 1937, with excellent results. His sponsorship for the course had been provided by certain American business people with philanthropic interests.

Banda now wished to use his qualifications in the service of his own people, but he required British licentiates for this. In 1938 he took ship to Scotland; after a brief period as an assistant to a general practitioner in Renfrew, he enrolled in Edinburgh at the School of Medicine of the Royal College of Physicians and Surgeons. He completed the course easily, having covered much of the ground already. In 1941 he obtained the qualifications L.R.C.P. (Edin.), L.R.C.S. (Edin.) and L.R.F.P.S. (Glas.).

It was thus during his Scottish medical studies that Banda became reacquainted with Young. Banda had by now rejoined the Church of

Scotland; he attended the church of the Revd Dr Hector MacPherson, who himself had African missionary interests. Banda was ordained by him as an Elder in 1941 and he took his duties very seriously. Outside the church, Banda's reaction to what he saw in Scotland was anything but enthusiastic. He was shocked that in a Christian nation whose missionaries had forbidden the use of alcoholic drink, there were numerous public houses. He was also shocked by ballroom dancing, and felt that the Chewa dances that many missionaries had condemned were much more morally acceptable. He was thus well prepared to reassert the values of his own traditional culture when the time became ripe. He also began to take an interest in the politics of Malawi. The Bledisloe Commission was considering the possibility of closer association between Nyasaland and the Rhodesias. Banda abhorred this proposal, since he had seen at first hand the racism that prevailed in Southern Rhodesia, and could not contemplate the possibility of its extension into his own country.

Banda was encouraged in his views by many Scottish missionaries. Cullen Young, as already noted, opposed the idea of federation, but at this stage he was not one of the most accessible contacts for Banda. In 1939 Young was still in London, employed there at the USCL offices. However, his work entailed numerous visits to Scotland and it was probably on one of these that Young and Banda met again in Edinburgh.

As has already been seen, Young returned to his native Scotland in 1946; but by then Banda had just taken up residence in London. Banda had hopes of returning home after qualifying, but prejudice against an African doctor prevented him from pursuing this ambition at Livingstonia. He was later offered a post as a government doctor in Malawi, but this was only upon unacceptable terms (such as a ban on social contacts with white doctors). He enrolled for a course in tropical medicine at Liverpool University, and subsequently worked as a general practitioner in that city. In 1943 he was directed to move to Tyneside, because of wartime requirements. He disliked his stay there, since he sometimes received requests (such as for abortions) which offended his puritan conscience. He succeeded in leaving hospital work there and entered private practice. He stayed in Tyneside till 1945, then moved to London as a general practitioner. Thus there were only a few months between his arrival in London and Cullen Young's departure.

The most significant fact about Banda's work in London is the degree to which he became successfully absorbed into English middle-class life. His practice prospered. He employed a white secretary, and bought himself a house in a fashionable area. He wore a three-piece suit and homburg hat, and carried a rolled umbrella. He drove a small car; and he even became a freemason. This degree of assimilation might at first sight tell against any suggestion that Banda could be a proponent of a strong belief in 'African tradition'. As Short points out:

> African friends who visited him at his home were impressed not only by the extent of his adjustment and by the ease with which he had assimilated British attitudes, but by the efficiency with which he ran his practice and the high standard of living which he had attained. Few other black men, and perhaps no other African, had achieved such total integration into a white community. Banda could boast a white secretary and a standard of living higher than that enjoyed by many of his white neighbours, and yet have those neighbours accept that this was no more than was right and proper.[33]

However, this is only one side of the story, as Short himself goes on to recognise. Short remarks that there was 'something incongruous in Banda's Englishness'.[34] His house on Sunday afternoons was a meeting-place for African nationalists and their European sympathisers; some of the nationalists, including Banda himself, were later to be imprisoned by the British. Kwame Nkrumah and Jomo Kenyatta were among Banda's associates during this period. Moreover, Banda may have been middle-class and he was certainly anti-communist, but he was no Tory. He joined the Willesden branch of the Labour Party, and the Fabian Colonial Bureau. He maintained a strong interest in pan-Africanism and in the nationalist movement in his home country.

Short suggests further that Banda's political activity in this direction could be explained in terms of compensation for failure to return home for such a long period. A further aspect of Banda's situation would no doubt have been a certain feeling of nostalgia, a kind of exaggerated support for the home culture such as affects

expatriates everywhere. It is true that Banda had left Malawi at a
fairly young age (apparently 16) but various aspects of traditional
Chewa culture had already left an impression upon him. Against the
rules of the mission, Banda had become initiated at the age of about
13, through the *Vinyau* rite. His uncle Hanock Msokera Phiri
maintained a keen interest in Chewa history, and told tales of the past
to his nephew. It was the custom for the old people to recount the
folk tales of the tribe in the evening, and this was a crucial part of a
Chewa child's education. A matter of some significance for future
events is that Banda was born around the border of two cultural areas:
that of the Tumbuka-speaking northerners, and that of the Chewa of
the Central Region. He was aware of matters of common tradition,
but also of the fact that the Tumbuka were patrilineal and the Chewa
matrilineal.

The meeting between Young and Banda was therefore destined to
lead to much discussion of matters of common concern. The
immediate sequel occurred in July 1939. The Government of
Nyasaland had agreed to send Chief Mwase Kasungu to England, to
assist a project on Chichewa which was being carried out at the
London School of Oriental and African Studies. Cullen Young wrote
to Dr Bargery of that institution, recommending Banda as chief
adviser for the project. Young maintained than Banda was a 'very
sound fellow of good judgement and character', and also pointed out
that Banda was acquainted with London. These comments are
themselves of interest; they suggest that Young had got to know
Banda better after their brief meeting in Edinburgh; also that Banda,
who was based in Scotland, had visited Young in London. Banda was
of course very suited for the Chichewa project; he had already
assisted with the work on Chichewa at Chicago, which Watkins had
undertaken. Moreover his village in Malawi lay a few miles east of
the trading centre at Kasungu, where Chief Mwase had his
headquarters. However, when Mwase arrived in London in the
autumn of 1939, Banda found communication somewhat difficult.
Mwase's Chichewa displayed some important differences from the
language that Banda had known as a boy, and contained numerous
English borrowings; and Banda was not pleased by the changes. In
the event Mwase stayed for only a few months in London, because of
the outbreak of the war.

Clear and positive proof of collaboration between Young and

Banda is to be found in the introduction to the collection *Our African Way of Life*, which was published in 1946. This appeared under the joint authorship of the two of them. An explanation of the story of their collaboration, covering the expulsion and later reunion, is presented there. But the main point made in this introduction is to the effect that there was much of value in traditional African culture, and the three short stories in the collection are presented as illustrations of this. There is also much discussion of the workings of a matrilineal society. Marriage procedures are explained, and there is discussion of the central importance of instruction to prepare young people up to parenthood. The initiation procedures for girls (*chinamwali*) and for boys (*vinyau*) are explained. There is also discussion of the purposes of traditional medicine. The procedures whereby a male guardian is responsible for a group of female relatives are outlined. The guardian is referred to as the 'responsible relative' in this particular text. (The vernacular term *nkhoswe* translates in modern anthropology as 'warden', and the group of female relatives [*mbumba*] would be known as a 'sorority group').[35]

The authors are concerned to stress that the system is not as rigid as many Westerners would like to think. Thus in the case of marriage, while they acknowledge that a large number of people are involved when such a step is taken, they add the following qualification:

Contrary to the prevailing idea, marriage among the Chewa people is not always the business of older people. Young people often make it their concern. As in the West, it is the young man who approaches the young woman. The young man may approach her by himself. But usually, he reveals the contents of his heart to her through the intermediary of his older sister or sister-in-law, more often, through the latter.[36]

They go on to discuss the procedures that can be followed in the event of persistent refusal, noting that escape routes exist in the form of elopement or marriage by capture. In such cases, however, negotiations would still have to take place, albeit retrospectively. As Banda and Young go on to point out:

When a Chewa youth enters upon his honeymoon via

elopement or capture, he does so fully and seriously aware that his action in doing so is illegal and reprehensible. But his mind is perfectly at peace. For he enters upon his illegal marital bliss with a sure knowledge that his uncle will unravel the legal tangle. Is it not just for such purposes and for such occasions that one has uncles and elder brothers?

Nor is he ever disappointed. However much the uncle may disapprove or deplore his nephew's actions, he never fails to straighten matters out. This is not so much from a sense of duty as from that of honour. He employs the services of an agent. And how sorely is he in need of them! The young bride's uncles and brothers are scandalized and indignant. They are in the worst of tempers, which only the silver tongue of a skilful and witty *chidindilo* (go-between) can calm.[37]

The three short stories in the collection all take various aspects of the life cycle and how it is dealt with by the Chewa as their main theme. Two of their authors (Kambalame and Chidzalo) also say that their stories have a didactic purpose, that is to ensure that the young will know about traditional values. The overall message of the collection is that Chewa society has clearly-articulated rules of conduct, which comprise a system that cannot as such be questioned; but that these rules still provide for manipulation, and for the realisation of individual ambition.[38]

Young and Banda acknowledge in their introduction that discussion between them of linguistic questions soon led to more far-ranging issues; Young had initially asked Banda to assist him on matters of translation, and broader concerns logically followed: 'What more fitting than that, the work accomplished, the two together should offer its results as a contribution towards more and fuller understanding of African thought and African longings?'.[39]

They also observe that it was only when this collaboration was agreed upon that Banda revealed himself as the boy whom Young had expelled from the examination room. Their work together continued in relation to other publications. Banda's assistance was particularly important in the preparation of the English text for Ntara's book *Headman's Enterprise*, which was published in 1949. Banda is also explicitly referred to in a postscript by Edwin Smith to Young's contribution to the collection *African Ideas of God* (1950).[40] Banda here confirms Young's view regarding a sharp distinction between God and the ancestral spirits. Banda points out that the word for God (*Mulungu*) was never used in the plural, whereas the spirits were normally referred to in the plural form (*mizimu*). Banda also confirms that he could remember appeals being made to God by his parents and grandparents in similar circumstances to those referred to by Young.

Banda could not have influenced the writing of *African Ways and Wisdom*, which had been published in 1937; and *Contemporary Ancestors* appeared in 1940, too soon after the reacquaintance for Banda to have had any impact. But it is interesting to entertain the hypothesis that there was an important influence of Young upon Banda. Banda's nostalgia would in his London years have been fuelled by the meetings of various African nationalists who came to his house. He would undoubtedly have been receptive to Cullen Young's perception of African culture: since, far from seeing it as disgusting, Young tended if anything to over-idealise it. Once they had become reacquainted, Young discussed all his subsequent work on Africa with Banda.[41]

Banda was a highly-assimilated African in England, but this does not preclude a concern for traditional culture; indeed, there are parallels to his experience. It has been noted for French-speaking Africa that a policy of assimilation could lead some of those who responded most successfully to reassert African cultural values eventually; thus Léopold Sédar Senghor, one of the most highly assimilated of French Africans, embraced the philosophy of *négritude*.[42] In West Africa even in the British colonies nationalism had a cultural dimension, adopting the notion of the 'African personality'.[43] But on the whole the British, unlike the French, discouraged Africans from attaining high levels of education and Westernisation; also, the policy of Indirect Rule had the aim of leaving largely intact the traditional culture and political organisation. Banda was exceptional for his times in his high levels of educational attainment, and significantly these were realised mainly in the United States, not Britain.

Although Banda had many acquaintances who were missionaries, he was by no means enthusiastic about all of them. He has in recent years charged some missionaries with an imperfect understanding of

African languages and cultures, and with issuing condemnations of
African tradition which lacked any scriptural justification. Moreover
for a considerable period of his life he was a member of the African
Methodist Episcopal Church, which is not of white missionary origin.
Banda may frequently have found himself on the defensive with
regard to his feeling that his own traditions had some value - until his
reacquaintance with Young. Many missionaries saw African culture
as disgusting, while others saw a cultural void into which European
ways could be poured successfully. An example of the latter view can
be seen in an unsigned editorial to a special Africa number of the
Scottish missionary periodical *Other Lands* (January 1927):

> Here we are dealing with an immense population, the
> majority of whom are still in a primitive stage of
> evolution - a huge, raw mass of human material, the
> potentialities of which for good or evil no man knows.
> Their whole future depends on how they are being taken
> in hand now, and how they are being taught and trained.
>
> While they possess, like other races, their own
> peculiar qualities, which they will retain, the evidence is
> that they will progress according to European examples
> and standards. They have no ancient civilization to
> conserve. They are imitative and adaptable ....
>
> Thus we have a plastic, impressionable people which,
> like clay in the hands of the potter, can be moulded as
> civilization wills. It is this fact which makes Africa so
> important in the eyes of the Christian statesman and
> missionary.[44]

This standpoint had been quite influential at Livingstonia. The
ambitious standards aimed at in the educational policies there had
the counterpart of downgrading traditional culture. This attitude
had its echoes even in some of the earlier African converts.
However Levi Mumba, mentioned in Chapter II, was one of a
number of the latter who resisted. His exposition of traditional
Tumbuka religion was received sympathetically by Cullen Young,
who sponsored its publication.[45] It is significant that for Mumba,
cultural nationalism led to political activity. He became president of
the North Nyasa Native Association in 1912; and by 1944 he was first

President-General of the Nyasaland African Congress Party, and in correspondence with Banda in that capacity. But for his untimely death the following year, Mumba's role in the independence movement would have continued to be highly significant.[46]

As has been shown, Young's attitude to African culture will certainly have been refreshing for Banda. Unlike many other missionaries, Young was prepared to defend both the significance of African historical tradition and the values enshrined in African culture. And in addition, Young and Banda had other experiences and attitudes in common. Young's period of service at Loudon had given him a feeling for Chewa language and culture as well as Tumbuka. Banda's own origins were in the border between the two culture-areas. Young was also conscious of his own ancestry on the Scottish borders, and this had helped him in developing sensitivity towards cultural differences. Banda had eventually succeeded in completing his education in Scotland, Young's native country. Both Young and Banda were members of the Church of Scotland. Finally, they both supported African nationalism and were particularly opposed to the proposed Central African Federation.

Banda became more active in politics as a consequence of the Federation policy, that the British government seemed destined to accept. He produced in 1949 a memorandum, written together with the Zambian nationalist Harry Nkumbula, refuting the claim that the Federation would provide for genuine partnership. and in particular suggesting that the standpoint of settlers on this subject was hypocritical.[47] It does not appear that Young took an active part in opposing the Federation, beyond the publication of his 1944 pamphlet. But it must be remembered that by the late 1940s Young became less active in general, since both he and his wife were beginning to suffer from health problems. The campaign against the Federation was in the event a failure at this particular juncture in history; Federation became a reality in August 1953. Following this even the Labour Party accepted the Federation as an accomplished fact. Banda now felt bitterly disappointed with life in Britain, and left to settle in Ghana.

While in Ghana Banda kept a very low political profile, both in relation to Ghanaian independence (which was achieved in 1957) and to the nationalist movement in Malawi. There is also no evidence of whether or not he kept in touch with the ailing Cullen Young until his

death in 1955. But it is necessary to make a brief digression
concerning the events leading to Banda's return to politics and
eventual autocractic leadership of Malawi. This will make possible
an examination of the way in which Banda's view of 'African
tradition', which Cullen Young influenced to some unknown degree,
became part of the Malawian state ideology after independence.

In the 1950s, the Malawian independence movement (the
Nyasaland African Congress) was led primarily by two young
educated men, Henry Chipembere and Kanyama Chiume. They
feared that their youth would count against them as potential leaders
of a country where old age was greatly revered. Banda on the other
hand was unusual in being both old and educated. Attempts were
made to encourage him to return to Malawi so as to lead the
nationalist movement to victory. Banda was initially non-committal;
but when moves were afoot to turn the Federation into an
amalgamation, he began to show more interest. He eventually agreed
to return, and first set foot again in Malawi on 6 July 1958. He
received a tumultuous welcome, as a messiah; his supporters in
Malawi had taken care to build up his image for some time.

His message concentrated upon opposition to the Federation. The
initial image which he presented was one of a local man who had
made good despite obstacles, in the white man's world. He retained
his English warm clothes despite the climate. He spoke in English
through an interpreter, his Chichewa now being halting and archaic.
The Nyasaland African Congress became more successful under his
leadership, and white resistance became correspondingly stronger.
Eventually in March 1959 a State of Emergency was declared. There
were 48 African deaths in this operation, and 1500 arrests, including
Banda and Chipembere (Chiume was outside the country and was
ordered by the British not to return). Banda was imprisoned, but
received comfortable treatment; he later referred to his stay in prison
as a holiday. He took the opportunity to make plans for an
independent Malawi. He also wrote an autobiography, which
unfortunately has not been published or otherwise made available.
Banda was released in 1960. In Britain, the Macmillan government
accepted that there was a 'wind of change' in Africa, and was in the
process of coming round to the idea of independence. Self-
government for Malawi was attained on 1 February 1963, with Banda
sworn in as the first Prime Minister (the Governor, Sir Glyn Jones,

remaining for the present). Full independence came on 6 July 1964, with Banda as President. In 1971 he was made President for Life, though as early as February 1963 he was made Life President of the Malawi Congress Party.

Banda was not yet in a sufficiently powerful position to stamp the Malawi political culture with ideas largely promulgated by himself. The personality cult was well developed, but still he was expected to rule as leader of a Cabinet in which discussion and criticism of policies were permitted.[48] But tensions soon arose between Banda and his ministers. Banda expected them to see him as a 'father', and to show gratitude and respect accordingly. Matters came to a head in the months immediately following independence, when disagreements occurred between Banda and various ministers, including Chiume and Chipembere: these related to sources of foreign aid, foreign policy, hospital charges, and civil service salaries. Banda appealed to, and obtained, a vote of confidence from rank-and-file MPs over the heads of ministers, and eventually dissenting ministers were forced to leave the country. Their replacements were those prepared to accept Banda's definition of the function of Cabinet, and the scene was set for dictatorship.

The relevance of these events for the present discussion lies in the way in which Banda constantly justified his actions in terms of their accordance with cultural values found in Malawi. As early as December 1962, he declared his opposition to cultural imperialism: 'It was not only politically that we were enslaved, colonised. We were also enslaved and colonised culturally. It became clear to me that the kind of Christianity we are being given here which condemns the people's national culture was not at all a true Christianity but something else.'[49]

Banda soon began to argue that Malawi could not be a carbon copy of any other country; thus democracy in Malawi would be distinctive in form, and would be 'based on the old African institutions'.[50] In accordance with this policy, the institution of chieftainship was retained. Banda's expectation that his orders would be obeyed without question was also based upon his view of what could have been traditionally expected by a chief.

Apart from the Cabinet Crisis, the first major break from the assumptions inherited from the British colonialists occurred in relation to the workings of the legal system. As early as November,

1963, Banda declared himself to be the ultimate source of all law: 'Anything I say is law. Literally law. It is a fact in this country.'[51] And in various ways, he attempted to mould the legal system so as to accord with his version of Malawi tradition. He strengthened the powers of the local (now 'traditional') courts; he saw them as being more appropriate for Malawi than the British system, since it was not possible in such courts to be acquitted on the basis of a clever defence or a legal technicality. He also condemned the strict rules of evidence required in the British system, and praised the Chewa law for taking a different view. In 1965 he commented upon a murder trial, saying that he knew that the defendants would be found guilty: remarks of this kind would be deemed in Britain to be prejudicial to the outcome.

Outside the more overtly political domain, Banda has expressed widely-reported views upon family relationships, and has stressed the importance of traditional values. In particular, he has stressed the subordination of the young to the old, and he has urged that parents, elders and chiefs be respected. He has constantly repeated this refrain, and has compared Malawi favourably to other societies with respect to ways in which such traditional patterns of obedience are safeguarded. A corollary of this has been the assertion that the traditional wisdom of the elders is of primary importance; and that school education serves only to supplement this. He stresses the value of character training from parents in the village, and the virtues of the common people. He has been particularly critical of the complex of attitudes and behaviour patterns characterised by Western 'permissiveness'. Throughout Malawi, 'good behaviour' is regarded as a prerequisite for continued participation in educational institutions.

Banda trusts the ordinary villager, rather than the educated elite, to respond appropriately to his message. He did find it necessary to create such an educated elite, so as to replace the departing expatriates. He was in fact already planning the university while in prison. However, he has made it clear that the educated should keep their proper place, and in particular that they should not promulgate subversive doctrines.

Throughout, Banda has displayed an image of personal concern for his subjects. Malawi is not a large country geographically, and is relatively densely populated by African standards; Banda frequently tours the country and it is not difficult for most of his subjects to see him in person. Banda pays with his own money for certain benefits to individual supporters; he provides houses for certain chiefs and members of women's organisations, and for trips abroad. The image of community benefactor is reminiscent of the ideal of 'open-handedness' of the chief, who acquires a personal following on such a basis. Banda's personal concern tends to be directed particularly at the women of Malawi. His policies aim at improvement of the position of women, but in some respect their status is still seen in traditional terms.[52] Malawian women are still under the guardianship of the *nkhoswe* (warden) of their *mbumba* (sorority-group), in the manner that was explained in *Our African Way of Life*. Banda has in fact gone further and has declared himself as 'Nkhoswe No. 1' of all Malawian women, implying that he is the overall guardian who is concerned for their interests.

One final aspect of tradition fostered by Banda which is worthy of mention is dancing. This is one aspect of culture which Banda definitely wished to reassert. Traditional dances both for men and for women have been adapted for modern political purposes (the women's dances being much more frequently performed). The dances are a crucial component of cultural nationalism in Malawi. The women's dances are performed on most occasions when Banda arrives to deliver an oration. A special uniform is worn by the women dancers, incorporating a picture of Banda; and songs of praise to Banda are sung during the dance.

Thus in numerous ways a particular version of 'African tradition' is incorporated into the political culture of modern Malawi. As Hobsbawm and Ranger have shown, 'tradition' is frequently an invented phenomenon.[53] In the post-colonial situation cultural nationalism involves a certain amount of selectivity. Since the aim is usually to preserve the 'best' of 'traditional culture', some judgement needs to be made as to what are the 'good' and the 'bad' components. There may also be problems of regional differences. This is a particularly serious problem in the post-colonial state which in Africa frequently does not have 'traditional' boundaries. It is easy in such circumstances for a tribal rather than a national culture to be proclaimed, and the danger of tribalism has sometimes led modern African leaders to tone down their cultural nationalism. In the case of Malawi, the question arises as to whether in fact Banda has promoted values shared by Malawians as a whole, or whether he has promoted

what are really Chewa values. The latter standpoint has been taken
by Vail and White. Vail has maintained as follows:

> Banda was a cultural prophet at a time when such seemed
> needed, but he emerged as a distinctly Chewa prophet,
> and not a national prophet. He tended to equate Chewa-
> ness with Malawian-ness, and the Chewa people with the
> soul of the country. During his years in Nyasaland after
> 1958, while campaigning against the Federation, he
> frequently denounced tribalism in others, yet often
> emphasised that he himself was a Chewa. In his
> speeches he was always at pains to paint a picture of a
> glorious Chewa past .... In short, Banda has emphasised
> Chewa ethnic standards, not Malawi nationalism.[54]

Vail and White have gone on to point out that recent students of
the Chewa. notably Linden and Schoffelers, have contributed to the
Chewa myth, and especially to the idea of the central significance of
the *Vinyau*.[55] Vail also noted the interest that Cullen Young aroused in
Banda with regard to Chewa culture; and it is true that *Our African
Way of Life* was an exposition of Chewa virtues. It has also been
observed that no Chewa was dismissed in the Cabinet Crisis. A
further apparently Chewa-oriented policy of Banda was the decision
in 1968 to declare Chichewa the sole official African language in
Malawi, side by side with English. This involved the discontinuance
of official use of Yao and Tumbuka, and the policy led to the violent
destruction of a radio post in the North.

There is, however, another side to this coin. When an attempt is
made to homogenise a culture, some aspects of a given area's culture
are bound to be highlighted more than others. The *Vinyau* are given
respectability in modern Malawi, but are not imposed upon areas
where previously they were not practised. The dialect of Chichewa
which is promoted as national is Banda's own. This is consequently
the dialect of the border with Tumbuka territory, and it is nearer to
Tumbuka than some other Chewa dialects. Chilivumbo has
maintained that success was achieved in Malawi in promoting 'unity
in diversity'. This he suggests is seen even in the dances, which are
an adaptation of traditional practices. Moreover, he argues, they can
be used to create a feeling of national unity, since dancers often dance

outside their own areas.[56] Malawians have a long history of travelling outside the country, as labour migrants or soldiers, and this has led to a consciousness of collective identity as 'Nyasas'. As Shepperson has suggested, external factors have had an important part to play in African nationalism: an alien environment can strengthen national consciousness and lessen the importance of ethnic differences.[57] In Banda's case this appears to have happened; and while it is true that his discussions with Cullen Young initially arose out of Chichewa translation, Young's major contributions to the study of culture in Malawi had been concerned with the Tumbuka. Moreover his general works on 'Africanity' had a strong bias towards Tumbuka material. Thus it is very likely that the Tumbuka culture will have influenced the amalgam that Banda later went on to develop.

Banda was praised by non-Chewa politicians, before the Cabinet Crisis, for his knowledge of custom. Chipembere bemoaned his own ignorance on the subject, having been born and brought up on a mission. Orton Chilwa, a Tonga political activist, had also praised Banda for his knowledge of 'what used to be good in our own society'.[58]

Thus Banda's emphasis on the importance of 'tradition' is a significant element in Malawian political culture. Some might have maintained that this was inconsistent with his Anglicisation, but Banda himself would not think so. In July 1969 Banda commented:

> I believe in tradition .... In Britain the people believe in tradition. In my view, the reason why Britain is the most stable country in the world .... is that the British people are sensible enough not to throw overboard their old and ancient institutions overnight. True, they change their system of government and their social ways of life, but not all of a sudden; not violently, but gradually and orderly, grafting on their own ancient traditions anything new that they might want to adopt.
>
> I want the same here. While I want to adopt new ways of life; while I want us to copy the good from other people, I do not want us to just throw away everything that is ours by tradition. We must change gradually.[59]

Banda is committed to development, which involves change, just like any other African leader. Malawians are exhorted by their media to show gratitude to the 'wise and dynamic leadership of His Excellency the Life President' - to a leadership which respects tradition but which responds to change, and which is powerful, too.

Having examined the way in which Banda has articulated his own version of African cultural nationalism, it is necessary to consider further Cullen Young's possible contribution to Banda's ideas. *Our African Way of Life* has already been mentioned, but there is much evidence, albeit circumstantial, of a further degree of influence. It cannot be denied that there is much in common between Banda's articulation of 'African tradition' and that put forward by Cullen Young. Some specific points have already been noted. But in more general terms, it can be seen that Banda's vision of the good state of affairs in Malawi is like Young's exposition of the Tumbuka notion of the 'good village'. Malawi is seen as a moral community, whose values are to be supported by all. People may be lax in living up to the community values, but must never rebel against them; and if they do, there is swift retribution. Young had shown how traditional moral communities had been confined to the limits of the clan; but he also argued that the community was capable of extension.

Banda has persisted with the view that European ways are not necessarily better than those of Africa; he has gone even further, seeing the older ways as often superior, and certainly as more suited to Malawi. The inflow of new ideas and book-learning is something that he welcomes, but only to 'complete' the ancient wisdom.

It should not of course be assumed that Cullen Young was the sole influence upon Banda, even in respect of cultural nationalism. Relevant topics of discussion will certainly have cropped up during discussions between African nationalists that had taken place at Banda's London home. Kenyatta was one of Banda's visitors, and in 1938 he had already written an account of his own Kikuyu people which was heavily stamped with nationalism.[60] Nkrumah was another London associate, and the notion of the 'African Personality' was a significant component of Nkrumah's anti-colonial message.[61] Other experiences, too, will have shaped Banda's outlook. His earliest university studies were in political science and history, leading him to be acquainted with much relevant material for his future role. The Church of Scotland will have helped to reinforce his puritanism and his work ethic, and the same will have been true of his medical training. As MacMaster suggests: 'Although generalizations about organizational attitudes must be subject to many qualifications, nevertheless, in the case of Dr Banda, membership of the BMA and the Church of Scotland is indicative of a view of society which places value on hard work, individual effort, and respect for authority'.[62]

Many would attribute the continued stability of Malawi to political repression, and there is no doubt that there is plenty of it in Malawi. Banda's regime has always been backed up by the necessary strong-arm organisations, and by the omnipresent secret police, to ensure that dissidents and rebels are identified and punished. Punishment can include detention without trial, or much worse. Yet it would be inadequate to explain his continued appeal in such terms alone. As Joffe has suggested, this is not a suitable explanation since many African regimes have been toppled in spite of powerful machinery for political repression; the answer must therefore be at least partly in terms of Banda's populist appeal.[63]

Banda's cultural nationalism seems therefore to be a natural sequel to earlier attempts to codify 'African tradition'. Ranger has documented some instances of this on the part of the British colonialists. He has shown how the British sometimes invented such 'tradition' on behalf of Africans, especially in the context of Indirect Rule. In such a process, even if a particular view of the past contained elements of distortion, it could become the basis for subsequent actions.[64] Cullen Young had shown himself adept at codifying tradition in his earlier Tumbuka studies, before the reunion with Banda. His subsequent discussion of 'tradition' in more general terms was a natural progression from this. African tradition has almost invariably been codified initially by Europeans, but this could scarcely have been otherwise in societies where previously there was no writing.

It would be fanciful to declare dogmatically that Cullen Young was the architect of cultural nationalism in modern Malawi. Yet it would be equally hard to deny that Cullen Young was a crucial influence upon Banda's thinking at a particular period in his life. The extent of such influence can however be only a matter for speculation. But what seems likely is that (using an analogy employed by Socrates) Cullen Young served a maieutic function; that is to say, he performed a midwife's services to Banda's thoughts and ideas.

Notes

Notes for pages 1 - 4

I   The Man and his Times

1.   For a discussion of missionary accounts see especially H.A.C. Cairns, *Prelude to Imperialism* (London, 1965); also R. Thornton, 'Narrative Ethnography in Africa, 1850-1920', *Man*, n.s. 8 (1973) 502-21.

2.   E.W. Smith and A.M. Dale, *the Ila-speaking Peoples of Northern Rhodesia* 2 vols (London, 1920; 2nd ed. New York, 1968). The second edition has a new introduction by E. Colson (pp.. i-vi).

3.   For a report of this conference see E.W. Smith, *The Christian Mission in Africa: a study based on the work of the International Conference at Le Zoute* (London, 1926).

4.   The extent of this is considered in A.C. Ross, 'Scottish Missionary Concern, 1874-1914: a golden era?', *Scottish Historical Review*, 51 (1972) 52-72.

5.   O. Ramsford, *David Livingstone: the dark interior* (London, 1978) p. 80.

6.   G. White, 'Highly Preposterous: origins of Scottish missions, *Records of the Scottish Church History Society*, 19 (1976) 111-24.

7.   J.A. Mangan, *Athleticism in the Victorian and Edwardian Public Schools* (Cambridge, 1981) p.47; R.J. MacKenzie, *Almond of Loretto* (London, 1905) Ch. IX.

8.   For the implications of this for missionary work see J. McCracken, *Politics and Christianity in Malawi: the impact of the Livingstonia Mission in the Northern Province*

Notes for pages 5 - 7

(Cambridge, 1977) pp. 180-1.

9. Ibid., p.30; see also Dow, Ch. I.

10. For details see McCracken, *Politics and Christianity*, esp. Ch. III; also H.W. Macmillan, 'The Origins and Development of the African Lakes Company, 1878-1908' (Edinburgh University, Ph.D., 1970).

11. A.C. Ross, 'The Origins and Development of the Church of Scotland Mission, Blantyre, Nyasaland, 1875-1926' (Edinburgh University, Ph.D., 1970).

12. A full description of these events is contained in J. Highet, *The Churches in Scotland Today* (Glasgow, 1950).

13. McCracken, *Politics and Christianity*, pp. 65-8; Dow, Appendix A; Ross, 'Origins and Development', Ch. III.

14. For a detailed biography see W.P. Livingstone, *Laws of Livingstonia* (London, 1921).

15. For Lord Overtoun (John Campbell White) see D. Carswell, *Brother Scots* (London, 1927) pp. 191-211; Dow, Ch. V; McCracken, *Politics and Christianity, passim.*

16. Personal information about T. Cullen Young has been obtained from his daughter, Mrs Margot Moffett (personal communications) and from many other members of the Young family; also from Young's former colleagues. Names of key informants are contained in the Bibliography and List of Sources. For a printed source see I. Nance, new introduction to T.C. Young, *Notes on the History of the Tumbuka-Kamanga Peoples in the Northern Province of Nyasaland*, 2nd ed. (London, 1970) pp. v-xiv. See also P.G. Forster, 'The Rev. T. Cullen Young: a preliminary note', *Bulletin of the Scottish Institute of Missionary Studies*, n.s. 2

Notes for pages 7 - 11

(1984) 13-14.

17.   For John Young (Cullen's father) information was obtained
        from 'Family Reminiscences: Father's notes and memories',
        unpublished typescript by John Young, in the possession of
        Dr Alastair Young (Edinburgh); see also references to him in
        S.J. Sjölinder, *Presbyterian Reunion in Scotland, 1907-1921*
        (Uppsala, 1962).

18.   See W. Barradell-Smith, 'The Glasgow Academy: a historical
        sketch' Ch. I (pp. 1-46) in [Anon.], *The Glasgow Academy:
        the first hundred years* (Glasgow, 1946) esp. p.2.

19.   For Rhodes's request see W.P. Livingstone, *Laws*, p. 267; for
        Cullen Young's response see *Livingstonia Mission
        Committee, Minutes*, 1903 no. 41, and 1904 no. 15.

20.   J.F. Daly, letter to John Young, 15 Apr. 1904, NLS 7864.

21.   For these preparatory steps see *United Free Church of
        Scotland Assembly Proceedings*, 1904, 74, 76; and Daly, letter
        to T.C. Young, 17 May 1904, NLS 7864.

22.   Macmillan, pp. 168-9.

23.   For correspondence about his early period see NLS 7865;
        Livingstonia Mission Report, 1904 ff.; MNA, Livingstonia
        Papers (letterbooks) LI/1/1/7-9, *passim*.

24.   *Livingstonia Mission Report*, 1905. p.9.

25.   W.A. Elmslie, *Among the Wild Ngoni* (Edinburgh, 1899).

26.   A.G. MacAlpine, 'Tonga Beliefs and Customs', *Aurora*, 8
        (1905) Apr., 13-16; June, 36-7; 9 (1906) Dec., 48-50.

27.   D. MacDonald, *Africana: or the heart of heathen Africa* 2

Notes for pages 11 - 12

vols (London, 1882); D.C. Scott, *A Cyclopaedic Dictionary of the Mang'anja Language* (Edinburgh, 1892).

28. Reports of these for the years 1900, 1904 and 1907 are bound together with Livingstonia Mission, Letters to the Sub-Committee, NLS. See also H. Feldman, 'Die allgemeine Missionskonferenz in Livingstonia in Britisch Central-Afrika', *Allgemeine Missions-Zeitschrift,* 28 (1901) 392-6.

29. For the 1905 syllabus see Livingstonia Mission, Letters to the Sub-Committee, NLS, year 1905, p. 42.

30. D. Fraser, 'The Zulu of Nyasaland: their manners and customs', *Proceedings of the Philosophical Society of Glasgow,* 32 (1900-1) 60-75: p. 75 contains one of his earliest pronouncements on the matter.

31. The system is sympathetically described in R.E. Gregson, 'Work, Exchange and Leadership: the mobilization of agricultural labor among the Tumbuka of the Henga valley' (Columbia University Ph. D., 1969) Ch. II.

32. Their different outlook is examined in T.J. Thompson, 'Fraser and the Ngoni' (Edinburgh University Ph.D., 1980).

33. Livingstonia Mission, Letters to the Sub-Committee, 1905, p. 54.

34. For the history of this qualification see R.N. Smart, 'Literate Ladies - a Fifty Year Experiment', *Alumnus Chronicle* (St Andrews University), no. 59 (June 1968) 21-31.

35. Livingstonia Mission, Letters to the Sub-Committee, year 1905, p. 83.

36. Reports quoted in *Women's Missionary Magazine,* no. 72 (Dec. 1906), 300.

Notes for pages 12 - 15

37.   NLS 7865; Daly to J. Fiddes, 23 Feb. 1906 and 22 Nov. 1906;
        Daly to T.C. Young, 26 Dec. 1906.

38.   Report in *Glasgow Academy Chronicle* 5 (1908) 111.

39.   NLS 7866; Daly to T.C. Young, 15 Nov. 1907, 21 Nov. 1907,
        and 29 Nov. 1907.

40.   *Livingstonia News*, 3 (Feb. 1910) 8-11; *Livingstonia Mission
        Reports*: 1909, p. 43; 1910. pp. 42-3; 1911, pp. 22-4. Also
        T.C. Young, 'The Peoples of the Karonga District',
        Missionary Record of the United Free Church of Scotland, 10
        (1910) 257-8.

41.   T.C. Young, 'Indian Experience in the Matter of Native
        Education', *Livingstonia News*, 2 (Feb. 1909) 5-8; this was a
        response to A.G. Fraser, 'Education in India and Ceylon in
        View of the National Movement', *The East and the West*, 6
        (1908) 28-42.

42.   T.J. Thompson, 'Ngoni'; A.R. Fraser, *Donald Fraser of
        Livingstonia* (London, 1934). Fraser's principal works are
        The Future of Africa (London, 1911); and *Winning a
        Primitive People* (London, 1914). See also the report of the
        1910 Mvera Nyasaland Missionary Conference [bound
        together with Livingstonia Mission: Letters to the Sub-
        Committee (NLS)]: see especially Fraser's contribution on
        'Heathenism' (pp. 30-4).

43.   For such details see *Livingstonia Mission Reports*: 1906, pp.
        13-14; 1910, pp. 42-3; 1911, pp. 22-4; and 1912, pp. 21-4.

44.   T.C. Young, 'Uzamba: a native initiation ceremony',
        Livingstonia News, 5 (Oct. 1912) 71-4.

45.   A detailed discussion of educational policies is contained
        in R.J. MacDonald, 'A History of African Education in

Notes for pages 15 - 17

Nyasaland, 1875-1945' (Edinburgh University Ph.D., 1969).

46. NLS 7787: 136, 488 and *passim.*

47. *United Free Church of Scotland Assembly Proceedings*, 1914, pp. 140-1.

48. *United Free Church of Scotland: Assembly Papers: Cases, Overtures*, 1914, pp. 157-60.

49. A history of this church is contained in [Anon.]. *Thirty Years of Broughton Place Church* (Edinburgh, 1914); also J. Wallace, *Broughton McDonald Church, 1785-1985* (Edinburgh, 1985).

50. *Life and Work in Broughton Place Church* nos 233 (Feb. 1914) 4; and 238 (Jul. 1914) 2.

51. Entry on T.C. Young, 'Register of Missionaries of the Free Church and subsequently of the United Free Church of Scotland'. MS, Church of Scotland.

52. T.C. Young, 'Stranded in British East Africa', *Kikuyu News* no. 52 (Nov.-Dec. 1914) 2.

53. MNA LI/1/1/10, p. 71.

54. The incident is described in P. Short, *Banda* (London, 1974) pp. 12-13; also T.C. Young and H.K. Banda (eds) *Our African Way of Life* (London, 1946) p. 26; R.J. MacDonald, 'African Education in Nyasaland', Ch. III.

55. The incidents surrounding the rising are described in detail in the classic work of G.A. Shepperson and T. Price, *Independent African: John Chilembwe and the origins, setting and significance of the Nyasaland Native Rising of 1915* (Edinburgh, 1958). For the general impact of the war

Notes for pages 18 - 22

see M.E. Page, 'Malawians in the Great War' (Michigan State University, Ph.D., 1977) and 'The War of Thangata: Nyasaland and the East African Campaign, 1914-18', *Journal of African History*, 19 (1978) 87-100; also B. Gardner, *German East* (London, 1963) and H.L. Duff, 'Nyasaland and the World War 1914-18', typescript, Imperial War Museum, London.

56.   Kew, PRO, CO 525/66.

57.   L. Vail, 'Ethnicity, Language and National Unity: the case of Malawi', in P. Bonner (ed.), *Working Papers on Southern African History* (Johannesburg, 1981) 121-63 (at p. 134).

58.   T.C. Young, 'Zovu', *Nyasaland Journal*, 6 (1953) 53-9.

59.   'Nyasaland Operations during the World War, 1914-18', typescript, Society of Malawi Library, Blantyre, Malawi.

60.   T.C. Young, 'Zovu'; and 'The Battle of Karonga', *Nyasaland Journal*, 8 (1956) 27-30.

61.   'Zovu' (ibid.).

62.   W.P. Young, *A Soldier to the Church* (London, 1919).

63.   NLS 7682 no. 414; 7684 no. 371; and 7885 no. 64.

64.   A.R. Fraser, pp. 230-2.

65.   Jessie Young, 'Camp Scenes in Central Africa', *Record of the Home and Foreign Mission Work of the United Free Church of Scotland*, 19 (1919) 93-4; T.C. Young, 'Africa's Women', *Missionary Record of the United Free Church of Scotland*, 14 (1914) 130.

66.   *United Free Church of Scotland Assembly Proceedings*, 1920,

Notes for pages 23 - 25

  p. 123.

67.   NLS 7885 no. 60 (Jessie Young to Webster).

68.   See E.W. Smith, *Aggrey of Africa: a study in Black and White* (London, 1929) pp. 214-16, for details of this visit.

69.   K. Mufuka, *Missions and Politics in Malawi* (Kingston, Ontario, 1977).

70.   C.M. Pauw, *Mission and the Church in Malawi: the history of the Nkhoma Synod in the Church of Central Africa Presbyterian* (Stellenbosch, 1980).

71.   McCracken, *Politics and Christianity*, pp. 263-4.

72.   T.C. Young, 'Zovu' pp. 55-7.

73.   A.C. Madan, *Living Speech* (Oxford, 1911).

74.   *Notes on the Speech and History of the Tumbuka-Henga Peoples* (Livingstonia 1923) p. 27. This comment is repeated in the reissue of the linguistic section in 1932, except that the word 'usual' is omitted: see *Notes on the Speech of the Tumbuka-Kamanga Peoples in the Northern Province of Nyasaland* (London, 1932) p. 38.

75.   I am grateful to Michael Mann of the London School of Oriental and African Studies for his comments on Young's linguistic works.

76.   McCracken, *Politics and Christianity*, pp. 287-9; Vail, 'Ethnicity'.

77.   Young eventually published this as a parallel text, as S. Nyirenda, 'History of the Tumbuka-Henga People' (translated and edited by T.C. Young), *Bantu Studies*, 5 (1931) 1-75. See

Notes for pages 25 - 27

also Young's comments in 'The African of Today', *World Dominion*, 30 (1952) 104-7.

78.   G.M. Sanderson. 'Some Marriage Customs of the Wa-Henga, Nyasaland', *Journal of the African Society*, 22 (1922-3) 131-8. For Young's comments see his 'The Wa-Henga of Northern Nyasaland', *Journal of the African Society*, 23 (1923-4) 188-93. See also Sanderson's 'Relationship Systems of the Wangonde and Wahenga Tribes, Nyasaland', *Journal of the Royal Anthropological Institute*, 53 (1923) 448-59; and M. Gelfand, *Lakeside Pioneers: a socio-medical study in Nyasaland, 1875-1920* (Oxford, 1974).

79.   Edinburgh University, New College, Faculty of Divinity: Caseby Papers, no. 17.

80.   See T.C. Young, 'Holiday Experiences', *Livingstonia News*, 11 (Jan.-Mar. 1924) 9-10 (at p.10).

81.   NLS 7689, no. 284; 7889, no. 23.

82.   See T.C. Young, *Contemporary Ancestors* (London, 1940) Ch. XIII; and 'The "Native" Newspaper', *Africa* 11 (1938) 63-72; there are numerous other references.

83.   NLS 7889, no. 1; see also Ch. IV of this book.

84.   Le Zoute is reported in Smith, *Christian Mission*; see also J.H. Oldham, 'The Christian Mission in Africa as seen at the International Conference at Le Zoute', *International Review of Missions*, 16 (1927) 24-35; K.J. King, *Pan-Africanism and Education* (Oxford, 1971) esp. Ch. V. For the preparatory papers see *International Review of Missions*, 15 special double number (July 1926). For High Leigh see SOAS: IMB/CBMS Joint Archive, Box 216.

85.   *Other Lands*, 7 (1927) 47-50.

Notes for pages 28 - 32

86.   Ibid., p. 48.

87.   MNA *Northern Province Annual Report*, 1930, p. 22; SOAS IMC/CBMS Box 230: Minutes of the Third Session of the Advisory Committee on Education in Nyasaland, held in Zomba on June 7 and 8, 1932. For the general problems associated with service in the Tropics that were faced by families with children, see C. Allen, *Tales from the Dark Continent* (London, 1979).

88.   T.C. Young, *Notes on the Customs and Folklore of the Tumbuka-Kamanga Peoples of the Northern Province in Nyasaland* (Livingstonia, 1931); and 'Some Proverbs of the Tumbuka-Nkamanga Peoples of the Northern Province in Nyasaland', *Africa*, 4 (1931) 345-51.

89.   NLS: Acc. 7548, C212: Forgan to Young, 7 June 1931.

90.   SOAS: RTS Minutes, 2 June 1931.

91.   SOAS: RTS Minutes, 18 June 1931.

92.   T.C. Young, *Notes on the History of the Tumbuka-Kamanga Peoples in the Northern Province of Nyasaland* (London, 1932); and *Notes on Speech* (see n. 74).

93.   T.C. Young, 'The Communal Bond in Bantu Africa', *International Review of Missions*, 22 (1933) 105-14.

94.   T.C. Young, 'A Good Village', *Africa*, 7 (1934) 89-96 (at p. 90).

95.   T.C. Young, 'How far can African Ceremonies be incorporated into the Christian System?', *Africa*, 8 (1935) 210-17.

96.   S.Y. Ntara, *Man of Africa* (translated by T.C. Young)

176   *T. Cullen Young*

Notes for pages 32 - 36

(London, 1934). For further details see Ch. IV.

97.   *St Columba's Church of Scotland, Pont St, Belgravia SW:*
        Church Magazine: no. 351 (June 1933) 115; no. 352 (July
        1933) 128; no. 381 (Dec. 1935) 229.

98.   Review of I. Schapera (ed.), *Western Civilization and the*
        Natives of South Africa (London, 1934), *Man* (1934) 178-80.

99.   For history see B. Hewitt, *Let the People read: a short*
        history of the United Society for Christian Literature
        (London, 1949). See also *USCL Annual Report*, year ended
        31 Mar. 1935; and SOAS: RTS Minutebook, 1934-5.

100.   T.C. Young, *African Ways and Wisdom: a contribution to*
        understanding (London, 1937: reissued, 1944); and
        Contemporary Ancestors (see n. 82).

101.   F. Melland and T.C. Young, *African Dilemma* (London,
        1931); F. Melland, *In Witchbound Africa* (London, 1923).
        For details about Melland see P. Hetherington, *British*
        Paternalism and Africa, 1920-1940 (London, 1978).

102.   T.C. Young, *The Genesis Mosaic* (Wallington, 1941).

103.   For further detail see Short, *Banda*, Chs. I-III.

104.   Young and Banda (eds), p. 27.

105.   T.C. Young, *Herrenvolk and Sahib-Log* (London, 1946).
        Similar material also appears in *World Dominion*, 22 (1944)
        43-8 and 80-4.

106.   SOAS: USCL Minutes, 27 Feb. 1945; Sept. 1945, and Mar.
        1946. See also *USCL Annual Report*, 1945-6.

107.   See J.M. Graham and R. Piddington, *Anthropology and the*

Notes for pages 37 - 38

Future of Missions (Aberdeen, 1940), *passim*; and for a more general discussion of the relationship between anthropology and missionaries, R. Piddington, *An Introduction to Social Anthropology* 2 vols (Edinburgh, 1950-7) vol. II, pp. 670-80.

108.   T.C. Young, 'Zovu', and 'The Battle of Karonga' (see n. 60).

109.   T.C. Young, 'The African of Today' (see n. 77); and 'Understanding the Old', *International Review of Missions*, 40 (1951) 450-5; also 'End of an Era in Livingstonia: death of two men who remembered Livingstone', *Other Lands*, 32 (1951) 83-4.

110.   *Nyasaland Journal*, 5 (1952) 61.

111.   SOAS: Scottish USCL Central Committee, Minutes, 7 Dec. 1955.

112.   *Life and Work*, 3s. 10 (1955) 199. For other obituaries see *Accountants Magazine*, 59 (1955) 437; *Other Lands* 36 (1955) 78; *Glasgow Academy Chronicle*, 29 (Oct. 1955) 9. See also *Edinburgh Evening Dispatch*, 9 Dec. 1955.

113.   SOAS: Scottish USCL Central Committee, Minutes: 26 July 1955; 3 and 25 Oct. 1955; 7 Dec. 1955; 2 July 1956. See also *The Highway* (Scottish USCL Annual Report) no. 84 (1956); *St Columba's Church of Scotland, Pont St, Belgravia SW: Church Magazine* no. 615 (Dec. 1955-Jan. 1956) 6.

114.   NLS Acc. 7548, C223: 'Retired and Former Missionaries, 1952-7'.

115.   SOAS: Scottish USCL Central Committee, Minutes: 6 Feb. 1958.

116.   She contributed a short article on her father's relationship with Banda, published as M. Moffett, 'The Story', *Monthly*

Notes for pages 40 - 43

> *Review* (Calcutta), 37 (Sept. 1973) 25-6.

II   The Anthropological Contribution

1.   This question is discussed further in P.G. Forster, 'Missionaries and Anthropology: the case of the Scots of northern Malawi', *Journal of Religion in Africa*, 16 (1986) 101-20.

2.   Elmslie, *Ngoni*; the revised edition (London, 1970) contains a new introductory note by I. Nance, with some biographical information on Elmslie.

3.   His publications on Yao are: G.M. Sanderson, *A Yao Grammar* (London, 1922); and *A Dictionary of the Yao Language* (Zomba, 1955).

4.   Information from Revd Dr Fergus MacPherson, British Council of Churches, London.

5.   This was done with the help of R.M. Nyirenda, of Karonga. The material was published in *Notes on Customs and Folklore*, and in 'Proverbs of the Tumbuka-Nkamanga' (see Ch. I, n. 88).

6.   W.P. Young published the following on the basis of his investigations: *The Rabbit and the Baboons, and other Tales from Northern Nyasaland* (London, 1933); *The Rabbit and the Lion, and other Tales from Northern Nyasaland* (London, 1933); *Why Rabbit and Hyena quarrelled, and other Tales from Northern Nyasaland* (London, 1933); and *Stories told to African Girls* (London, 1938).

7.   'Camp Scenes'; and "The Unchartered Lake', *Record of the Home*

Notes for pages 43 - 59

and Foreign Mission Work of the United Free Church of Scotland, 26 (1926) 447-8.

8. 'An African' [L. Mumba], 'The Religion of my Fathers', *International Review of Missions*, 19 (1930) 362-71.

9. See, for instance, T.C. Young, *Contemporary Ancestors*, Ch. XIII, *passim* and *African Ways and Wisdom*, 54-65.

10. T.C. Young, *Notes on History*, pp. 37-8; and 'A Note on Iron Objects of Unknown Origin from Northern Nyasaland', *Man*, 29 (1929) 189-90.

11. T.C. Young; 'Tribal Intermixture in Northern Nyasaland', *Journal of the Royal Anthropological Institute*, 63 (1933) 1-18; also 'Tribal Intermixture in Northern Nyasaland' [Royal Anthropological Institute Communication Report], *Man*, 32 (1932) 142.

12. T.C. Young, 'Three Medicine-Men in Northern Nyasaland', *Man*, 32 (1932) 229-34.

13. T.C. Young, 'The Idea of God in Northern Nyasaland', in E.W. Smith (ed.), *African Ideas of God* (London, 1950) 36-60.

14. Ibid., p. 40.

15. Melland and Young, Ch. X.

16. T.C. Young, *Notes on Customs and Folklore*, p. 102.

17. Ibid., p.60.

18. D. Kidd, *Kafir Socialism and the Dawn of Individualism: an introduction to the study of the native problem* (London, 1908). This is mentioned by Young in Melland and Young,

Notes for pages 60 - 61

p. 99.

19.   E.W. Smith, 'Indigenous Education in Africa', in E.E. Evans-Pritchard, R. Firth, B. Malinowski and I. Schapera (eds), *Essays presented to C.G. Seligman* (London, 1934) 319-334.

20.   R.S. Rattray, *Akan-Ashanti Folk-tales* (Oxford, 1930) p. xiii.

21.   E. Torday, 'The Principles of Bantu Marriage', *Africa 2* (1929) 255-90.

22.   C.W. Hobley, *Bantu Beliefs and Magic* (London, 1922).

23.   D. Fraser, *Winning a Primitive People*; see note in Young's *Notes on Customs and Folklore*, p. 106.

24.   W.C. Willoughby, *The Soul of the Bantu: a sympathetic study of the magico-religious practices and beliefs of the Bantu tribes of Africa* (Garden City, 1928).

25.   See pp. 67-8 of Young's *Notes on Customs and Folklore*.

26.   W.P. Johnson, *My African Reminiscences 1875-1895* (London, 1926).

27.   F.L. Moir, *After Livingstone: an African trade romance* (London, 1923).

28.   D.R. Mackenzie, *The Spirit-ridden Konde* (London, 1925).

29.   See Young's tribute to him in T.C. Young, 'Thirty Years on Lake Nyasa', *Life and Work* n.s. 3' (1932) 30.

30.   See T.C. Young, *Notes on Speech*, p.7.

31.   Since Young never refers to Malinowski in print, the point at which he made contact with Malinowski either personally or

in writing remains a matter for speculation. However, by 1929 Malinowski was expounding some of his ideas in articles in the *Encyclopaedia Britannica,* an accessible source even for those outside academic circles. For an overall view of Malinowski's work see R. Firth (ed.), *Man and Culture: an evaluation of the work of Bronislaw Malinowski* (London, 1957).

32. One work of Emile Durkheim appeared in English in 1915 as *The Elementary Forms of the Religious Life* (London). Durkheim's other major works appeared in English as follows: *The Division of Labor in Society* (New York, 1933); *The Rules of Sociological Method* (Chicago, 1938); and *Suicide* (Glencoe, 1951).

33. J.G. Frazer's best-known work is *The Golden Bough* full ed., 12 vols (London, 1907-15); also abridged ed. (London, 1922).

34. T.C. Young, *Notes on Customs and Folklore*, pp. 146-7.

35. Edinburgh University Faculty of Divinity, Caseby Papers nos 8 and 27.

36. J.G. Steytler, *Educational Adaptations with Reference to African Village Schools with Special Reference to Central Nyasaland* (London, 1939).

37. G.W. Broomfield, review of *Contemporary Ancestors, East and West Review,* 7 (1941) 60-1 (at p.61).

38. Gregson, 'Work, Exchange and Leadership' (See Ch. I, n. 31).

39. Ibid., pp. 51-2; D.M. Schneider, 'Introduction: the distinctive features of matrilineal descent groups', in D.M. Schneider and K. Gough, *Matrilineal Kinship* (Berkeley, 1961) 1-29.

Notes for pages 65 - 69

40.   J. Van Velsen, *The Politics of Kinship* (Manchester, 1964).

41.   S.S. Ncosana, 'Spirit Possession and Tumbuka Christians' (Aberdeen University Ph.D., 1985). As this is written by an ordained minister of the Church of Central Africa, Presbyterian, it follows logically as a development of the 'missionary anthropology' tradition in Malawi.

42.   Thompson's 'Fraser and the Ngoni' has a full discussion of this question.

43.   M. Tew, *Peoples of the Lake Nyasa Region* (London, 1950) (Ethnographic Survey of Africa: East Central Africa part II).

44.   R. Redfield, *The Little Community: viewpoints for the study of the human whole* (Chicago, 1955).

45.   T.C. Young, *Contemporary Ancestors*, p.61: *Notes on Customs and Folklore*, p.22.

46.   T. Scudder and E. Colson, 'Long-term Field Research in Gwembe Valley, Zambia', in G.M. Foster, T. Scudder, E. Colson and R.V. Kemper, *Long-term Field Research in Social Anthropology* (London, 1979) 227-54.

47.   Redfield, *The Little Community*, p. 164.

48.   See A. Kuper, *Anthropology and Anthropologists: the modern British school* (London, 1983) Ch. I.

49.   A.R. Radcliffe-Brown's chief general works are *Structure and Function in Primitive Society* (London, 1952); and *A Natural Science of Society* (Glencoe, 1964).

50.   References to these are included in the Bibliography of Works by T. Cullen Young (see Appendix).

Notes for pages 69 - 72

51. A.I. Richards, *Hunger and Work in a Savage Tribe: a functional study of nutrition among the southern Bantu* (London, 1932).

52. Contributions to this debate appear in *Man* as follows (a) by T.C. Young: 29 (1929) 189-90, 32 (1932) 80, 35 (1935) 80; (b) by other contributors: 30 (1930) 72-3, 31 (1931) 42, 32 (1932) 41-3 and 139-40, 34 (1934) 184, 35 (1935) 30-2 and 95-6, 36 (1936) 39, 38 (1938) 30-1 and 80.

53. For contributions to the debate on bridewealth in *Man* see (a) by T.C. Young: 30 (1930) 75-6, 31 (1931) 202-3 and 260; (b) by other contributors: 29 (1929) 5-7, 131-2, 148, 180 and 215; 30 (1930) 74-5 and 92: 31 (1931) 36-9, 75-6, 163-4, 190, 235-6 and 284: 32 (1932) 54-5, 80 and 128; 33 (1933) 191-6; 34 (1934) 32 and 172-5; 35 (1935) 93-4; 36 (1936) 38-9 and 127-8.

54. *Man*, 31 (1931) 119.

55. Kuper, *Anthropology and Anthropologists*, p. 125.

III   The Historical Contribution

1. T.C. Young, *Notes on Speech and History*, pp. 137-223.

2. T.C. Young, *Notes on History*.

3. Vail, 'Ethnicity', 130; Vail and White, 'Tribalism', 156.

4. John Young, 'Family Reminiscences' [typescript].

5. D. and C. Livingstone, *Narrative of an Expedition to the*

Notes for pages 72 - 73

> *Zambezi and its Tributaries* (London, 1865). The Tumbuka
> are referred to on pp. 438, 524 and 526-7.

6. Elmslie, *Wild Ngoni* (see Ch. I, n. 25). Young definitely had a
   copy of this since he is recorded in the *Nyasaland Journal* [5
   (1952) 61] as having donated his copy to the library of the
   Nyasaland Society.

7. L.M. Fotheringham, *Adventures in Nyasaland* (London,
   1891).

8. Fraser, 'Zulu of Nyasaland' (see Ch. I, n. 30).

9. Elmslie, *Wild Ngoni*, p. 261.

10. G. Steele, 'History of the Tambuka', *Nyasa News* no. 1
    (1893) 17-19.

11. J. Rebman, *Dictionary of the Kiniassa Language* (Basle,
    1877).

12. F.J.M. de Lacerda e Almeida, *The Lands of Cazembe*,
    translated by R.F. Burton (London, 1873); published together
    with translations of accounts of journeys by P.J. Baptista and
    A. José, and résumé of journeys by Monteiro and Gamitto.
    A.C.P. Gamitto also mentions the Tumbuka in his full
    personal record of his journey in *O Muata Cazembe* (Lisbon,
    1854), but this was not accessible to Young since it was in
    Portuguese. It was eventually translated by I. Cunnison, as
    *King Kazembe and the Marave, Cheva, Bisa, Bemba, Lunda,
    and other Peoples of Southern Africa* (Lisbon, 1960).

13. G.M. Theal, *Records of South Eastern Africa* 9 vols (Cape
    Town, 1898-1903).

14. Ibid., vol. 3, pp. 415-19.

Notes for pages 73 - 79

15.   R.N. Hall, *Prehistoric Rhodesia* (London, 1909).

16.   T.C. Young, *Notes on Speech and History*, p. 145; also in the revised *Notes on History*, p.27.

17.   Ibid., pp. 147-8, earlier ed.; pp. 22-3, revised ed. (slightly different wording).

18.   D. and C. Livingstone, *Narrative of an Expedition*, Ch. XXVII.

19.   Y.B. Abdallah, *The Yaos/Chiikala cha Wayao* (Zomba 1919); parallel text, English and Yao, edited and translated by G.M. Sanderson.

20.   *Notes on Speech and History*, p. 150; *Notes on History*, p. 27.

21.   Nyirenda, 'History of the Tumbuka-Henga' (see Ch. I, n. 77).

22.   Ibid., 4-29.

23.   Ibid., 4.

24.   For these events in their broader context of the history of the Bemba see A.D. Roberts, *A History of the Bemba: political growth and change in north eastern Zambia before 1900* (London, 1973).

25.   *Notes on Speech and History*, 139-92.

26.   This was published with the support of A.D. Easterbrook, DC for Lilongwe. See 'A Native Account' [A. Nkonjera], 'History of the Kamanga Tribe of Lake Nyasa', *Journal of the African Society*, 10 (1910-11) 331-41; and 11 (1911-12) 231-4. Information on Nk(h)onjera is contained in Vail, 'Ethnicity', 126, and Vail and White, 'Tribalism', 155, 186.

Notes for pages 80 - 90

27.   See especially Fraser, *Winning a Primitive People*, Chs II, X.

28.   *Notes on Speech and History*, pp. 174-5; *Notes on History*, p.81.

29.   Ibid., p. 177 (earlier ed.); p. 83 (revised ed.).

30.   Ibid., p. 183 (earlier ed.); p. 100 (revised ed., slightly different wording).

31.   Nyirenda, 'History of the Tumbuka-Henga', 28-75.

32.   Ibid., 74.

33.   Ibid.

34.   *Notes on Speech and History*, pp. 192-216.

35.   Elmslie, *Wild Ngoni*, Ch. I.

36.   W.P. Johnson, *Nyasa, the Great Water* (London, 1922) pp. 93-4, 102-112.

37.   H.H. Johnston, *British Central Africa* (London, 1897); F.D. Lugard, *The Rise of our East African Empire* vol. 1 (Edinburgh, 1893); Fotheringham, *Adventures;* Moir, *After Livingstone*.

38.   Fraser, *Winning a Primitive People*, Chs II, XVIII.

39.   Nkonjera 'A Native Account', 339.

40.   'Nyasaland Operations during the World War', pp. 9-10; *Notes on Speech and History*, p. 212; *Notes on History*, p.133.

41.   *Notes on Speech and History*, pp. 212-13; *Notes on History*,

Notes for pages 91 - 97

p. 133 (slightly different wording).

42.   *Notes on History*, p.5.

43.   Ibid., pp. 155-92.

44.   Ibid., p. 9.

45.   Ibid., Chs VI (pp. 56-61); IX (pp. 90-7); and XII (pp. 127-30).

46.   McCracken, *Politics and Christianity*, pp. 199, 200. Chirwa contributed Ch. IX to *Notes on History*.

47.   *Notes on History*, pp. 155-6.

48.   Ibid., p. 136.

49.   See, for instance, Young to (?) DC, Mzimba, 13 Mar. 1931 (found inserted in Mzimba District Book, 1907, MNA); Fraser to T.C. Young, 19 Nov. 1929, NLS 7690 no. 284.

50.   T.C. Young, 'The Wa-Henga of Northern Nyasaland'.

51.   Sanderson, 'Some Marriage Customs of the Wa-Henga'.

52.   T.C. Young, *Notes on Speech*.

53.   Ibid.

54.   L. Vail, review of 1970 republication of *Notes on History*, in *African Studies*, 30 (1971) 67-8 (at p. 67).

55.   Ibid.

56.   L. Vail, 'Suggestions towards a reinterpreted Tumbuka History', in B. Pachai (ed.), *The Early History of Malawi*

Notes for pages 97 - 102

(London, 1972) 148-67. The argument is developed further in Vail, 'Religion, Language and the Tribal Myth: the Tumbuka and Chewa of Malawi', in M. Schoffelers (ed), *Guardians of the Land* (Gwelo, 1978) 209-33.

57.   Vail, 'Tumbuka History', 149-50; Tew, *Peoples of the Nyasa Region*; M. Wilson, *The Peoples of the Nyasa-Tanganyika Corridor* (Cape Town, 1958) 38-40; J.G. Pike, *Malawi: a political and economic history* (London, 1968) 48-50; J. Omer-Cooper, *The Zulu Aftermath* (London, 1966) 80-3.

58.   G. Wilson, *The Constitution of Ngonde* (Livingstone, 1939).

59.   Vail, 'Ethnicity', 155 n. 55; Vail and White, 'Tribalism', 186 n. 33.

60.   'Ethnicity', 131-2; 'Tribalism', 159.

61.   L. Vail, personal communication.

62.   See, for instance, correspondence in MNA: NNM/1/10/9 (DC Mzimba to PC Northern Province, Lilongwe, 23 Apr. 1931); 1/14/6 (DC Isoka [Northern Rhodesia] to DC Mzimba 22 Jan. 1937; and DC Mzimba to DC Isoka 27 Feb. 1937).

63.   This notion is suggested in the collection edited by E. Hobsbawm and T. Ranger, *The Invention of Tradition* (Cambridge, 1983).

64.   J. Van Velsen, 'Notes on the History of the Lakeside Tonga of Nyasaland', *African Studies*, 18 (1959) 105-11; and 'The Establishment of Administration in Tongaland', Leverhulme Inter-Collegiate History Conference, *Historians in Tropical Africa* (Salisbury, 1962) 177-96.

65.   O.J.M. Kalinga, *A History of the Ngonde Kingdom of Malawi* (Berlin, 1985).

Notes for pages 103 - 110

66. Gregson, 'Work, Exchange and Leadership', Ch. II.

67. Van Velsen, *The Politics of Kinship*.

68. S.Y. Ntara, *Mbiri ya Achewa* (Nkhoma, 1945); English translation, *History of the Chewa*, by W.S.K. Jere (Wiesbaden, 1973). This contains an introduction by H. Langworthy (pp. ix-xvii).

69. For his obituary see *Nyasaland Journal*, 11 (1958) 7.

70. Blantyre, Society of Malawi Library, Rangeley papers, 1/2.

71. Ntara, *History of the Chewa*, p. xix.

72. Rangeley to T.C. Young, 30 Apr. 1952 (Rangeley Papers).

73. W.H.J. Rangeley, 'Bocarro's Journey', *Nyasaland Journal*, 8 (1954) 15-23 (at p. 15).

74. Y.M. Chibambo, *My Ngoni of Nyasaland*, translated by Charles Stuart (London, [1942]).

75. Y.M. Chibambo, *Midauko* (Livingstonia, 1946).

76. Vail, 'Ethnicity', 137; Vail and White, 'Tribalism', 162.

77. 'Ethnicity', 135-6; 'Tribalism', 163.

78. L. Vail, 'The Making of the "Dead North": a study of the Ngoni rule in northern Malawi, c. 1885-1905', in J. Peires (ed.), *Before and after Shaka: papers in Ngoni history* (Grahamstown, 1981).

79. M. Read, *The Ngoni of Nyasaland* (London, 1956); *Children of their Fathers* (London, 1959); 'Songs of the Ngoni People', *Bantu Studies* 11 (1937) 1-35; 'The Moral Code of

Notes for pages 110 - 113

the Ngoni and their Former Military State', *Africa*, 11 (1938) 1-24; 'The Ngoni and Western Education', in V. Turner (ed.), *Colonialism in Africa 1870-1960* vol. III, 346-92.

80.   Young to Rangeley, 11 May 1952 (Rangeley Papers).

81.   W.H.J. Rangeley, 'Mtwalo', *Nyasaland Journal*, 6 (1952) 55-70.

82.   E.H. Lane Poole, *The Native Tribes of the Eastern Province of Northern Rhodesia* (Lusaka, 1949); earlier eds 1934 and 1938.

83.   T.J. Thompson, 'Fraser and the Ngoni'; and 'The Origins, Migration and Settlement of the Northern Ngoni', *Society of Malawi Journal*, 38 (1985) 6-35.

84.   J.K. Rennie, 'The Ngoni States and European Intrusion', in E. Stokes and R. Brown (eds.), *The Zambezian Past: studies in Central African history* (Manchester, 1966) pp. 302-31.

85.   J.A. Barnes, 'The Fort Jameson Ngoni', in E. Colson and M. Gluckman, *Seven Tribes of British Central Africa* (London, 1951) 194-252; *Marriage in a Changing Society* (London, 1951); *Politics in a Changing Society* (Cape Town, 1954). The latter work relies particularly heavily upon historical material.

86.   J.A. Barnes, 'History in a Changing Society', *Rhodes-Livingstone Journal*, 11 (1951) 1-9.

87.   R.G. Collingwood, *The Idea of History* (Oxford, 1946).

88.   I. Cunnison, *History on the Luapula: an essay on the historical notions of a Central African tribe* (London, 1951).

89.   J. Vansina, *Oral tradition: a study in historical methodology*.

Notes for pages 114 - 119

English translation (London, 1961).

90. B. Pachai, *Malawi: the history of the nation* (London, 1973) pp. 225-30.

91. T. Ranger, 'The Invention of Tradition in Colonial Africa', in Hobsbawm and Ranger, pp. 211-262.

IV   Educational and Literary Concerns

1. Thompson, 'Ngoni' (see Ch. I, n. 32), Ch. IV.

2. See, for instance, *African Ways and Wisdom*, p. 62.

3. T.C. Young, 'A Lion Hunt in Nyasaland', *Glasgow Academy Chronicle*, 7 (1913) 198-200.

4. See, for instance, 'Bride-Price' (letter) *Man*, 30 (1930) 75-6; also *Men, Women and Things* (London, 1944).

5. See especially *Livingstonia Mission Report*: 1905, p. 9, and 1906, pp. 13-14.

6. NLS 7888: T.C. Young to Ashcroft, 18 Feb. 1925.

7. See especially T.C. Young, 'Africa's Women'.

8. A.G. Fraser, ' Education in India and Ceylon in View of the National Movement' (see Ch. I, n. 41).

9. John Young, 'Family Reminiscences' [typescript].

10. Fraser (see n. 8) p. 31.

Notes for pages 120 - 123

11.   T.C. Young, 'Indian Experiences' (1909).

12.   Kew, PRO, CO 525/66.

13.   McCracken, *Politics and Christianity*, pp. 235-6.

14.   King, *Pan-Africanism and Education, passim.*

15.   J. McCracken, 'Underdevelopment in Malawi: the missionary contribution', *African Affairs*, 76 (1977) 195-209.

16.   McCracken, *Politics and Christianity*, Ch. VIII.

17.   Ibid, pp. 139-40, 236-42.

18.   SOAS: IMB/CBMS Joint Archive, Box 1209; T.C. Young to Oldham, 19 Dec. 1927; and to Miss B.D. Gibson, 26 Sept. 1931. See also R.J. MacDonald, 'History of African Education in Nyasaland', Ch. V.

19.   SOAS: IMC/CBMS Joint Archive, Box 1209; T.C. Young to Miss B.D. Gibson, 3 Oct. 1931.

20.   A.T. Lacey, 'Notes on a Recent Anti-Witchcraft Movement in Nyasaland' (Thesis, Cambridge University Diploma in Anthropology, 1934).

21.   SOAS: IMC/CBMS Joint Archive, Box 1209: Folder 'Director of Education A.T. Lacey, 1931-2'.

22.   Report in *East Africa*, 10 (15 Mar. 1934), 544.

23.   T.C. Young, 'The "Native" Newspaper'; and 'Vyaro na Vyaro: virimika kumi', *Vyaro na Vyaro*, 6 (May 1940) 101-2.

24.   This went through various editions. Full details as available are contained in the Appendix.   This information, which is

Notes for pages 124 - 126

not necessarily complete, is taken from S.S. Mwiyera, 'Vernacular Literature of Malawi, 1845-1975: an annotated bibliography' (F.L.A. Fellowship Thesis, 1978).

25.   NLS 7888: T.C. Young to Ashcroft, 30 Apr. 1926. For the preceding communication see *United Free Church of Scotland Foreign Mission Committee Minutes* (NLS no. 599, 20 Apr. 1926).

26.   SOAS: RTS *129th Annual Report* (Year ending 31 Mar. 1928) pp. 71-2.

27.   NLS: Acc. 7548, C212: Forgan to T.C. Young, 7 Jan. 1931.

28.   For a historical study of the RTS see Hewitt, *Let the People read.*

29.   For the origin of the literature competitions see *Africa*, 2 (1929) 195.

30.   For further details of the competition see B. Pachai, 'Samuel Josiah Ntara: writer and historian', *Society of Malawi Journal*, 21 (1968) 60-6.

31.   For further information on Ntara see Ibid; also C.M. Pauw, *Mission and the Church*, pp. 226-8.

32.   T.C. Young, preface to Ntara, *Man of Africa*, p. 10.

33.   Pauw, *Mission and the Church*, Ch. III.

34.   T.C. Young, *Contemporary Ancestors*, p. 62. Young's ethnographic notes on Ntara's text are on pp. 66-7, 86, 92, 96-7, 102, 109-10, 116, 117, 127, 143, 150, 151-2, 158, and 164.

35.   Blantyre, Society of Malawi Library, Rangeley Papers, I/2; see especially T.C. Young to Rangeley, 29 Mar. 1952.

Notes for pages 126 - 131

36.   Young and Banda, *Our African Way of Life.*

37.   S.Y. Ntara, *Headman's Enterprise* (London, 1949).

38.   J. Jahn, *Schwarzer Orpheus* (Munich, 1954).

39.   The story is told in A. Calder, 'The Making of *Schwarzer Orpheus*: Jahnheinz Jahn and George Shepperson', *Journal of Commonwealth Literature*, 15 (1980) 5-14.

40.   Jahn, pp. 41-3, 174, and 187.

41.   *African New Writing: short stories by African authors* (London, 1947). T.C. Young is mentioned as the anonymous editor of this collection in J. Jahn and C.P. Dressler (eds), *Bibliography of Creative African Writing* (New York, 1973).

42.   He reviewed F. Brownlee's *Corporal Wanzi* in *Man*, 38 (1938) 112; and T. Mofolo's *Chaka: a historical romance* in *International Review of Missions*, 20 (1931) 599-600.

43.   E.g. for Ch. I cf. *Africa*, 7 (1934) 89-96; for Ch. II cf. *Student Movement*, 36 (Oct. 1933, 8-9; and Nov. 1933 36-7).

44.   G.A. Gollock and T.C. Young, *God's Family in the World* (London, 1936).

45.   'The Padre's Talk: fear and cowardice', *Boy's Own Annual*, 58 (1935-6) p. 212; 'The Padre's Talk: the headman's wisdom', *Boy's Own Annual*, 58 (1935-6) p. 304; 'The Padre's Talk: carols', *Boy's Own Annual*, 60 (1937-8) p. 148; 'The Padre's Talk: what do you think?', *Boy's Own Annual*, 62 (1939-40) p. 73. (The *Boy's Own Annual* consists of a year's issues of the *Boy's Own Paper* bound together).

46.   J. Cox, *Take a Cold Tub, Sir!: the story of the Boy's Own Paper* (Guildford, 1982) esp. pp. 70 and 107.

Notes for pages 131 - 134

47. 'Padre's Talk: the headman's wisdom'.

48. 'Padre's Talk: what do you think?'.

49. *Other Lands* 4 (1927) 47-50.

50. J. Merle Davis, *Modern Industry and the African* (London, 1933).

51. Ibid., Part V.

52. A.L. Epstein, *Politics in an Urban African Community* (Manchester, 1958) Ch. II; see also H.L. Berger, *Labour, Race and Colonial Rule; the Copperbelt from 1924 to Independence* (Oxford, 1974) esp. Ch. III.

53. SOAS: IMC/CBMS Joint Archive: UMCB Papers. See also J.V. Taylor and D.A. Lehmann, *Christians of the Copperbelt* (London, 1961).

54. T.C. Young, 'The "Native" Newspaper', p. 63.

55. T.C. Young, 'Christian Literature and the Madras Meeting', *International Review of Missions*, 31 (1942) 308-14.

56. SOAS: IMC/CBMS Joint Archive, UMCB Papers Folder C.

57. Ibid., Folder E.

58. Epstein, p. 67. (The Revd George Fraser who is referred to here was, incidentally, the son of Donald Fraser of Livingstonia).

59. SOAS: IMC/CBMS Joint Archive, UMCB Papers, Folder H. See especially the letter from A.W. Goodbody (Roan Antelope and Mufulira Mines) to T.C. Young, 16 June 1943; and the reply from Miss B.D. Gibson, 28 July 1943. See also

Notes for pages 134 - 137

   Taylor and Lehmann, p. 16.

60. For an examination of this process see H. Msiska, 'The
     Development of Popular Literature in Malawi', *Inter-Arts*
     (Edinburgh) 1 pt 4 (1987) 13-14, 22.

61. W.J. Noble, A.S. Kydd, G.W. Broomfield and T.C. Young,
     'The Copperbelt Report' (letter to *The Times*, 3 Apr. 1941).
     The debate in question began with the leading article in *The
     Times* for 18 Feb. 1941. Sir William McLean's contributions
     are found in *The Times* for 11 and 14 Mar. 1943. See also
     contributions from H. Moody (13 and 24 Mar.); M. Perham (5
     Mar.), and E.S.B. Taggart (12 Mar.).

62. T.C. Young, 'African talking', *African Affairs*, 47 (1948) 215-
     20 at 219.

63. Taylor and Lehmann, Ch. II.

64. SOAS: IMC/CBMS Joint Archives, UMCB 1214 Folder H:
     Minutes of UMCB British Committee, 17 July 1939. Also
     Cross, letter to Young, 4 Aug. 1939.

65. Hewitt, p. 91.

66. T.C. Young, 'Christian Literature and the Madras Meeting'
     (see n. 55).

67. See E.A. Nida (ed.), *The Book of a Thousand Tongues*
     (London, 1972) p. 439. Also obituary of T.C. Young in *Other
     Lands*, 36 (1955) 78.

68. R. Hoggart, *The Uses of Literacy* (London, 1957).

69. For a general discussion of the media on the Copperbelt see
     H. Powdermaker, *Copper Town* (New York, 1967).

Notes for pages 138 - 141

70. See especially *United Free Church of Scotland Assembly Proceedings*, 1914, pp. 140-1.

71. T.C. Young, 'Those African Barbarians', *Other Lands*, 34 (1953) 27-9.

72. T.C. Young, *Contemporary Ancestors*, p. 138.

73. T.C. Young, 'Understanding the Old', *International Review of Missions*, 40 (1951) 450-5 at p. 454: 'I can never forget the illuminating experience of a colleague down among his Lake-shore folk. One day, in a group of old headmen and counsellors which he very wisely gathered around him at regular intervals for talk and debate, he was told, "Sir, don't think that the things you are telling us contradict what we used to believe, no, but they *complete* what the old folk taught us"'.

74. See especially 'Rooting or Planting: continued', *Student Movement*, 36 (Nov. 1933) 36-7.

V   The Political Dimension

1. John Young, 'Family Reminiscences' [typescript].

2. NLS 7885 no. 60 (Jessie Young to Webster).

3. Mufuka, *passim*.

4. McCracken, *Politics and Christianity*, pp. 257-73.

5. *United Free Church of Scotland Assembly Proceedings*, 1920, p. 123.

Notes for pages 141 - 145

6.   Kew, PRO, CO 525/66.

7.   See *East Africa*, 8 (2 Jan. 1932) 976 (paper to Royal Anthropological Institute); 10 (15 Mar. 1934) 544 (comments on talk by A. Travers Lacey); *East Africa and Rhodesia*, 13 (17 Dec. 1936) 442 (talk to British Commonwealth League Conference); and 15 (23 Feb. 1939) 713 (talk on 'Christianity and the African Mind').

8.   Report of a speech by Godfrey Huggins, *East Africa*, 10 (19 July 1934) 909-10, 922; also editorial, 907-8.

9.   'East Africa in 1970: need for deep thinking' (letter), *East Africa* 10 (6 Sept. 1936) 1054-5.

10.   Editorial, *East Africa*, 11 (20 Sept. 1934) 23; *East Africa*, 10 (6 Sept. 1934) 1054-5.

11.   'Imperial Dilemma', in F. Joelson (ed.), *East Africa Today and Tomorrow* (London, 1934) pp. 115-18.

12.   Ibid., pp. 117-18.

13.   Ibid., p. 116; *East Africa*, 11 (1 Nov. 1934) 147 (pseudonym 'Afer').

14.   Summary of J.H. Oldham's speech 'Racial Problems' in *East Africa*, 11 (8 Nov. 1934) 166; Editorial, 164.

15.   See J.H. Oldham, *Christianity and the Race Problem* (London, 1925); cf. also J.W. Cell (ed.), *By Kenya possessed: the correspondence of Norman Leys and J.H. Oldham* (London, 1976).

16.   *East Africa and Rhodesia*, 21 (22 Mar. 1945) 664-5.

17.   See Ch. IV., n. 61, for full details.

Notes for pages 145 - 148

18. McCracken, 'Underdevelopment in Malawi'.

19. McCracken, *Politics and Christianity*, 139-40, 235-41; Mufuka, Ch. II.

20. R.B. Boeder, 'The Effects of Labour Migration on Rural Life in Malawi', *Rural Africana*, 20 (1973) 37-46; J. Van Velsen, 'Labour Migration as a Positive Factor in the Continuity of Tonga Tribal Society', in A. Southall (ed.), *Social Change in Modern Africa* (London, 1961) 230-41; W. Watson, *Tribal Cohesion in a Money Economy: a study of the Mambwe of Northern Rhodesia* (Manchester, 1958).

21. *Report of the Committee to Enquire into Emigrant Labour 1935* (A. Travers Lacey, Chairman; Zomba, 1936).

22. 'The Over-taxed Native', *Spectator*, 159 (28 Aug. 1936) 342.

23. 'East African Tax Method Revision', *Journal of the Royal African Society*, 35 (1936) 381-5.

24. 'Taxation', in F. Melland (ed.), *African Survey surveyed* (London, 1938) pp. 30-3.

25. T.C. Young, *Herrenvolk and Sahib-Log*, p. 8; cf. also 'Africa Talking', *African Affairs*, 47 (1948) 215-20.

26. *Herrenvolk and Sahib-Log*, esp. pp. 11, 14, 30.

27. 'Africa Talking'.

28. *Herrenvolk and Sahib-Log*, pp. 31-7.

29. C. Kadalie, *My Life with the I.C.U.* (London, 1970) pp. 116-17.

30. Biographical details of Banda are derived mainly from

Notes for pages 149 - 155

P. Short, *Banda* (London, 1974).

31.   R.J. MacDonald, 'Reverend Hanock Msokera Phiri and the Establishment of the African Methodist Episcopal Church', *African Historical Studies*, 3 (1970) 75-87.

32.   M.H. Watkins, *A Grammar of Chichewa: a Bantu language of British Central Africa*. (Language Dissertations No 24 [supplement to *Language*]; Philadelphia, 1937).

33.   Short, p. 52.

34.   Ibid.

35.   For a discussion of this system in terms of modern social anthropology see M. Marwick, *Sorcery in its Social Setting: a study of the Northern Rhodesian Chewa* (Manchester, 1965) pp. 128-9.

36.   Young and Banda, *Our African Way of Life* (preface, pp. 16-17).

37.   Ibid., pp. 18-19.

38.   Cf. also J. Maquet, *Africanity* (English translation, New York, 1972) p. 79: 'Without causing the elders to lose face by opposing them openly, the ordinary villagers ... can make the whole weight of their disagreement felt by the incomplete execution of unanimously approved measures'.

39.   Young and Banda, p. 27.

40.   T.C. Young, 'The Idea of God in Northern Nyasaland', p. 60.

41.   Dr H.K. Banda, personal communication.

42.   Cf. M. Crowder, *Sénégal: a study of French assimilation*

Notes for pages 155 - 161

   policy (London, 1962).

43.   See R.W. July, *The Origins of Modern African Thought* (London, 1968) esp. Ch. XI (on E.W. Blyden); and A. Quaison-Sackey, *Africa Unbound: reflections of an African statesman* (London, 1963) Ch. II.

44.   Unsigned editorial, *Other Lands*, 6 (1 Jan. 1927: special Africa number) p. 41.

45.   An African [L. Mumba], 'The Religion of my Fathers' (see Ch. II, n.8).

46.   For Mumba see R.K. Tangri, 'The Development of Modern African Politics and the Emergence of a Nationalist Movement in Colonial Malawi, 1891-1958' (Edinburgh University Ph.D., 1970) Chs V, VI; Short, *Banda*, pp. 44-5; McCracken, *Politics and Christianity*, pp. 260-82.

47.   H.K. Banda and H. Nkumbula, *Federation in Central Africa* (London, 1949).

48.   S.H. Joffe, 'Political Culture and Communication in Malawi: the hortatory regime of H. Kamuzu Banda' (Boston University, Ph.D., 1970) Chs V and VI.

49.   Ibid., p. 332 (quoted from *Malawi News*, 7 Dec. 1962, p.1).

50.   Short, *Banda*, p. 260.

51.   Ibid., p. 254.

52.   See entry 'Women' in C.A. Crosby, *Historical Dictionary of Malawi* (London, 1980) pp. 113-16.

53.   Hobsbawm and Ranger, *The Invention of Tradition*.

Notes for pages 162 - 164

54.   Vail, 'Ethnicity', 146: see also Vail and White, 'Tribalism'
       181-2.

55.   Vail and White, 'Tribalism'. The chief works referred to are:
       I and J. Linden, *Catholics, Peasants and Chewa Resistance in
       Nyasaland 1889-1939* (Berkeley, 1974); M. Schoffelers, 'The
       Meaning and Use of the Name *Malawi* in Oral Tradition and
       Pre-colonial Documents' in B. Pachai (ed.), *Early History of
       Malawi* 91-103; and 'Towards the Identification of Proto-
       Chewa Culture; a preliminary contribution', *Journal of
       Social Science* (Malawi) 2 (1973) 47-60; also M. Schoffelers
       and I. Linden, 'The Resistance of the Nyau Societies to the
       Roman Catholic Missions in Colonial Malawi', in T. Ranger
       and I.M. Kimambo (eds.), *The Historical Study of African
       Religion* (London, 1972) 252-73.

56.   A.V. Chilivumbo, 'Malawi's Culture in the National
       Integration', *Présence Africaine* no. 98 (1976) 234-42.

57.   G.A. Shepperson, 'External Factors in the Development of
       African Nationalism, with Particular Reference to British
       Central Africa', *Phylon*, 22 (1961) 207-25.

58.   M.L. Chanock, 'Ambiguities in Malawian Political
       Tradition', *African Affairs*, 74 (1975) 326-46 (see esp. 344-5).
       But contrast Chipembere's comments after the Cabinet Crisis:
       H. Chipembere, 'Malawi in Crisis, 1964', *Ufahamu* 1, pt. 2
       (1970) 1-21 (at p. 24).

59.   Address at the installation of Paramount Chief Lundu, July
       1969. Quoted in Joffe, p. 426.

60.   J. Kenyatta, *Facing Mount Kenya: the tribal life of the
       Gikuyu*. With an introduction by B. Malinowski. (London,
       1938).

61.   Quaison-Sackey, Ch. II.

Notes for page 165

62. C. McMaster, *Malawi: foreign policy and development* (New York, 1974) p. 17.

63. Joffe, Ch. X.

64. T. Ranger, 'The Invention of Tradition in Colonial Africa', Hobsbawm and Ranger, 211-82.

204

Bibliography of Works by T. Cullen Young

1909   'Indian Experience in the Matter of Native Education', *Livingstonia News*, 2, pp. 5-8.
'Karonga', Ibid., 2, pp. 51-2.
'A Possible Side-light on the Name *Tumbuka*, Ibid., 2, pp. 60-2.

1910   'Report from Karonga', Ibid., 3, pp. 8-11.
'The Peoples of the Karonga District' [report], *Missionary Record of the United Free Church of Scotland*, 10, pp. 257-9.

1912   'Uzamba: a native initiation ceremony', *Livingstonia News*, 5, pp. 71-4.

1913   'A Lion Hunt in Nyasaland', *Glasgow Academy Chronicle*, 7, pp. 198-200.

1914   'Africa's Women', *Missionary Record of the United Free Church of Scotland*, 14, p. 130.
'Stranded in British East Africa', *Kikuyu News*, no. 52, Nov-Dec., pp. 8-9.

1921   'The Call for Missionaries' [letter], *Record of the Home and Foreign Mission Work of the United Free Church of Scotland*, 21, p. 285.

1923   *Notes on the Speech and History of the Tumbuka-Henga Peoples* viii + 223 pp. (Livingstonia: Mission Press).
'The wa-Henga of Northern Nyasaland; *Journal of the African Society*, 23 (1923-4) pp. 188-93.

1924   'Holiday Experiences', *Livingstonia News*, 11, pp. 9-10.
'Overtoun Institute Schools 1923', Ibid., 11, pp. 12-15.

'Some Impressions of Conference', Ibid., 11, pp. 42-5.
'District Travel', Ibid., 11, pp. 64-6.
'The House of the Dream', *Other Lands*, 3, p. 65.

1925   'Overtoun Institution 1924', *Livingstonia News*, 12, pp. 6-8.

1927   'The New African', *Other Lands*, 7, pp. 47-50.
Review of W.J. Roome, *A Great Emancipation: a missionary survey of Nyasaland, Central Africa* in *International Review of Missions*, 16, pp. 135-6.

1929   'A Note on Iron Objects of Unknown Origin from Northern Nyasaland', *Man*, 29, pp. 189-90.
'Is it Zambezi or Zambesi?', *East Africa*, 5 (2 May), p. 1064.
Makuriro gha Mahara na Maluso Mukati mu W̃anthu pt 1 (Blantyre: Hetherwick Press).

1930   'Bride-price' (letter), *Man*, 30, pp. 75-6.
'The Religion of my Fathers' [by 'An African' (L. Mumba), introduced by T.C. Young], *International Review of Missions*, 19 pp. 362-76.

1931   'History of the Tumbuka-Henga People' [by S. Nyirenda; translated and edited by T.C. Young], *Bantu Studies*, 5, pp. 1-75 [parallel text, English and Tumbuka].
'The Meaning of the Word "Family"' [letter], *Man*, 31, p. 119.
'Bride-price: another alternative' [letter], Ibid., 31, pp. 202-3.
'Equilibrium Guarantee: translate and explain' [letter], Ibid., 31, p. 260.
Makuriro gha Mahara na Maluso mukati mu W̃anthu pt II (88 pp.) (Blantyre: Hetherwick Press).
Makuriro gha Mahara na Maluso Mukati mu W̃anthu (Livingstonia: Mission Press).

Notes on the Customs and Folklore of the Tumbuka-Kamanga Peoples 284 pp. (Livingstonia: Mission Press).

Review of T. Mofolo, *Chaka: an historical romance*, in *International Review of Missions*, 20, pp. 599-600.

'Some Proverbs of the Tumbuka-Nkamanga Peoples of the Northern Province of Nyasaland', *Africa*, 4, pp. 343-51.

1932   *Notes on the History of the Tumbuka-Kamanga Peoples in the Northern Province of Nyasaland* 194 pp. (London: RTS).

Notes on the Speech of the Tumbuka-Kamanga Peoples in the Northern Province of Nyasaland 181 pp. (London: RTS).

'Thirty Years on Lake Nyasa', *Life and Work*, n.s. 3, p. 30.

'Three Medicine-men in Northern Nyasaland', *Man*, 32, pp. 229-34.

'Tribal Intermixture in Northern Nyasaland' [Royal Anthropological Institute Communication Report], Ibid., 32, p. 142.

'Trident Sceptres from West Africa' [letter], Ibid., 32, p. 80.

1933   'The Communal Bond in Bantu Africa', *International Review of Missions*, 22, pp. 105-14.

'Developing a Reading Sense', *Books for Africa* 3 (Jan. pp. 5-7).

Review of I.A. Richards, *Hunger and Work in a Savage Tribe*, in *Man*, 33, pp. 19-20.

'Rooting or Planting, *Student Movement*, 36 (Oct.) pp. 8-9; (Nov.) pp. 36-7.

'Tribal Intermixture in Northern Nyasaland', *Journal of the Royal Anthropological Institute*, 63, pp. 1-18.

1934   'A Reader's Appreciation' [letter], *East Africa* 10 (29 Mar.) p. 582.

'East Africa in 1970: need for deep thinking' [letter],

Ibid., 10 (6 Sept.), pp. 1054-5.

'Kenya's Natives' [letter], *The Times*, 6 Sept., p. 8.

'Building a Native Policy' [letter], *East Africa*, 11 (11 Oct.) p. 86.

'The Wasokile' [letter], *Man*, 34, p. 32.

'Imperial Dilemma', in F. Joelson (ed.), *Eastern Africa Today and Tomorrow* (London: East Africa) pp. 115-18.

Man of Africa 180 pp. [by S.Y. Ntara; translated and arranged by T.C. Young] (London: RTS).

Review of A. Werner, *Myths and Legends of the Bantu*, in *Man*, 34, p. 12.

Review of E.D. Earthy, *Valenge Women*, Ibid., 34, pp. 111-12.

Review of I Schapera (ed.), *Western Civilization and the Natives of South Africa*, Ibid., 34, pp. 178-80.

1935   'Bow-stand or Trident' [letter], Ibid., 35, p.80.

'Bush Schools and Evangelism', *World Dominion*, 13, pp. 407-13.

'How Far can African Ceremonials be incorporated into the Christian System?', *Africa*, 8, pp. 210-17.

Review of H.G. Luttig, *The Religious System and Social Organisation of the Herero: a study in Bantu culture*', in *Man*, 35, pp. 158-9.

Review of I. Schapera (ed.), *Western Civilization and the Natives of South Africa*, and E. Brookes, *The Colour Problems of South Africa*, in *East and West Review*, 1, pp. 180-1.

'The Padre's Talk: fear and cowardice', *Boy's Own Annual* [1935-6] 58, p. 212.

'The Padre's Talk: the headman's wisdom', *Boy's Own Annual* [1935-6] 58, p. 304.

1936   'East African Tax Method Revision', *Journal of the African Society*, 35, pp. 381-5.

[G.A. Gollock and T.C. Young] *God's Family in the World* 80 pp. (London: USCL).

'Habits and Customs of the Olden Days among the

Tumbuka-Kamanga People' [author anonymous,
translation by T.C. Young], *Bantu Studies*, 10, pp.
314-57 [parallel text, English and Tumbuka].
'The Over-taxed Native', *Spectator*, 159 (28 Aug.) p.
342.
'Letter to the Editor' [letter] *East Africa and
Rhodesia*, 13, (24 Dec.), p. 487.
Review of R.H.W. Shepherd, *Literature for the South
African Bantu: a comparative study of Negro
achievement* in *International Review of Missions*, 25,
pp. 559-60.
Review of M. Perham, *Ten Africans*, in *Man*, 36, pp.
213-14.
Review of A.T. and G.M. Culwick, *Ubena of the
Rivers*, Ibid., p. 214.

1937   [F. Melland and T.C. Young] *African Dilemma* 172
pp. (London: USCL).
*African Ways and Wisdom: a contribution to
understanding* 144 pp. (London: USCL).
Review of E.J. Krige, *The Social System of the Zulus*,
and H.P. Junod and A.A. Jaques, *The Wisdom of the
Tonga-Shangaan People* in *Man*, 37, p. 15.
Review of M. Hunter, *Reaction to Conquest*, Ibid.,
37, pp. 15-16.
Review of F.W.T. Posselt, *Fact and Fiction: a short
account of the natives of Southern Rhodesia*, Ibid.,
37, p. 197.
Review of D. Westermann, *Africa and Christianity*,
in *East And West Review*, 3, pp. 372-3.
'The Padre's Talk: carols', *Boy's Own Annual* [1937-
8] 60, p. 148.

1938   'The "Native" Newspaper', *Africa*, 11, pp. 63-72.
'Taxation', in F. Melland (ed.), *African Survey
surveyed* (London: Royal African Society) 30-3.
Review of I. Schapera (ed.), *The Bantu-speaking
Tribes of South Africa: an ethnographical account*,
Man, 38, pp. 11-12.

Review of F. Brownlee, *Corporal Wanzi*, Ibid., p. 112.

1939   *The Christian Message of Completion* 12 pp. (London: UMCA).
'Experiment in Distribution', *Books for Africa*, 9 (Oct.) pp. 58-61.
Review of W.H. Macmillan, *Africa Emergent*, in *Man*, 39, p. 113.
Review of H.P. Junod, *Bantu Heritage*, Ibid., pp. 115-16.
Review of G.T. Basden, *Niger Ibos*, Ibid., p. 132.
Review of G. Hoyningen-Heuse, *African Mirage*, Ibid., p. 134.
Review of D.W.T. Shropshire, *The Church and Primitive Peoples* and G. Callaway, *Pioneers in Pondoland*, in *International Review of Missions*, 28, pp. 284-7.
[1939-40] 'The Padre's Talk: what do you think?', *Boy's Own Annual*, 62, p. 73.

1940   *Contemporary Ancestors* 190 pp. (London: RTS).
'Vyaro na Vyaro: virimika kumi' [letter], *Vyaro na Vyaro*, 6 (May) pp. 101-2.

1941   *The Genesis Mosaic* 88 pp. (Wallington: Religious Education Press).
[W.J. Noble, A.S. Kydd, G.W. Broomfield, T. Cocker Brown and T.C. Young] 'The Copperbelt Report' [letter], *The Times* 3 Apr., p. 5; reprinted in *Central Africa*, 59, pp. 59-60.
'The Late Mrs Vera Black, B.Sc.', *Other Lands*, 20, p. 52.

1942   'Christian Literature and the Madras Meeting', *International Review of Missions*, 31, pp. 308-14.
Review of N. Leys, *The Colour Bar in East Africa* and J. Cary, *The Case for African Freedom*, in *International Review of Missions*, 31, pp. 122-5.

1943   *Makuriro gha Mahara na Maluso Mukati mu Ŵantu*
            (Blantyre: Hetherwick Press).
            'The Backward Peoples', *World Dominion*, 21, pp.
            269-75.
            Review of M. Perham and J. Simmons, *African
            Discovery. International Review of Missions*, 32, pp.
            350-1.
            –

1944   *African Ways and Wisdom: a contribution to
            understanding* (2nd ed., London, USCL).
            Herrenvolk and Sahib-log 47 pp. (London, USCL).
            Also in *World Dominion*, 23, pp. 43-8., and 80-4
            [wording similar but not identical].
            Men, Women and Things 64 pp. (London: USCL).
            'The Challenge of the Colonial Office to the
            Missionary', *Books for Africa*, 14 (Apr.) pp. 17-24.

1946   [Translated, edited and with a preface by T.C. Young
            and H.K. Banda] *Our African Way of Life* 152 pp.
            (London, USCL).
            'Welfare Planning in Africa', *World Dominion*, 24,
            pp. 163-5.
            'A Shaking of Nations', Ibid., 24, pp. 353-7.
            'Spoken in our Ear', *Life and Work* 3s. 1, p. 230.
            'Overseas Mail', *Other Lands*, 26 (Oct.) p.22.

1947   'A Turning Point in History', *Other Lands* 32, pp. 35-
            6.
            Review of R. Ure, *The Highway of Print*, in
            International Review of Missions, 36, pp. 285-7.
            [ed., anonymously] *African New Writing; short
            stories by African authors* (London: USCL).

1948   'Africa Talking', *African Affairs*, 47, pp. 215-20.
            'Britain's Imperial Greatness: is it declining?', *Life
            and Work*, 3s., 3, pp. 127-8.
            'Henry Morton Stanley: missionary', *World
            Dominion*, 26, pp. 157-60.

1949   *Makuriro gha Mahara na Maluso Mukati mu Ŵantu*
        88 pp. (Blantyre; Hetherwick Press).
        Headman's Enterprise 213 pp. [by S.Y. Ntara;
        translated, edited and with a preface by T.C. Young]
        (London: Lutterworth).
        'Africa at the Talking-place', *World Dominion*, 27,
        pp. 107-10.
        'Stories around the Fire', *Africana*, 1, pt 3, pp. 21-2.

1950   'The Idea of God in Northern Nyasaland', in E.W.
        Smith (ed.), *African Ideas of God* (London:
        Edinburgh House) pp. 36-60.
        'Kinship among the Chewa of Rhodesia and
        Nyasaland', *African Studies*, 9, pp. 29-31.
        'Letter to the Editor', *African Studies*, 9, pp. 92-4.

1951   'End of an Era in Livingstonia', *Other Lands*, 32, pp.
        83-4.
        'Understanding the Old', *International Review of
        Missions*, 40, pp. 450-5.

1952   'The African of Today', *World Dominion*, 30, pp.
        104-7.
        'The "Henga" Peoples in Northern Nyasaland',
        Nyasaland Journal, 5, pp. 33-7.
        'The Maravi People in Central Africa' [letter],
        African Studies, 11, p. 91.

1953.   [G.A. Gollock and T.C. Young] *God's Family in the
        World* (new ed., revised, London: USCL).
        [with B. Malekebu] 'African Playtime', *Nyasaland
        Journal*, 6, pp. 34-44.
        'Place-names in Nyasaland', Ibid., 6, pp. 35-6.
        'Zovu', Ibid., 6, pp. 53-9.
        'Those African "Barbarians"', *Other Lands*, 33, pp.
        27-9.
        'Why do they call us Jim?', *World Dominion*, 31, pp.
        19-20.

1954   'Africa, imagined and real', *Nyasaland Journal*, 7,
            pp. 30-5.
            'Tribute' (memorial to Thomas Cochrane), *World
            Dominion*, 32, pp. 92-3.

1955   'The Battle of Karonga', *Nyasaland Journal*, 8, pp.
            27-38.

1965   *Makuriro gha Mahara na Maluso Mukati mu W̃antu*
            (88 pp.) (Blantyre: Hetherwick Press).

1970   *Notes on the History of the Tumbuka-Kamanga
            Peoples in the Northern Province of Nyasaland* xiv +
            192 pp. (2nd ed., with an introduction by I. Nance.
            London: Cass).

General Bibliography

1.   Archival Sources.

Great Britain:

Edinburgh: National Library of Scotland (NLS)

United Free Church of Scotland (MSS 7556-7980):
> Foreign Letterbooks of the Secretaries and other Officials of the Foreign Mission Committee, 1901-1931.
> Home Letterbooks of the Secretaries of the Foreign Mission Committee, 1910-1923.
> Letterbooks of the Secretary of the Livingstonia Committee, 1901-1934.
> Letterbooks of the Secretary of the Foreign Mission Committee 1911-1929
> Letterbooks of the Convenor of the Foreign Mission Committee and of the Secretary and other Officials for Women's Foreign Missions, 1897-1920.
> Letters from Missionaries in Livingstonia to the Secretary of the Foreign Mission Committee, 1874-1926.

Note: the above items are all fully catalogued and indexed in:
National Library of Scotland, *Catalogue of Manuscripts acquired since 1925: Vol. 6, Manuscripts 7530-8022, Scottish Foreign Mission Records 1827-1929.* (Edinburgh, 1984).

Nyasaland Missionary Conference Reports (1900, 1904, 1910).
United Free Church of Scotland General Assembly, Foreign Missions Committee, Annual Report of the Livingstonia Mission, 1901-13.

Archive of the Church of Scotland Foreign Mission Committee, 1929-64, together with much 19th and earlier 20th Century Material, and some Items relating to Jewish and Continental Missions (Acc. 7548),
especially:

Rev. Dr R. Forgan (miscellaneous) (C212)
Retired and Former Missionaries, 1952-7 (C223)
Livingstonia: Letters to the Sub-Committee 1898-1910 (D69-71)

Church of Scotland Overseas Council, Minutebooks of the various Committees and Associations now subsumed in the Overseas Council (Dep. 298):
United Free Church of Scotland Foreign Missions Committee, 1900-29 (nos 126-37).
United Free Church of Scotland, Livingstonia Mission, [Sub-] Committee 1901-14 (nos 140-43).

Edinburgh: Church of Scotland, George Street
Register of Missionaries of the Free Church of Scotland and subsequently of the United Free Church of Scotland

Edinburgh: Main University Library
Robert Laws: Notebooks and Papers mainly relating to the Work of the Livingstonia Mission in Nyasaland, c. 1875-1934.
Alexander Gillon MacAlpine: African Papers, including Diaries 1893-1910, Folklore Notebooks, Lectures, Articles etc.

Edinburgh University, Faculty of Divinity, New College: Centre for the Study of Christianity in the Non-Western World:
Alexander Caseby: Missionary Work in Livingstonia, Central Africa (Miscellaneous papers).

Aberdeen: University of Aberdeen, Department of Religious Studies
Personal Papers of Robert and Amelia Laws of Livingstonia (MS. 3290).

London: London University, School of Oriental and African Studies (SOAS)
International Missionary Council/Conference of British Missionary Societies: Joint Archives (IMC/CBMS): Minutes, Reports, Correspondence concerning Africa, 1910-45, especially:
Box 1207: Central Africa and Nyasaland

Box 1208: Nyasaland
Boxes 1209-10 Nyasaland: Education
Boxes 1213-20: Northern Rhodesia, United Missions in the
Copperbelt (UMCB).
United Society for Christian Literature, Minute-books, Letterbooks,
and Miscellaneous Papers, 1921-57.

London: Imperial War Museum
Duff, H.L., 'Nyasaland and the World War 1914-18' (typescript, n.d.)

Material in Private Hands
Miscellaneous correspondence in the possession of Mrs Sheila
Partington, Newcastle upon Tyne
Young, John, 'Family Reminiscences: Father's notes and memories',
typescript in the possession of Dr Alastair Young, Edinburgh

Malawi:

Zomba: Malawi National Archives (MNA)

Livingstonia Papers:

Letterbooks, 1905-31 (LI 1/1/7-46)
Minutes of Meetings of Livingstonia Mission Council, 1922-
31 (LI 1/3/17-23)

Official Publications:

Mzimba District Books, 1928-32
Native Authorities: Henga, Chikulamayembe, 1930-1
Northern Province Annual Report, 1930

Blantyre: Society of Malawi Library

Papers of W.H.C. Rangeley, 1950-52
Young, T.C., 'Nyasaland Operations during the World War,
1914-18' [typescript, n.d.]

2.   Personal Recollections

Interviewed only:

His Excellency the Life President of the Republic of Malawi, Ngwazi
Dr H. Kamuzu Banda (interviewed in London).

Correspondents, also interviewed:

Revd Dr Fergus Macpherson (London)
Mrs M. Moffett (Dehra Dun)
Revd W.D. Moyo (Ekwendeni)
Mrs S. Partington (Newcastle upon Tyne)
Miss M. Senior (Scarborough)
Professor G.A. Shepperson (Edinburgh)
Mr R.B.C. Young (Cheltenham)

Correspondents not interviewed:

Revd J.H. Alexander (Peebles)
Mr G.A. Anderson (London)
Revd D. Campbell (Edinburgh)
Revd A. Caseby (Glenrothes)
Miss E. Charleson (Godstone)
Revd S. Kauta Msiska (Rumphi)
Revd Dr C. Northcott (Cambridge)
Mr T. Price (Glasgow)
Mrs C. Robertson (Anstruther)
Mr A. Rumble (Epping)
Mrs J.C. Todd (Montrose)
Revd Dr W.H. Watson (Aberdeen)
Dr A. Young (Edinburgh)
Mr J.A. Young (Shorehampton)
Mrs J.M. Young (Lairg)
Mrs S. Young (Nethy Bridge)

3. Official Sources

Public Record Office, Kew (PRO)

Nyasaland: Original Correspondence (CO 525/66).

Nyasaland Protectorate Official Publications

[R.W. Lyall Grant, Chairman] *Report of the Commission appointed by His Excellency the Governor to inquire into the Various Matters and Questions concerned with the Native Rising within the Nyasaland Protectorate* (Zomba: Government Printer, 1916).

[A. Travers Lacey, Chairman] *Report of the Committee to enquire into Emigrant Labour* (Zomba: Government Printer, 1936).

4. Theses and Dissertations

Dow, D.A., 'Domestic Response and Reaction to the Foreign Missionary Enterprises of the Principal Scottish Presbyterian Churches, 1873-1929' (Edinburgh University Ph.D., 1977).

Gregson, R.E., 'Work, Exchange and Leadership: the mobilization of agricultural labour among the Tumbuka of the Henga valley' (Columbia University Ph.D., 1969).

Joffe, S.H., 'Political Culture and Communication in Malawi: the hortatory regime of H. Kamuzu Banda' (Boston University Ph.D., 1973).

Lacey, A. Travers, 'Notes on a Recent Anti-Witchcraft Movement in Nyasaland' (Cambridge University Diploma in Anthropology, 1934).

MacDonald, R.J., 'A History of African Education in Nyasaland, 1875-1945' (Edinburgh University Ph.D., 1969).

Macmillan, H.W., 'The Origins and Development of the African Lakes Company' (Edinburgh University Ph.D., 1970).

Mwiyera, S.S., 'Vernacular Literature of Malawi, 1845-1975: an annotated bibliography' (F.L.A., 1978).

Ncosana, S.S., 'Spirit Possession and Tumbuka Christians' (Aberdeen University Ph.D., 1985).

Page, M.E. 'Malawians in the Great War' (Michigan State University Ph.D., 1977).

Ross, A.C., 'The Origins and Development of the Church of Scotland Mission, Blantyre, Nyasaland, 1875-1926 (Edinburgh University Ph.D., 1968).

Tangri, R.K., 'The Development of Modern African Politics and the Emergence of a Nationalist Movement in Colonial Malawi, 1891-1958 (Edinburgh University Ph.D., 1970).

Thompson, T.J., 'Fraser and the Ngoni' (Edinburgh University Ph.D., 1980).

5.   Periodical Publications

Note: Unless otherwise stated, these are listed in the *British Union Catalogue of Periodicals*, which should be consulted regarding their availability in libraries.

(a)   Publications of Churches and Missionary Societies

The Aurora
Books for Africa
Central Africa
The East and the West
East and West Review
International Review of Missions
Life and Work
Life and Work in Broughton Place Church (available at Broughton McDonald Church)
Livingstonia News
Missionary Record of the United Free Church of Scotland
Nyasa News
Other Lands
Record of the Home and Foreign Mission Work of the United Free Church of Scotland
St. Columba's Church of Scotland, Pont St Belgravia SW/SW1: Church Magazine (available at St Columba's Church)
Student Movement
United Free Church of Scotland: Assembly Papers, Cases, Overtures

(New College Library, Edinburgh University)
United Free Church of Scotland: Assembly Proceedings (New College Library, Edinburgh University).
Vyaro na Vyaro (MNA)
Women's Missionary Magazine
World Dominion

(b)   Academic Periodicals

Africa
African Affairs
African Studies
Bantu Studies
Journal of the (Royal) African Society
Journal of the Royal Anthropological Institute
Journal of Social Science (Malawi)
Man
Nyasaland Journal
Society of Malawi Journal

(c)   Miscellaneous

Boy's Own Paper
East Africa (and Rhodesia)
Glasgow Academy Chronicle (available at the Glasgow Academy)

6.   Printed Sources.

[Anon.] *The Glasgow Academy: the first hundred years* (Glasgow: Blackie & Son, 1946).
[Anon.] *Thirty Years of Broughton Place Church* (Edinburgh: Howie and Seath, 1914).
Abdallah, Y.B., *The Yaos/Chiikala cha Wayao*, ed. and trans. by G.M. Sanderson (Zomba: Government Printer, 1919).
Allen, C., *Tales from the Dark Continent* (London: Deutsch, 1979).
Banda, H.K., and Nkumbula, H., *Federation in Central Africa* (London: privately published 1949).
Barnes, J.A., 'The Fort Jameson Ngoni', in E. Colson and M.

Gluckman (eds), *Seven Tribes of British Central Africa* (London: Oxford University Press, 1951) 194-252.

Barnes, J.A., 'History in a Changing Society', *Rhodes-Livingstone Journal*, 11 (1951) 1-9.

Barnes, J.A., *Marriage in a Changing Society* (London: Oxford University Press, 1951).

Barnes, J.A., *Politics in a Changing Society* (Cape Town: Oxford University Press, 1954).

Berger, E.L., *Labour, Race and Colonial Rule: the Copperbelt from 1924 to independence* (Oxford: Clarendon Press, 1974).

Boeder, R.B., 'The Effects of Labor Migration on Rural Life in Malawi', *Rural Africana*, 20 (1973) 37-46.

Bonner, P. (ed.), *Working papers in Southern African History* (Johannesburg: Rawan Press, 1981).

Bretton, H.L. *The Rise and Fall of Kwame Nkrumah* (London: Pall Mall Press, 1967).

Broomfield, G.W., Review of T.C. Young, *Contemporary Ancestors* in *East and West Review*, 7 (1941) 60-1.

Cairns, H.A.C., *Prelude to Imperialism* (London: Routledge and Kegan Paul, 1965).

Calder, A., 'The Making of *Schwarzer Orpheus:* Jahnheinz Jahn and George Shepperson', *Journal of Commonwealth Literature*, 25 (1980) 5-14.

Carswell, D., *Brother Scots* (London: Constable, 1927).

Cell, J.W. (ed.), *By Kenya possessed: the correspondence of Norman Leys and J.H. Oldham* (London: Chicago University Press, 1976).

Chanock, M.L., 'Ambiguities in the Malawian Political Tradition', *African Affairs*, 74 (1975) 326-46.

Chanock, M.L., 'The New Men revisited: an essay on the development of political consciousness in colonial Malawi', in R.J. Macdonald (ed), *From Nyasaland to Malawi* (Nairobi: East African Publishing House, 1975) 235-353.

Chibambo, Y.M., *Midauko* (Livingstonia: Mission Press, 1946).

Chibambo, Y.M., *My Ngoni of Nyasaland*, trans. by C. Stuart (London: USCL, [1942]).

Chilivumbo, A.B., 'Malawi's Culture in the National Integration', *Présence Africaine*, no. 96 (2e trimestre, 1976) 234-42.

Chipembere, H., 'Malawi in Crisis, 1964', *Ufahamu* 1, pt 2 (1970) 1-

24.

Collingwood, R.G., *The Idea of History* (Oxford: Clarendon Press, 1946).

Colson, E., and Gluckman, M. (eds), *Seven Tribes of British Central Africa* (London: Oxford University Press, 1951).

Coser, L.A., *Masters of Sociological Thought: ideas in historical and social context* (New York: Harcourt Brace, 1971).

Cox, J., *Take a Cold Tub, Sir!: the story of the Boy's Own Paper* (Guildford: Lutterworth Press, 1982).

Crosby, C.A., *Historical Dictionary of Malawi* (London: Scarecrow Press, 1980).

Crowder, M., *Sénégal: a study of French assimilation policy* (London: Methuen, 1962).

Cunnison, I., *History on the Luapula: an essay in the historical notions of a Central African tribe* (London: Oxford University Press, 1951).

Davis, J. Merle, *Modern Industry and the African* (London: International Missionary Council, Department of Social and Economic Research and Counsel, 1933).

Donaldson, G., *The Scots Overseas* (London: Hale, 1966).

Durkheim, E., *The Division of Labor in Society* English trans. (New York: Macmillan, 1933).

Durkheim, E., *The Elementary Forms of the Religious Life* English trans. (London,: Allen and Unwin, 1915).

Durkheim, E., *The Rules of Sociological Method* English trans. (Chicago: University Press, 1938).

Durkheim, E., *Suicide* English trans. (Glencoe: Free Press, 1951).

Elmslie, W.A., *Among the Wild Ngoni* (Edinburgh: Oliphant and Ferrier, 1899).

Epstein, A.L., *Politics in an Urban African Community* (Manchester: University Press, 1958).

Evans-Pritchard, E.E. Firth, R., Malinowski, B., and Schapera, I. (eds), *Essays presented to C.G. Seligman* (London: Kegan Paul, Trench, Trubner, 1934).

Feldmann, H., 'Die allgemeine Missionskonferenz in Livingstonia in Britisch Central-Afrika', *Allgemeine Missions-Zeitschrift*, 27 (1901) 392-6.

Firth, R. (ed), *Man and Culture: an evaluation of the work of Bronislaw Malinowski* (London: Routledge and Kegan Paul,

1957).

Forster, P.G., 'Missionaries and Anthropology: the case of the Scots of northern Malawi', *Journal of Religion in Africa*, 16 (1986) 101-20.

Forster, P.G., 'The Rev. T. Cullen Young: a preliminary note', *Bulletin of the Scottish Institute of Missionary Studies* n.s. 2 (1984) 13-14.

Foster, G.M.; Scudder, T.; Colson, E; and Kemper, R.V., *Long-term Field Research in Social Anthropology* (London: Academic Press, 1979).

Fotheringham, L.M., *Adventures in Nyasaland* (London: Sampson Low, Marston, Searle and Rivington, 1891).

Fraser, A.G., 'Education in India and Ceylon in view of the National Movement', *The East and the West* 6 (1908) 28-42.

Fraser, A.R., *Donald Fraser of Livingstonia* (London: Hodder and Stoughton, 1934).

Fraser, D., *The Future of Africa* (London: Young People's Missionary Movement, 1911).

Fraser, D., *Winning a Primitive People* (London: Seeley Service, 1914).

Fraser, D., 'The Zulu of Nyasaland: their manners and customs' *Proceedings of the Philosophical Society of Glasgow* 32 (1900-1) 60-75.

Frazer, J.G., *The Golden Bough*, 12 vols (London: Macmillan, 1907-15); .... (abridged ed., 1 vol.; London: Macmillan, 1922).

Gamitto, A.C.P., *King Kazembe and the Marave, Cheva, Bisa, Bemba, Lunda, and other Peoples of Southern Africa* trans. by I. Cunnison, 2 vols (Lisbon: Junta de Investigações do Ultramar, Centro de Estudos Políticos e Sociais, 1960).

Gardner, B., *German East* (London: Cassell, 1963).

Gelfand, M., *Lakeside Pioneers: a socio-medical study in Nyasaland, 1875-1920* (Oxford: Blackwell, 1974).

Gollock, G.A., and Young, T.C., *God's Family in the World* (London: USCL, 1936).

Graham, J.M., and Piddington, R., *Anthropology and the Future of Missions* (Aberdeen: University Press, 1940).

Hall, R.N., *Prehistoric Rhodesia* (London: Leipsic, 1909).

Hetherington, P., *British Paternalism in Africa, 1920-1940* (London: Cass, 1978).

Hewitt, G., *Let the People read: a short history of the United Society for Christian Literature* (London: Lutterworth, 1949).

Highet, J., *The Churches in Scotland today* (Glasgow: Jackson, 1950).

Hobley, C.W., *Bantu Beliefs and Magic* (London: Witherby, 1922).

Hobsbawm, E., and Ranger, T. (eds), *The Invention of Tradition* (Cambridge: University Press, 1983).

Hoggart, R., *The Uses of Literacy* (London: Chatto and Windus, 1957).

Holding, E.M., *A Good Village* (London: USCL, 1949).

Horton, R., 'African Conversion', *Africa* 41 (1971) 85-108.

Jack, J.W., *Daybreak in Livingstonia* (New York: Young People's Missionary Movement, 1900).

Jahn, J., *Schwarzer Orpheus* (Munich: Carl Hanser, 1954).

Jahn, J., and Dressler, C.P. (eds), *Bibliography of Creative African Writing* (New York: Kraus, 1973).

Joelson, F. (ed.), *East Africa today and tomorrow* (London: East Africa, 1934).

Johnson, W.P., *My African Reminiscences, 1875-1895* (London: UMCA, 1926).

Johnson, W.P., *Nyasa, the Great Water* (London: Milford, 1922).

Johnston, H.H., *British Central Africa* (London: Methuen, 1897).

Jones, T.J., *Education in East Africa* (New York: Phelps Stokes Fund, 1925).

July, R.W., *The Origins of Modern African Thought* (London: Faber, 1968).

Kadalie, C., *My Life with the I.C.U.* (London: Cass, 1970).

Kalinga, O.J.M., *A History of the Ngonde Kingdom of Malawi* (Berlin: Mouton, 1985).

Kauta, S., 'Traditional Religion among the Tumbuka and other Tribes', *Ministry* (Lesotho) 9, no.1 (1979) 3-11.

Kenyatta, J., *Facing Mount Kenya: the tribal life of the Gikuyu*, introduction by B. Malinowski (London: Secker and Warburg, 1938).

Kidd, D., *Kafir Socialism and the Dawn of Individualism: an introduction to the study of the Native Problem* (London: Black, 1908).

King, K.J., *Pan-Africanism and Education* (Oxford: Clarendon Press, 1971).

Kuper, A., *Anthropology and Anthropologists: the modern British school* 2nd ed. (London: Routledge and Kegan Paul, 1983).

Lacerda e Almeida, F.J.M. de, *The Lands of Cazembe: Lacerda's journey to Cazembe in 1798* [trans. and annotated by R.F. Burton]; also includes *'Journey of the "Pombeiros"'* [trans. by B.A. Beadle]; and a *'Resume of the Journey of MM. Monteiro and Gamitto'* by Dr C.Y. Beke (London: Murray, 1873).

Lamb, J.A. (ed.), *The Fasti of the United Free Church of Scotland 1900-29* (Edinburgh: Oliver and Boyd, 1956).

Leverhulme Inter-Collegiate History Conference, *Historians in Tropical Africa* (Salisbury, University of Rhodesia and Nyasaland, 1962).

Linden, I. and J., *Catholics, Peasants and Chewa Resistance in Nyasaland, 1889-1939* (Berkeley: University of California Press, 1974).

Livingstone, D. and C., *Narrative of an Expedition to the Zambezi and its Tributaries* (London: Murray, 1865).

Livingstone, W.P., *Laws of Livingstonia: a narrative of missionary adventure and achievement* (London: Hodder and Stoughton, 1921).

Lugard, F.D., *The Rise of our East African Empire*, 2 vols (Edinburgh: Blackwood, 1893).

McCracken, J., *Politics and Christianity in Malawi, 1875-1940: the impact of the Livingstonia Mission in the Northern Province* (Cambridge: University Press, 1977).

McCracken, J., 'Underdevelopment in Malawi: the missionary contribution, *African Affairs* 76 (1977) 195-209.

MacDonald, D., *Africana: or the heart of heathen Africa*, 2 vols (London: Simpkin Marshall, 1882).

Macdonald, R.J., *From Nyasaland to Malawi* (Nairobi: East African Publishing House, 1975).

Macdonald, R.J., 'Reverend Hanock Msokera Phiri and the Establishment of the African Methodist Episcopal Church', *African Historical Studies* 3 (1970) 75-87.

Macgregor, A.A., *The Buried Barony* (London: Hale, 1949).

Mackenzie, D.R., *The Spirit-ridden Konde* (London: Seeley Service, 1925).

Mackenzie, R.J., *Almond of Loretto* (London: Constable, 1905).

McMaster, C., *Malawi: foreign policy and development* (New York:

St Martin's Press, 1974).

Macpherson, F., *Anatomy of a Conquest: the British occupation of Zambia, 1884-1924* (Harlow: Longman, 1981).

Macpherson, F., *One Finger* (Lusaka: Neczam, 1974).

Madan, A.C., *Living Speech* (Oxford: Clarendon Press, 1911).

Mangan, J.A., *Athleticism in the Victorian and Edwardian Public Schools* (Cambridge: University Press, 1981).

Maquet, J., *Africanity*, English trans. (New York: Oxford University Press, 1972).

Marwick, M., *Sorcery in the Social Setting* (Manchester: University Press, 1965).

Melland, F. (ed), *African Survey surveyed* (London: Macmillan, 1938)

Melland, F., *In Witchbound Africa* (London: Seeley Service, 1923).

Melland, F., and Young, T.C., *African Dilemma* (London: RTS, 1931).

Moffett, M., 'The Story', *Monthly Review* (Calcutta), 38, no. 9 (1973) 25-6.

Moir, F.L., *After Livingstone: an African trade romance* (London: Hodder and Stoughton, 1923).

Mufuka, K., *Missions and Politics in Malawi* (Kingston [Ohio]: Limestone Press, 1977).

[Mumba, L] ('An African'), 'The Religion of my Fathers', *International Review of Missions*, 19 (1930) 362-71.

National Library of Scotland, *Catalogue of Manuscripts acquired since 1925: Vol. 6, Manuscripts 7530-8022, Scottish Foreign Mission Records 1827-1929* (Edinburgh: HMSO, 1984).

Nida, E.A., *The Book of a Thousand Tongues* (London: United Bible Society, 1972).

Nkhwazi, D., *Presidential Leadership in Malawi* (Hamburg: Hamburg University, 1971).

Nkonjera, A., 'A Native Account: History of the Kamanga Tribe of Lake Nyasa' (published with the support of A.D. Easterbrook), *Journal of the African Society*, 10 (1910-11) 331-41, and 11 (1911-12) 231-4.

Ntara, S.Y., *Headman's Enterprise*, English trans. and preface by T.C. Young (London: Lutterworth, 1949).

Ntara, S.Y., *History of the Chewa*, English translation of *Mbiri ya Achewa* by W.S.K. Jere, with introduction by H. Langworthy (Wiesbaden, Franz Steiner, 1973).

Ntara, S.Y., *Man of Africa* English trans. by T.C. Young (London:

RTS, 1934).

Ntara, S.Y., *Mbiri ya Achewa* (Nkhoma: Mission Press, 1945).

Nyirenda, S., 'History of the Tumbuka-Henga People' trans. and ed. by T.C. Young, *Bantu Studies* 5 (1931) 1-75.

Oldham, J.H., *Christianity and the Race Problem* (London: SCM Press, 1925).

Oldham, J.H., 'The Christian Mission in Africa as seen at the International Conference at Le Zoute', *International Review of Missions*, 16 (1927) 24-35.

Oliver, R., *The Missionary Factor in East Africa* (London: Longman, 1952).

Omer-Cooper, J., *The Zulu Aftermath* (London: Longman, 1966).

Pachai, B. (ed.), *The Early History of Malawi* (London: Longman, 1972).

Pachai, B., *Malawi: the history of the nation* (London: Longman, 1973).

Pachai, B., 'Samuel Josiah Ntara: writer and historian', *Society of Malawi Journal*, 21 (1968) 60-6.

Page, M.E., 'The War of Thangata: Nyasaland and the East African Campaign, 1914-18', *Journal of African History*, 19 (1978) 87-100.

Pauw, C.M. *Mission and the Church in Malawi: the history of the Nkhoma Synod in the Church of Central Africa Presbyterian* (Stellenbosch: Stellenbosch University, 1980).

Peires, J. (ed.), *Before and after Shaka: papers in Nguni history* (Grahamstown: Rhodes University Press, 1981).

Piddington, R., *An Introduction to Social Anthropology*, 2 vols (Edinburgh: Oliver and Boyd, 1950-7).

Pike, J.G., *Malawi: a political and economic history* (London: Pall Mall Press, 1968).

Poole, E.H. Lane, *The Native Tribes of the Eastern Province of Northern Rhodesia* (Lusaka: Government Printer, 1949).

Powdermaker, H., *Copper Town* (New York: Harper and Row, 1967).

Pretorius, J.L., 'An Attempt at Christian Initiation in Nyasaland', *International Review of Missions* 34 (1950) 284-91.

Pretorius, J.L., 'An Introduction to the History of the Dutch Reformed Church Mission in Malawi 1889-1914', in B. Pachai (ed.), *Early History*, 365-82.

Quaison-Sackey, A., *Africa Unbound: reflections of an African statesman* (London: Deutsch, 1963).

Radcliffe-Brown, A.R., *A Natural Science of Society* (Glencoe: Free Press, 1964).

Radcliffe-Brown, A.R., *Structure and Function in Primitive Society* (London: Cohen and West, 1952).

Ramsford, O., *David Livingstone: the dark interior* (London: Murray, 1978).

Rangeley, W.H.J. 'Bocarro's Journey', *Nyasaland Journal*, 7 (1954) 15-23.

Rangeley, W.H.J. 'Mtwalo', *Nyasaland Journal*, 5 (1952) 55-70.

Ranger, T., 'The Invention of Tradition in Colonial Africa', in E. Hobsbawm and T. Ranger, *The Invention of Tradition*, 211-62.

Ranger, T., and Kimambo, I.N. (eds), *The Historical Study of African Religion* (London: Heinemann, 1972).

Rattray, R.S., *Akan-Ashanti Folk-Tales* (Oxford: Clarendon Press, 1930).

Read, M., *Children of their Fathers* (London: Methuen, 1959).

Read, M., 'The Moral Code of the Ngoni and their Former Military State', *Africa*, 11 (1938) 1-24.

Read, M., 'The Ngoni and Western Education', in V.W. Turner (ed.) *Colonialism in Africa, 1870-1960* vol. 3 (Cambridge: University Press, 1971), 346-92.

Read, M., *The Ngoni of Nyasaland* (London: Oxford University Press, 1956).

Read, M., 'Songs of the Ngoni People', *Bantu Studies*, 11 (1937) 1-35.

Rebman, J., *Dictionary of the Kiniassa Language* (Basle, Church Missionary Society, 1877).

Redfield, R., *The Little Community: viewpoints for the study of the human whole* (Chicago: University Press, 1955).

Rennie, J.K., 'The Ngoni States and European Intrusion', in E. Stokes and R. Brown (eds), *The Zambezian Past*, 302-31.

Richards, A.I., *Hunger and Work in a Savage Tribe: a functional study of nutrition among the southern Bantu* (London: Routledge, 1932).

Roberts, A.D., *A History of the Bemba: political growth and change in north eastern Zambia before 1900* (London: Longman, 1973).

228 T. Cullen Young

Ross, A.C., 'Scottish Missionary Concern, 1874-1914: a golden era?', *Scottish Historical Review*, 51 (1972) 52-72.

Rotberg, R.I., *Christian Missionaries and the Creation of Northern Rhodesia 1880-1924* (Princeton [N.J.]: Princeton University Press, 1965).

Rotberg, R.I., *The Rise of Nationalism in Central Africa* (London: Oxford University Press, 1966).

Sanderson, G.M., *A Dictionary of the Yao Language* (Zomba: Government Printer, 1955).

Sanderson, G.M., 'Relationship Systems of the Wangonde and Wahenga Tribes, Nyasaland', *Journal of the Royal Anthropological Institute*, 53 (1923) 448-59.

Sanderson, G.M., 'Some Marriage Customs of the Wahenga, Nyasaland', *Journal of the African Society*, 22 (1922-3) 131-8.

Sanderson, G.M., *A Yao Grammar* (London: SPCK, 1922).

Schneider, D.M., and Gough, K. (eds), *Matrilineal Kinship* (Berkeley: University of California Press, 1962).

Schoffelers, J.M. (ed.), *Guardians of the Land* (Gwelo: Mambo Press, 1978).

Schoffelers, J.M., 'The Meaning and Use of the Name *Malawi* in Oral Tradition and Pre-Colonial Documents', in B. Pachai (ed.), *Early History* 91-103.

Schoffelers, J.M., 'Towards the Identification of Proto-Chewa Culture: a preliminary contribution'. *Journal of Social Science* (Malawi), 2 (1973) 47-60.

Schoffelers, J.M., and Linden, I., 'The Resistance of the Nyau Societies to the Roman Catholic Missions in Colonial Malawi', in T. Ranger and I.N. Kimambo (eds), *The Historical Study of African Religion* 252-273.

Scott, D.C., *A Cyclopaedic Dictionary of the Mang'anja Language* (Edinburgh: Church of Scotland, 1892).

Scudder, T., and Colson, E., 'Long-term Research in Gwembe Valley, Zambia', in G.M. Foster *et al.*, *Long-term Field Research in Social Anthropology*, 227-54.

Shepperson, G.A., 'David Livingstone the Scot', *Scottish Historical Review*, 39 (1960) 113-21.

Shepperson, G.A., 'External Forces in the Development of African Nationalism, with Particular reference to British Central

Africa', *Phylon*, 22 (1961) 207-25.

Shepperson, G.A., *Myth and Reality in Malawi* (Evanston: Northwestern University Press, 1966).

Shepperson, G.A., 'Nyasaland and the Millennium', in S.L. Thrupp (ed.), *Millennial Dreams in Action*, 144-59.

Shepperson, G.A., and Price. T., *Independent African: John Chilembwe and the origins, setting and significance of the Nyasaland Native Rising of 1915* (Edinburgh: University Press, 1958).

Short, P., *Banda* (London: Routledge and Kegan Paul, 1974).

Sjölinder, S.J., *Presbyterian Reunion in Scotland, 1907-1921* (Uppsala: Almqvist and Wiksell, 1982).

Smart, R.N., 'Literate Ladies: a fifty-year experiment', *Alumnus Chronicle* (St Andrews University), (June 1968) 21-31.

Smith, E.W. (ed.), *African Ideas of God* (London: Edinburgh House, 1950).

Smith, E.W., *Aggrey of Africa: a study in Black and White* (London: SCM, 1929).

Smith, E.W.,*The Christian Mission in Africa: a study based on the work of the International Conference at Le Zoute* (London: International Missionary Council, 1926).

Smith, E.W., 'Indigenous Education in Africa', in E.E. Evans-Pritchard *et al.*, *Essays presented to C.G. Seligman*, 319-34.

Smith, E.W., *Knowing the African* (London: Lutterworth, 1946).

Smith, E.W., and Dale, A.M., *The Ila-speaking Peoples of Northern Rhodesia*, 2 vols (London: Macmillan, 1920); 2nd ed., [with new introduction by E. Colson] (New York: University Books, 1968).

Southall, A. (ed.), *Social Change in Modern Africa* (London: Oxford University Press, 1961).

Steele, G., 'History of the Tambuka', *Nyasa News* 1 (1893) 17-19.

Steytler, J.G., *Educational Adaptations with Reference to African Village Schools with Special Reference to Central Nyasaland* (London: Sheldon Press, 1939).

Stokes, E., and Brown, R. (eds), *The Zambezian Past: studies in Central African History* (Manchester: University Press, 1966).

Tangri, R.K., 'The Rise of Nationalism in Colonial Africa: the case of colonial Malawi', *Comparative Studies in Society and*

History, 10 (1967-8) 142-61.

Taylor, J.V., *The Primal Vision* (London: SCM, 1963).

Taylor, J.V., and Lehmann, D.A., *Christians of the Copperbelt* (London: SCM, 1961).

Tew, M., *Peoples of the Lake Nyasa Region* (London: Oxford University Press, 1950).

Theal, G.M., *Records of South Eastern Africa*, 9 vols (Cape Town, Government of Cape Colony, 1898-1903).

Thompson, T.J., 'African Leadership in the Livingstonia Mission, 1875-1900', *Journal of Social Science* (Malawi), 2 (1973) 76-91.

Thompson, T.J., 'The Origins, Migration and Settlement of the Northern Ngoni' *Society of Malawi Journal*, 38 (1985) 6-35.

Thomson, T.D., 'Place-names in Nyasaland', *Nyasaland Journal*, 6 (1953) 64-6.

Thornton, R., 'Narrative Ethnography in Africa, 1850-1920: the creation and capture of an appropriate domain for anthropology', *Man* n.s., 8, 1973, 502-21.

Thrupp, S.L. (ed.), *Millennial Dreams in Action: essays in comparative study* (The Hague: Mouton, 1962).

Torday, E., 'The Principles of Bantu Marriage', *Africa*, 2 (1929) 255-90.

Turner, V. (ed.), *Colonialism in Africa*, vol. 3, 1870-1960 (Cambridge: University Press, 1971).

Vail, L., (ed.), *The Creation of Tribalism in Southern Africa* (London: Currey, 1989).

Vail, L., 'Ethnicity, Language and National Unity: the case of Malawi', in P. Bonner (ed.), *Working Papers on Southern African History* 121-63.

Vail, L., 'The Making of the Dead North: a study of the Ngoni rule in northern Malawi', in J. Peires (ed.), *Before and after Shaka*, 230-67.

Vail, L., 'Religion, Language and the Tribal Myth: the Tumbuka and Chewa of Malawi', in J.M. Schoffelers (ed.), *Guardians of the Land*, 209-33.

Vail, L., Review of T.C. Young, *Notes on the History of the Tumbuka Kamanga Peoples in the Northern Province of Nyasaland* 2nd ed., in *African Studies*, 30 (1971) 67-8.

Vail, L., 'Suggestions towards a reinterpreted Tumbuka History', in

B. Pachai (ed.), *The Early History of Malawi* 148-67.

Vail, L., and White, L., 'Tribalism in the Political History of Malawi', in L. Vail (ed), *The Creation of Tribalism in Southern Africa* 151-92.

Van Velsen, J., 'The Establishment of Administration in Tongaland', in Leverhulme Inter-Collegiate History Conference, *Historians in Tropical Africa* 177-96.

Van Velsen, J., 'Labour Migration as a Positive Factor in the Continuity of Tonga Tribal Society', in A. Southall (ed.), *Social Change in Modern Africa*, 230-41.

Van Velsen, J., 'The Missionary Factor among the Lakeside Tonga of Nyasaland', *Rhodes-Livingstone Journal*, 26 (1960) 1-22.

Van Velsen, J., 'Notes on the History of the Lakeside Tonga of Nyasaland', *African Studies*, 28 (1959) 105-11.

Van Velsen, J., *The Politics of Kinship* (Manchester: University Press, 1964).

Van Velsen, J., 'Some Early Pressure Groups in Malawi', in E. Stokes and R. Brown (eds), *The Zambezian Past* 376-412.

Vansina, J., *Oral Tradition: a study in historical methodology* English trans. (London: Routledge and Kegan Paul, 1961).

Wallace, J.M., *Broughton McDonald Church, 1785-1985* (Edinburgh: Broughton McDonald Church, 1985).

Warren, M., *Social History and Christian Mission* (London: SCM, 1967).

Watkins, M.H., *A Grammar of Chichewa: a Bantu language of British Central Africa* (Language Dissertations no. 24, supplement to *Language*; Philadelphia, Pennsylvania University, 1937).

Watson, W., *Tribal Cohesion in a Money Economy: a study of the Mambwe people of Northern Rhodesia* (Manchester: University Press, 1958).

Weber, M., *The Protestant Ethic and the Spirit of Capitalism* English trans. (London: Allen and Unwin, 1930).

Weber, M., *The Theory of Social and Economic Organization* English trans. (New York: Oxford University Press, 1947).

White, G., 'Highly Preposterous: origins of Scottish missions', *Records of the Scottish Church History Society*, 19 (1976) 111-24.

Who was Who?, 1929-40 (London: Black, 1941), and 1961-70

(London: Black, 1972).

Willoughby, W.C., *The Soul of the Bantu: a sympathetic study of the magico-religious practices and beliefs of the Bantu tribes of Africa* (Garden City: Doubleday Doran, 1928).

Wilson, G., *The Constitution of Ngonde* (Rhodes-Livingstone Paper no. 3; Livingstone: Rhodes-Livingstone Institute, 1939).

Wilson, M., *The Peoples of the Nyasa-Tanganyika Corridor* (Cape Town: University Press, 1958).

Young, T.C., and Banda, H.K. (eds), *Our African Way of Life* (London: Lutterworth, 1946).

Young, W.P., *The Rabbit and the Baboons, and other Tales from Northern Nyasaland* (London: Sheldon Press, 1933).

Young, W.P., *The Rabbit and the Lion, and other Tales from Northern Nyasaland* (London: Sheldon Press, 1933).

Young, W.P., *A Soldier to the Church* (London: SCM, 1919)

Young, W.P., *Stories told to African Girls* (London: Sheldon Press, 1938).

Young, W.P., *Why Rabbit and Hyena quarrelled, and other Tales from Northern Nyasaland* (London: Sheldon Press, 1933).

233

Index of Personal Names
(Clan Names are to be found in the Subject Index)

Abdallah, Revd Yohanna Barnaba, 75
Aggrey, Dr James Emman Kwegyir, 23
Arthur, Dr J.W., 16
Bamantha, Fig. 1, facing p. 82
Banda, Ngwazi Dr Hastings Kamuzu (His Excellency the Life
     President of the Republic of Malawi), and 'African tradition',
     150-65; and Chewa Language, 34, 149, 152, 154, 158, 162-3; and
     Cullen Young, 17, 34-5, 126, 148-50, 152-8, 164-5; (with Cullen
     Young) *Our African Way of Life*, 34-5, 65, 126, 152-5, 162, 164;
     early years, 17, 148-9; in England, 150-2, 155, 157; in Ghana,
     157; medical practice, 150-1; medical studies, 148-9, 165;
     political activities after Malawian independence, 17, 115, 139,
     158-65; political activities before Malawian independence, 151,
     157-8; in Scotland, 149-50, 152; in South Africa, 148-9; in
     U.S.A., 149, 152; in Zimbabwe, 148
Bargery, Dr George Percy, 152
Barnes, Professor John Arundel, 111-13
Barton, Captain, 19
Baza Mdokowe, 89, 103, 108
Bocarro, Gaspar, 75, 106
Booth, Joseph, 17
Broomfield, Revd Canon Gerald Webb, 63
Bwati, 79, Fig. 1, facing p.82
Chawara, 80, 81, 91
Chayeka, Fig. 1, facing p. 82
Chepere: *see* Kyepere
Chibambo, Revd Yesaya Mloneyi, 23, 96, 106-11, 115
Chidzalo, E.P., 154
Chilembwe, John, 17-18, 120-1, 141; *Commission of Inquiry into
     Nyasaland Native Rising* (1916), 18, 141
Chilivumbo, Dr Alifeyo, 162-3
Chimtunga, Paramount Chief, 18-19
Chiparamoto, 87

236   *T. Cullen Young*

241

Index of Place-names

Subject Index
(Names of African ethnic groups [e.g. Bemba] are indicated with an asterisk)